The Phenomenology of Religious Belief

BLOOMSBURY POLITICAL THEOLOGIES

Edited by Ward Blanton (University of Kent), Arthur Bradley (Lancaster University), Michael Dillon (Lancaster University), and Yvonne Sherwood (University of Kent)

This series explores the past, present, and future of political theology. Taking its cue from the ground-breaking work of such figures as Derrida, Agamben, Badiou, and Žižek, it seeks to provide a forum for new research on the theologico-political nexus, including cutting-edge monographs, edited collections, and translations of classic works. By privileging creative, interdisciplinary, and experimental work that resists easy categorization, this series not only re-assets the timeliness of political theology in our epoch but seeks to extend political theological reflection into new territory: law, economics, finance, technology, media, film, and art. In *Bloomsbury Political Theologies*, we seek to reinvent the ancient problem of political theology for the twenty-first century.

International Advisory Board

Agata Bielik-Robson (University of Nottingham)
Howard Caygill (Kingston University)
Simon Critchley (New School of Social Research)
Roberto Esposito (Scuola Normale Superiore)
Elettra Stimilli (Sapienza University of Rome)
Miguel Vatter (University of New South Wales)

Titles in the series:

Massimo Cacciari, *The Withholding Power: An Essay on Political Theology*
Michel de Certeau, *The Weakness of Belief*
Charlie Gere, *Unnatural Theology*
Andrew Gibson, *Modernity and the Political Fix*
Elettra Stimilli, *Debt and Guilt*
Thomas Lynch, *Apocalyptic Political Theology*
Agata Bielik-Robson, *Another Finitude: Messianic Vitalism and Philosophy*
Antonio Cerella, *Genealogies of Political Modernity*
Colby Dickinson, *Theological Poverty in Continental Philosophy*

The Phenomenology of Religious Belief

Media, Philosophy, and the Arts

Michael J. Shapiro

BLOOMSBURY ACADEMIC
LONDON • NEW YORK • OXFORD • NEW DELHI • SYDNEY

BLOOMSBURY ACADEMIC
Bloomsbury Publishing Plc
50 Bedford Square, London, WC1B 3DP, UK
1385 Broadway, New York, NY 10018, USA
29 Earlsfort Terrace, Dublin 2, Ireland

BLOOMSBURY, BLOOMSBURY ACADEMIC and the Diana logo are
trademarks of Bloomsbury Publishing Plc

First published in Great Britain 2021
This paperback edition published in 2023

Cover image: Winter Light, (aka Nattvardsgästerna), Gunnar Bjornstrand, 1962
Cover image © Everett Collection Inc / Alamy Stock Photo

A catalogue record for this book is available from the British Library.

Library of Congress Cataloging-in-Publication Data
Names: Shapiro, Michael J., author.
Title: The phenomenology of religious belief: media, philosophy, and the arts / Michael J. Shapiro.
Description: London; New York: Bloomsbury Academic, [2021] |
Series: Bloomsbury political theologies |
Includes bibliographical references and index. |
Identifiers: LCCN 2020055540 (print) | LCCN 2020055541 (ebook) |
ISBN 9781350164307 (hb) | ISBN 9781350164314 (epdf) | ISBN 9781350164321 (epub)
Subjects: LCSH: Experience (Religion) in motion pictures. |
Experience (Religion) in literature. | Religion–Philosophy. |
Christianity–Philosophy. | American fiction–20th century–History
and criticism. | Phenomenological theology.
Classification: LCC PN1995.9.R4 S53 2021 (print) |
LCC PN1995.9.R4 (ebook) | DDC 791.4/3682–dc23
LC record available at https://lccn.loc.gov/2020055540
LC ebook record available at https://lccn.loc.gov/2020055541

ISBN: HB: 978-1-3501-6430-7
PB: 978-1-3502-4398-9
ePDF: 978-1-3501-6431-4
eBook: 978-1-3501-6432-1

Series: Bloomsbury Political Theologies

Typeset by Integra Software Solutions Pvt. Ltd.

To find out more about our authors and books visit
www.bloomsbury.com and sign up for our newsletters.

*To Mick Dillon, with gratitude for his friendship
and the inspiration of his passion for knowledge*

Table of Contents

List of Figures

Preface and Acknowledgments

The Prototype

The topic of this monograph was initiated by an invitation to present a keynote address in Prague at a November 2018 conference: "Image, Phenomenon, and the Imagination in the Phenomenology of Religious Experience." The paper I delivered, "The Phenomenology of Belief: Media Technologies and Communities of Sense," provided the prototype for Chapter 1. Reflecting on the conversation I entered as I prepared and delivered that paper, it became evident that to contemplate religious experience is to join a history of conversations about life that have persisted in a wide variety of disciplines and media genres, populated by notable artists, writers, and protagonists. Some of them were featured in my Prague keynote and several additional ones receive attention in the book's chapters. Here I want to rehearse briefly one who doesn't, Spinoza, because of the passion and intensity with which he pursued a conversation about life and because he is an exemplar of the kind of critical thinking that I reference in each chapter. Those features of Spinoza's philosophy are noted by Gilles Deleuze, who refers to the way Spinoza exemplifies "the power of thinking," which "the best society" exempts "from the obligation to obey."[1] Heeding that insight, I want to summarize the Spinoza effect that inspires much of my investigation.

Spinoza and Life

> If the force of authority has an extra-human origin, societies cannot freely choose to structure themselves in one way or another: they must observe obsequiously the dictates of a transcendent will.
>
> Carlo Grassi

For purposes of illustration, I refer here to the obliged obedience featured in Leonard Padura's novelistic reprise of the assassination of Leon Trotsky in

Mexico in August 1940. It's a triple biography—of Trotsky, of the assassin, Ramón Mercader, and of the Cuban author who is writing the story. The novel exemplifies "the power of thinking," as it reviews the costs of the obedience of many to the zealous dreams of the few. The story of the assassination, Padura writes,

> was the very chronicle of the debasement of a dream and the testimony of one of the most abject crimes ever committed, because it not only concerned the fate of Trotsky, at the end of the day a contender in that game of power and the protagonist in various historical horrors, but that of many millions of people dragged—without their asking, many times without anyone ever asking them what they wanted—by the undertow of history and by the very fury of their patrons, disguised as benefactors, messiahs, chosen ones, as sons of historical necessity and of the unavoidable dialectics of the class struggle.

While "messiahs" and other "chosen ones," abound in the history of theology, it is nevertheless important to concede that "thinking"—in the critical sense in which it is embraced by Deleuze, who famously distinguishes thinking from mere recognition[2]—has been practiced by both those who embrace and those who oppose theologies. "The important thing," writes Deleuze (in his engagement with Spinoza), "is to understand life."[3] Inasmuch as understanding life is central to my focus on the theology-political relationship, I want to heed Spinoza's complex and ambivalent connection with theology and reflect on the implications of his intervention in the conversation about life. The Spanish Holocaust survivor, Jorge Semprún, another gifted writer intrigued by the assassin Ramón Mercader, has put the force of Spinozism succinctly. After reviewing world dynamics in 1654 when, "Things were happening in the world, alliances were formed and then broken again, strategic positions changed hands, and all across Europe, although the consequences of this development could still not be foreseen by anyone, the bourgeoisie was slowly taking over the managerial incentives of an expanding universe," he updates his observation to two years later:

> In Amsterdam that year Spinoza, everlastingly suspect and even more so because his philosophy was reducing to smithereens ... all the ideological refuges of that new social order which was advancing over Europe but

which could still not recognize its own newness, its historic essence even its power and necessary brutality, could not mirror its own clarity and was still incapable of adopting the theoretical reasons for its overwhelming impetus.[4]

Spinoza juxtaposed his critical "philosophy of life" to the model of transcendence derived from Judeo-Christian theology. Deleuze puts it this way: "There is ... a philosophy of 'life' in Spinoza; it consists precisely in denouncing all that separates us from life, all these transcendent values that are turned against life, these values that are tied to the conditions and illusions of consciousness."[5] However, Spinoza offers more than denunciation. His philosophy of life is among other things a celebration of the human body's vitality: it affects joys, sorrows, and potentials for action.[6] Promoting "naturalism against supernaturalism," while at the same time favoring "reason against both faith and revelation,"[7] Spinoza entered humanity's ongoing negotiation of the nature of vitality by offering a view of life as "the force through which things persevere in their own being."[8] Especially relevant to the textual features of my investigation is Deleuze's suggestion that "Writers, poets, musicians, filmmakers—painters too, even chance readers—may find they are Spinozists."[9] To be a Spinozist, I want to add is to heed the media genres and historical contexts within which religion encounters a person's sensibilities. As a media theorist as well as a philosopher, Spinoza argued that the bible was not an adequate stand-alone medium. Phenomenologically, what it can mean to a reader is mediated by the "time and culture" within which it is approached.[10] An anti-theocratic thinker, Spinoza regarded nature and the body as more reliable media than scriptures. Accordingly, in the chapters that follow, I assemble and intervene critically in a textual montage that features a wide variety of philosophically and theologically attuned cultural texts, while emphasizing the mediating effects of both the texts and the phenomenologies through which they are received and interpreted.

Acknowledgments

I am especially indebted to Martin Nitsche from the Institute of Philosophy in the Czech Academy of Sciences for the invitation to deliver the paper that ultimately inspired my project as a whole, and I am grateful to him and his colleagues Petr Kouba and Vit Pokorný, whose thought-provoking papers at the conference helped me to orient my thinking about the phenomenology of experience. I want to extend special thanks for invitations to deliver versions of some of my chapter drafts: Lars Tønder from the Department of Political Science at the University of Copenhagen (where I delivered a draft of Chapter 1 in October 2018), and Geoffrey Whitehall from the Department of Politics, Acadia University (where I delivered a draft of Chapter 2 in August 2019). I want also to extend special thanks to Mick Dillon who solicited the project for the Political Theology series he coedits for Bloomsbury, and to his coeditors, Arthur Bradley, Ward Blanton, and Yvonne Sherwood who welcomed the project. I am grateful to William Connolly, Brian Massumi, Sam Opondo, and John Rieder, who provided useful comments on chapter drafts.

Finally, I want to thank the acquisitions editors and production staff at Bloomsbury [Lucy Russell and Liza Thompson] and Karthiga Sithanandam from Integra - PDY for excellent management of the last stages of the production process.

The Phenomenology of Belief: Media Technologies and Communities of Sense

Contending Communities of Sense: Toni Morrison's *Paradise*

The textual engagements in this chapter are focused on the way media shape and sustain religious communities of sense. Borrowing Jacques Rancière's concise formulation, "a community of sense is a certain cutting out of space and time that binds together practices, forms of visibility, and patterns of intelligibility ... a partition of the sensible."[1] As I proceed, I emphasize the critical capacity of fictional texts, implicitly endorsing Gayatri Spivak's suggestion, "The protocols of fiction give us a practical simulacrum of the graver discontinuities inhabiting ... the ethico-epistemic and ethico-political ... an experience of the discontinuities that remain in place in 'real life.'"[2] And because I inaugurate the investigation with analyses of novels, I want also to summon the words of M. M. Bakhtin because no one has more effectively illustrated how that fictional genre provides access to "real life." Bakhtin points out that while "[i]n ancient literature it is memory and not knowledge that serves ... the creative impulse ... the novel by contrast, is determined by experience, knowledge and practice."[3] "From the very beginning," he adds, "the novel, ... was structured not by the distanced image of the absolute past [which was the case with the epic] but in the zone of direct contact with the conclusive present-day reality."[4] Most essentially, the novel's critical take on "present-day reality," according to Bakhtin, is the way it stages contention among diverse speech types; its "heteroglossia" or many contending voices have it resisting any verbal/ideological center.[5]

Heeding Bakhtin's characterization of the critical capacity of the genre, I begin with a novel that stages a theologically oriented, verbal/ideological contention, Toni Morrison's *Paradise*, which narrates a story about an all-Black community in the American West (of which there were many, founded by former slaves seeking a more comfortable venue than what was available in the South after The Emancipation in 1865). The community in the novel is first established in a town the founders name Haven, where they build a material manifestation of their spiritual covenant, a communal oven bearing an inscription about fearing God's wrath: "Beware the furrow of his brow." Because things don't go well in Haven (bad omens abound), the community moves and reestablishes itself in a new town they name Ruby. In an earlier discussion of the novel, I wrote:

> The Rubyites too have an "ark of the covenant" which in their case is [the same] communal oven, which they had made originally in Haven … It was a "flawlessly designed oven that both nourished them and monumentalized what they had done." To hold their past as a fixed monument, they took it apart brick by brick as they left Haven and reassembled it in Ruby. The oven/ark's original text, inscribed on the oven's iron plate reads, "Beware the furrow of His brow."[6]

All seems to be going smoothly as regards communal peace in Ruby until a younger generation pushes back against the founding elders' version of the community's theological binding. Wanting to alter Ruby's foundational commitment, they paint a Black power symbol on the oven and militate to change the text to, "*Be* the furrow of his brow," the sense of which is a radically different, more activist approach to the nation's white dominance.[7]

There follows a contentious community-wide discussion about the oven's role in conveying their ongoing history, as an emerging "fraternal community" is in "combat against the paternal community."[8] The elder "antagonists" allege that "they" [the younger generation] want to kill the oven's message, change it into something they made up. "That oven already has a history. It doesn't need you to fix it," one of the elders asserts, implying that the community's sacred text must be eternally unaltered in order to honor those who initiated the community's historical coherence. Immanuel Kant's remarks about ideational coercion as opposed to enlightenment are apropos here. The elders, in order to hold onto what amounts to their ecclesiastical power, are committed "to a certain unchangeable symbol in order to enjoy an unceasing guardianship over each of the [community's] members."[9] And the sci-fi writer Philip Dick (whose writing receives more attention below) captures the essence of such generational conflicts: "As the children of our world fight to develop their new individuality, their almost surely disrespect for the verities we worship, they become for us—and by 'us' I mean the establishment—a source of trouble."[10]

I have made the case elsewhere that Morrison's account of the younger generation's interpretative intervention renders the oven's text as Talmudic, i.e., as a living text open to continual re-inscription by the constantly changing textual community to which it belongs. That model has textual support. For example, in response to an elder, Mr. Deek's suggestion that the younger generation is disrespecting the oven, Ruby's Reverend Misner sides with the younger generation's interpretive challenge: "Seems to me Deek, they are respecting it. It's because they do know the oven's value that they want to give it a new life."[11] In effect, the younger generation was pushing for an enlightened view of the town's theology. As Kant's view of enlightenment implies, "An age cannot bind itself and ordain to put the succeeding one to such a condition that it cannot extend its knowledge."[12]

The Jewish theologian Jacob Taubes affirms that Kantian perspective while locating it within a Talmudic framing. He suggests, "It would be iconoclastic to deny a community the right of development, to outlaw all transformation, to declare all commentary as fake, and to argue that only the text is valid, ... to overlook the perennial conflict between text and commentary."[13] To develop that Talmudic perspective on the contentious episode in the fictional town of Ruby, I want to note that although there is a variety of Talmudic practices that have emerged over the centuries, produced by interpretive practices of generations of Jewish textual communities, one version in particular resonates well with the generational conflict that Morrison's novel explores. It's a radical philosophical approach to the text by the French philosopher-Rabbi, Marc-Alain Ouaknin, who identifies the essence of the Talmud as its resistance to closure. He indicates that from the point of view of one of its commentators, Rabbi Nahman of Breslav (b. 1772), the purpose of adding commentary to the Talmud is to undermine entrenched authority. As understood by Rabbi Nahman, the Talmud is an "open work" that seeks renewal rather than "reconciliation";[14] it "seeks to undo any mastery."[15] Put figuratively, Rabbi

Nahman insisted that to undo its textually reinforced mastery the book must be burnt, i.e., older textual traditions must be effaced in order to allow the community to move on to new self-understandings. That figuration emerges in Morrison's novel as well. Ruby's archivist, Patricia, who disparages the town's founding story of the purity of the community's bloodlines (continually reiterated by the elders) as a stultifying fiction, reports that she "burned the papers" in which that fiction is inscribed.

Textual Communities

The inability of the oven's initial inscription and the town of Ruby's oral tradition to maintain their hold over succeeding generations—as Patricia says, "Did they really think they could keep this up? The numbers, the bloodlines, the who fucks who?"[16]—testifies to the enduring contentiousness within textually mediated communities. In many venues and in many different historical epochs, we can witness ideational conflicts that have disrupted collectivities bound together and energized by media-influenced actualizations of what William James famously calls "the will to believe." What I want to pursue in the textual montage that follows is what we can learn about the phenomenology of religious belief by heeding media-involved disruptive events, either actual or imagined.

I begin with the actual, an extended event that occurred in late antiquity as described by the historian Peter Brown. It was a time in which exemplary persons were identified as the media through which spirit manifested itself. In the early fifth century, Brown points out, "the locus of the supernatural had come to shift significantly ... what changed between the second and fifth centuries were ... views as to where exactly this 'divine power' was to be found on earth, and consequently, on what terms access to it could be achieved."[17] Between 200 and 400 AD Mediterranean people believed "in increasing numbers and with increasing enthusiasm, the idea that 'divine power' did not only manifest itself to the average individual or through perennially established institutions: rather: 'divine power' was represented on earth by a limited number of exceptional human agents."[18] Late antiquity's society was "ever vigilant," watching "each other closely for those signs of intimacy with the supernatural."[19] What is therefore distinctive about the classical world "is the overwhelming tendency to find what is exemplary in persons rather than in more general entities."[20]

The exemplars were regarded as "Christ-carrying" men.[21] And crucially for purposes of this analysis, the writing medium that emerged to celebrate those exemplars of intimacy with the divine was "literary portraiture [;] ... biography and auto-biography flourished ... [for example] *Acts of the Martyrs*, [and] Eusebius' *Life of Constantine*."[22] The context for the importance of such exemplars was "the unprecedented weight of a providential monotheism which ... placed an exceptional weight on the joining points between God and men, and which in the case of Christianity, proposed as its central figure the Exemplar of all exemplars, a being, Christ, in whom human and divine had come to be joined."[23] Subsequently each (albeit lessor) exemplar has been located in the story of "the good news" as a "man of God" or a "righteous man" with a "revelatory quality about him," one who has the effect of "bringing God Himself back from exile in the hearts of those who doubted His abiding presence is a darkening world."[24]

I take "presence" to be a key term here. Given that the realm of the supernatural is beyond witnessing, it has been brought into the world during the "*longue durée* of Jewish and Christian imaginative structures"[25] through two practices of the imaginary, one internal, which I will call (after Gilles Deleuze's reading of Proust), the "*Tableux Vivants* [of a believer's] inner theater"[26] and the other external, a theater on display in homes and churches, specifically the statuary, icons and other decorative religious motifs through which a religious community displays what Brown refers to as "the intractable reality in which it finds itself."[27] Insofar as spirituality-relevant events are phenomenologically experienced, they are necessarily inflected by the way peoples' thought worlds emerge and thereafter how they inhabit and engage those internal and external theaters. W. G. Sebald also constructs an inventive perceiving/believing subject within a theatrical metaphor: "What manner of theater," he asks, "is it, in which we are at once playwright, actor, stage manager, scene painter and audience?"[28]

Because believers' inner and outer theaters contain and animate religious signs, it is through their sensitivity to signs that believers project "the world as an object to be deciphered"[29] in their search for the presence of the divine. In order to provide an elaborate illustration of that combination of phenomenology and semiology, I turn to a pair of Robert Coover novels, *The Origin of the Brunists* and *The Brunist Day of Wrath*, which narrate a trajectory from event, to belief, to institutionalized religion in a story that begins with a small town's mine disaster, which precipitates a collective apocalyptic movement after a person has been designated as one through whom spirit speaks (in *The Origin of the Brunists*) and follows with the scene five years later (in *The Brunist Day of Wrath*) with what has become a widespread religious movement inspired by the way media have figured and broadcast the initiating event.[30]

The Origin and Subsequent Establishment of the Brunists

In his gloss on the history of "Christ-carrying men," Peter Brown provides the basis for the name of the novel's object of spiritual veneration, Giovanni Bruno. Coover's Bruno has a prototype in Dante's *Inferno*, "Bruno Latini," to whom Brown refers in his discussion of the exemplars drawn from ancient mentorships, or "men of *paidea*." Brunetto Latini (*c.* 1220–1294), "a prominent [and erudite] Guelph who spent many years living in exile in Spain and France," played a "part in Dante's education, which was steeped in ancient religious and philosophical texts, most likely as a mentor."[31] As for the *novel's* Bruno, the back cover of the paperback version provides a convenient synopsis:

> Giovanni Bruno—hawk-faced, silent, some say deranged—is the only survivor [of a mine explosion]. A lapsed Catholic, given to peculiar visions, Bruno is adopted as a prophet by a group of secretive small-town mystics. 'Exposed' by the town newspaper editor, the Brunist cult gains international notoriety and the ranks swell. As members gather on the Mont of Redemption—above the site of the mine disaster—to await the apocalypse, and the fabric of the community begins to unravel, Robert Coover lays bare the madness of religious frenzy and the sometimes greater madness of 'normal' citizens.

For purposes of my analysis what the novel also lays bare are the interpersonal relations, media technologies, and ideational susceptibilities that trigger the underlying wills to believe—all elements of what Brian Massumi refers to as an "event potential"[32]—and spur the development and expansion of the Brunist cult. Because the original Greek sense of apocalypse (*Apokalupto*) means

"I disclose, I uncover, I unveil,"[33] Coover is confronting a fictional apocalyptic event—an inspired gathering expecting the *Dies Irae*—with an authorial apocalypse, a disclosure of the way an encounter between media and particular subjective susceptibilities becomes the phenomenological basis for the success of the Brunist recruitment as it unfolds within a contentious atmosphere of competing spiritual allegiances in the fictional mining town of West Condon.

The vehicles for the spiritualization of Coover's Bruno are the modern media, which have prepared the believers for receiving Bruno as a person through whom the divine speaks. One relevant medium, radio, shows up near the beginning of the novel. In a passage that follows a description of the men who are still alive in the collapsed mine, the narration cuts to two people trying to tune in a ballgame on their car radio. Flipping through the dial, they have instead tuned in an evangelical Christian broadcast with an apocalyptic message:

She is spreadin' her wings for a journey,
And is goin' to journey by and by,
And when the trumpet sounds in the mornin',
She will meet her dear lord in the sky![34]

Thereafter other media prepare the way for the belief explosion involved in the assembling of the Brunist cult. Some are observed at one point by Justin Miller, the editor of the town's newspaper, as he surveys the home of the Nazarine preacher Ely Collins, who has died in the mine accident: "A sentimental religiosity prevailed: evangelical pamphlets, dimestore plaques, cheap biblical prints."[35]

As the drama unfolds, new subject positions develop as some characters who had been minor players in the town's spiritual life vie for being privileged interpreters of the significance of the mine disaster. Miller observes a "prayer meeting" led by a preacher, "Abner Baxter," who

lacked eloquence and subtlety, but had a compact bullying style of his own and a volcanic delivery. '*Serve the Lord with Fear!*' he cried. '*With trembling kiss his feet!*' Their prayers defined the disaster as a judgment upon West Condon and a trial for God's faithful. What massed them up and charged them, apparently, was the expectation that Ely Collins—their man of tested faith—would emerge with messages, and it was with no small awe that they now awaited him.[36]

Those occurrences convince the cynical non-believer Miller that his newspaper can create a story that nominates Bruno as a chosen representative of the divine (because it turns out that a more obvious candidate, the charismatic reverend Ely Collins, has not survived the disaster). After Miller and his news cohort, Carl Jones ponder how to frame the survival of Giovanni Bruno, they "decided to banner it 'Miracle in West Condon,' just to wow the home folks." The story has an immediate impact, testifying to the power of print media compared with that of small-town prayer groups.[37] As a canny purveyor of a modern version of "the good news," Justin Miller is the novel's apostle Paul surrogate. To appreciate the proliferation of believers in both cases—those who are allegiant to the original, biblical good news and those moved by the version that emerges in West Condon—we can contrast the different sales missions of Paul and Miller and the alternative media they employ.

In a counter-reading of Paul's Epistle to the Romans, Jacob Taubes has famously addressed himself to the case of the former. He suggests that Paul, a self-described zealot, was an apostle of the Jews to the gentiles. Approaching Paul's epistle to the Romans "in the light of the Jewish experience,"[38] Taubes constructs Paul's delicate political agenda. His political task in Romans is geopolitical as well as spiritual inasmuch as rather than concerning himself only with the relationship of "man" to God, Paul was concerned with inter-nation dynamics. Paul's task unfolded at a historical moment in which two worlds were confronting each other, that of the ethnic community to which he, Paul, belonged and the imperial order in which it was located.

Certainly, the history of Christendom has since been one of change-inducing encounters. In addition to the ways Christianity has been historically ordered within its ranks, it has also been shaped by exotic encounters. To appreciate that aspect of its history, we have to heed a variety of post-Paul confrontational events. One described by Birget Rasmussen is exemplary. It is a dialogue that occurred in 1524—in the "recently conquered Tenochtitlan, now known as Mexico City"—attended by twelve Spanish friars who sought to convert indigenous Mexicans and by several Mexican scholar-priests. That encounter between "radically dissimilar worlds" created, according to Rasmussen, a "shared world—violently transformed [so that] epistemological, geopolitical and cosmological maps would be changed forever,"[39] "with," as I have put it elsewhere, "subtle effects on the way the Christian textual community subsequently evolved."[40]

In some cases, however, encounters involving Christianity's proselytizing outreach to cultural formations with incommensurate belief systems have been disastrous for both sides of the encounter rather than creating a shared consensual world. For example, roughly a century later the encounter between French Jesuits and the Huron people in North American was, in Brian Moore's terms, "the strange and gripping tragedy when Indian belief in a world of night and in the power of dreams clashed with the Jesuits' preachments of Christianity and a paradise after death." His novel *Black Robe* is designed to show how "each of these beliefs inspired in the other fear, hostility, and despair, which later would result in the destruction and abandonment of the Jesuit missions, and the conquest of the Huron people by the Iroquois, their deadly enemy."[41]

To return to Paul's encounter with the Roman imperial order, the version of the gospel that he sought to disseminate is marketed differently to the two worlds (As Gore Vidal sardonically puts it, "You don't get to be a major Saint without street smarts").[42] Taubes puts it this way: to Israel Paul offers a new solidarity-encouraging version of their messianic commitment and to Rome he suggests that the new messianic teaching is unthreatening to the Roman imperial order, as long as Rome is willing to tolerate less conformity and embrace a looser version of the way it conceives the integration of diverse nationalisms into one imperial state. Focusing on the epistle's literary structure to discern its political force, Taubes reads it as a carefully crafted polemical letter, delivered simultaneously to a congregation to which Paul does not belong and to an imperial order wary of competing kingships. He gives us a political Paul whose medium is a letter aimed at both challenging and seeking an accommodation between two estranged worlds. It's a missive with a "format," as Alain Badiou puts it, "in which the opportunity for action takes precedence over the preoccupation with making a name for oneself through publications."[43] Paul is selling a messiah to one and a reassurance to another. He is urging believers, who already have the license to resist participation in the cult of the emperor, to remain obedient to state authority.[44] Nietzsche is doubtless correct about the legitimating effect of Paul's "Romans": "At last the church was complete; it sanctioned even the existence of the state."[45]

Coover's Justin Miller is also a salesman. However, while Paul was a zealot, Miller is an opportunist. Utterly without religious commitment, Miller's project of promoting a new religious movement is an investment in practicing a journalism that sells newspapers. His medium is more the banner headline than the intricate and nuanced literary strategy, undertaken in an age in which print journalism has more impact than religious tracts. While Paul saw the "good news" as a story that effectively began with the crucifixion and would end with the post Parousia redemption of all believers, Miller, as befits a journalist whose temporal focus is the daily newspaper, saw all news episodically; "Miller perceived existence as a loose concatenation of separate and ultimately inconsequential instants, each colored by the actions that preceded it but each possessed of a small wanton freedom of its own."[46] Although he was selling Bruno's survival as a miracle, he was zealous only about earthly intimacies. He had become enamored of Bruno's sister Marcella, whom he saw almost daily and was taken with the "grace about everything she did … she was beautiful … Coming or going she caught a man's eye."[47] The eruption of Miller's desire is one moment among many in which Coover has interpersonal intimacies entangled with religious commitments throughout both novels.

As for his work on inventing a righteous Bruno, "Miller's interest in the man soon dissipated. What he saw was the browbeaten child turned egocentric psychopath, now upstaging it with his sudden splash of glory—a waste of time. But he made good copy."[48] Bruno himself aided the spiritualizing of the story. Adding spiritual credibility to Bruno's seemingly miraculous survival are his strange hallucinations about a "white bird." He frequently utters a six-word passage that sounds vaguely spiritual: "Hark ye to the white bird." The phrase adds enough creditability to the case for Bruno as a medium of the spirit for Miller to sell the story "nationally," while locally, the "white bird" remark is picked up by the cult as its apocalyptic slogan. As one believer, Clara Collins, says, "We must listen always to the white bird in our hearts. Abide in grace! The Son of God, *He is comin'! We will stand.*"[49]

While Miller, exploiting a latent communal will to believe, is selling his miracle, others in West Condon are involved in a different modality of community solidarity. One is a banker, Ted Cavanaugh, who "has faith in spirit" but resists "the little cult at the miner Bruno's house [which to him] seems too negative."[50] Entrepreneurial like Miller but civic-minded as well, Cavanaugh is also seeking to sell something. Joining the perennial battle between reason and revelation, but inflecting it within a marketing sensibility, he wants to promote "a community of good will … a third force … something to bring a little common sense to the community," which he explicitly figures as a sales issue: "Start with a specific problem, get the town enthused, as many people into the thing as possible, then subtly convert it into something positive, a kind of all-community WPA and sales team so to speak."[51]

Nevertheless, as key community leaders (among whom are Cavanaugh and the preacher Baxter with his own evangelical congregation) are resisting the cult while depending mainly on the medium of "word-of-mouth," cult members are deepening their commitments with symbiotic encounters in which the local dynamics of identity/difference serve to strengthen the hold of the cult. Illustrative of that effect—the way belief constitutes an event as it arises from an undercurrent of will—is the developing relationship between two characters, Ralph Himebaugh and Eleanor Norton. This passage is worthy of extensive quotation because it articulates the mediating effect of interpersonal encounters on the ability of print technology to shape events:

> The blossoming spiritual affair between Ralph Himebaugh and Eleanor Norton ... a disaster had thrown them together, two innocents surprised by fever and now their logbooks, their respective systems, were drawing their timid soils together in holy intercourse. In fact their two systems did fit together in the mating posture, one embracing from above, the other reaching up from below ... they both share ... hope for perfection. For final complete knowledge, and their different approaches actually complemented each other ... Eleanor's practical difficulty ... was in relating her inexpressible vision of the One to the tangible particulars of the in-the-world existence. And it was here where Himebaugh's constructions and proofs, founded on the cold data of newspaper reports, seemed to be of value, proving shortcuts ... to the relevant material within the impossible superfluity of sense data and enriching her own vision with useful kinds of imagery.[52]

Sociologist Edward Shils explains how such symbiotic moments enable spiritual belief systems to be "lived up to ... intermittently and only in an approximate way ... The ideals of prophets and saints can take root." He suggests, "only when they are attenuated, moderated, and compromised with other contradictory ideals ... Ideals and beliefs can only influence conduct alongside of personal ties."[53]

In short, as Coover's *The Origin of the Brunists* attests, the emergence of the town of West Condon's moment of a spiritual being-in-common, which has been precipitated by the mine disaster and the survival of Giovanni Bruno, is best considered as a contingent moment, mediated by what I have called the inner and outer religious theaters that have prepared the community for the print media's spiritualizing of an event. It also makes evident that the print media's construction of the event is subject to *re*mediation in interpersonal encounters.

As is often the case, such moments inspire collective attachments that persist beyond the interactions of a small affected community. Once such an event is widely disseminated to connect with broadly distributed susceptibilities, what begins as a small cult turns into a full-fledged religious movement. Coover pursues that transition. Having decided to imagine a situation in which the Brunist event has developed well beyond its origins, his follow-up novel (almost fifty years later), *The Brunist Day of Wrath*, begins back in West Condon, five years after the mine disaster. When the novel opens, the Brunists, thanks to the way media has disseminated their message, are well established. Although the newsman responsible for the original spread of the cult, Justin Miller, has moved to a new medium (he's a television broadcaster elsewhere), he's left behind the fruit of his work. Giovanni Bruno is the cult's prophet, and thanks to subsequent missionary work (for example, that of "Reverend Clegg, President of the International Council of Brunist Bishops" and "the most successful of the Brunist missionaries"),[54] the Brunists are now a geographically dispersed, institutionalized religious sect.

Their survival and expansion testify to an "extraordinary resilience": "Apocalypse can be disconfirmed [the experience of the original Brunists who waited in vain for the apocalypse] without being discredited."[55] There's an International Brunist Headquarters and an International Council of Brunist Bishops (2366); Bruno's "white dove" remark has been incorporated into a Brunist hymn; there are groundbreaking ceremonies underway for a new Brunist tabernacle; and the "Mount of Redemption," where the original Brunist cult had gathered for the apocalypse, has become a sacred place. As for the novel's drama: As the returned, much expanded cult faces both ideational and violent forms of opposition, it is not left to its own devices. While it tries to maintain its focus on rapture, chaotic forces turn West Condon into a battlefield. The figures, intrigues, and resources mobilized create an event that reproduces something like the Thirty Years' War, squeezed into a much smaller geographic space.

What Coover's follow-up treatment of the Brunists (involved in preparing for their second *Dies Irae*) animates is a contentious ideational atmosphere facing a contemporary apocalyptic religious movement. The novel's "normative mentality"[56] (resident in Coover's mediated voice) is doubtless articulated through Sally Elliott who (in a Hobbes-like soliloquy) explains to "Tommy," who is recently "home from university," that the Brunist religion is typical.

> What other kind of religion is there ... The plain truth, Tommy, is life is mostly crap, is very short, and ends badly. Not many people can live with that, so they buy into a happier setup somewhere else, another world where life's what you want it to be and nothing hurts and you don't die. That's religion.[57]

And in a later (Nietzschean) reflective moment, she says, "there's only now. And when that's insupportable, there isn't even that ... The hardest thing in life is to face the fact of nothingness without a consoling fantasy."[58]

Sally's voice contends with others as the novel's polyphonic form mobilizes what Bakhtin ascribes to the genre, the centrifugal force of competing sociolects. In this case, what occupies the town's space are the juxtapositions of the pious talk of the Brunists, the vernacular talk of some impious returnees to the town with secular (in some cases erotic) agendas, and the talk of the spiritually exhausted remnants of long-term residency, the religious (Baptists, Catholics, Lutherans, and Presbyterians) and non-religious, among whom are those seeking to maintain the basis for a common life (e.g., "the town banker Ted Cavanaugh [who has] created the Common Sense Committee to try to put the brakes on").[59] All are vying for ideational traction in the midst of chaos.

The arrival of the Brunists is for many experienced as another detonation in a town "still mourning its dead from the mine disaster of five years ago."[60] Ultimately what the novel realistically imagines is an episode of religious zeal competing for its share of communal sense in a fractionated town where alternative media genres shape competing world views. As for the returning Brunists: Although they have their texts (e.g., Giovanni Bruno's "white bird" utterance), "the Brunist faith rests wholly on historical events,"[61] while in contrast, the Presbyterian minister, John Wesley, whose religious commitment is more a career than a faith, seeks to stabilize his perspective on life by reading the philosophico-religious texts in "his old course notes [running] from Augustine and Abelard to Kierkegaard, Kant, Buber, and Tillich,"[62] and another character "gets all her advice from trashy romance rags."[63]

By way of transition, I want to suggest that Coover's novelistic focus on a belief-inspiring moment and its follow-up trajectory—an extended story in which a small cult becomes a global religion that has been spurred by both print and broadcast media (and is persisting in the midst of competing world views)—is an encouragement to explore the way alternative media technologies can exploit the will to believe and effectuate different ways of being "in common." In the next section, I pursue that exploration.

Technologies of Common Sense

My heading opens up a vast historical trajectory from which I will select one event, Martin Luther's revolt, which created, among other things, the *reading* "congregation," which displaced religious authority from the church hierarchy to the assemblage of believers.[64] As is well known, because of the coincidence of the development of printing technology his rebellion achieved a rapid dissemination. Luther's reform precipitated "the West's first large-scale media campaign."[65] It unfolded "with a rapidity that had been impossible before its invention."[66] Crucial to that rapid dissemination was the form of the publication. "[T]he small booklet or pamphlet as a tool of propaganda and agitation" had been perfected. The pamphlets were "handy, relatively cheap, readily concealed and transported, and accordingly well suited for delivering their message to a large popular audience ... They were ideal for circulating a subversive message right under the noses of the opponents of reform."[67] Luther's writing strategy also contributed to the influence of his message. As Andrew Pettegree points out in his contemporary figuring of the Luther effect (his *Brand Luther*), Luther "invented a new form of theological writing: short, clear, direct, speaking not only to his professional peers but to the wider Christian people ... [a] style, purpose, and form [that was] at the heart of the Reformation."[68]

Fredric Jameson picks up on that figuration: "After Luther," he writes, "religion comes in competing brands [at least as far as Christendom is concerned]."[69] To put it more elaborately, much of the rapid spread of the "brand" was owed to the variety of printed literatures Luther's rebellion instigated: "The increased availability of vernacular bible translations, the controversies called forth by the production of editions of older theological and philosophical texts, and the simultaneous evolution of theological disputes through pamphlets and printed books were accompanied by a growing diversification in Christian communities, which ... developed a variety of 'literary cultures.'"[70] The aftermath of the Reformation was among other things a historically extended encounter between alternative "conceptual worlds," based on two binaries—an "opposition between oral tradition and written word" and between symbolic icons and texts.[71]

With the roles of both "brands" and "texts" in mind, I want to point to a contemporary advertising text with broad distribution. The "True Religion" jeans company, doubtless aware of the proliferation of religious brands, has printed on the inside of the left leg of all their jeans, the slogan, "There are many religions in the world, but everybody wears jeans." Their implicit argument is that if there is any force that nurtures a global community of sense, it is the worldwide, enduring appeal of jeans as a clothing style. Inspired by the relationships among personal styles, commerce and religion, and the effect of that interrelationship on belief, I turn to a science fiction text, Philip Dick's *The Three Stigmata of Palmer Eldritch*, which draws on the almost universally recognized, fashion-exhibiting icons, the Mattel Toy company's Barbie and Ken dolls, reinventing them as Perky Pat and her boyfriend Walt. The couple, the main products in Leo Bulero's P. P. Layouts (a business design strategy company), appear as a shared hallucination within an illusory world that is entered by all those—in an exilic community living on Mars—who take the drug Can-D.

The pharmaceutical Can-D has replaced traditional community-creating and consolidating technologies, for example, scriptures, which thanks to printing technologies and vernacular translations had become "[f]or Catholics and Evangelicals ... *the* premier authority. All parties agreed that the church and its beliefs rested ultimately on Scripture."[72] Alert to the influence of scriptures and at the same time ambivalent about traditional religious transcendence (e.g., Sam, a Mars-dwelling character in the novel refers to, "Spirituality [as a] ... A denial of reality"), Dick's novel juxtaposes scripture-based religion to pharmaceutical technology and stages a clash on Mars between alternative communities of sense. Religion enters the narrative on two fronts. One involves a chemical war between Leo Bulero's manufactured pharmaceutical, Can-D, and Palmer Eldritch, an aspiring theocrat's competing hallucinogenic, Chew-Z. The other involves a clash between old and new media, between a textual community, Christianity, whose adherents find themselves in Dick's futuristic epoch as "Neo-Christians" that have become a "cognitive minority,"[73] embracing a venerable media platform (sacred texts), and a futuristic community ideationally fused by a bio-semiotic medium that penetrates bodies rather than merely proliferating signs aimed at inducing belief. The new media in the novel are pharmaceutically altered mentalities that fuse into an affective symbiosis among users, a shared sensuality rather than a shared spirituality. Community among the Can-D users eventuates because of the way the drug seizes mentality and imposes affect.

The speculative nature of Dick's imaginative construction of a futuristic community-creating technology is a critical intervention into historical time. His invention of an alternative community-creating technology effectively renders the entire historical trajectory of shared temporal experience radically contingent. It is in accord with Bernard Stiegler's observation that the bases of communities of sense are fragile. Over time they form and reform as a result of the continual "adoption" of a new technology, which "constructs communities" as it connects people in new ways.[74]

Philip Dick's Drug-Induced Community of Sense

To elaborate the theological clashes that Dick's novel stages on Mars: First, as I have noted, Dick's novel draws on the consumption-inspiring social contexts evoked in the Mattel toy company's Barbie and Ken doll variations and articulates those banal fashion icons with a drug-induced communal bonding. Specifically, the drug, Can-D, creates a fusion/translation experience that forges a community among a group of colonists on Mars by projecting them into the Barbie and Ken type dolls Perky Pat and her boyfriend Walt. The experience constitutes the planet's singular collective religious experience, which is disrupted by two uninvited interventions. One is by the above-noted aspirational tyrant, Palmer Eldritch, who intervenes with a competing pharmaceutical, Chew-Z, a drug that produces a psychosis-like reaction, an intensification of the Can-D fantasy. Rather than forging a consensual community with the consensual hallucinations that Can-D induces, Eldritch's product enslaves the minds of the colonists, placing their shared hallucinations under his domination.

Whether bonded through Can-D or Chew-Z, the Mars colonists are constructed to mimic Christian sects. They identify themselves in pseudo-religious terms as believers and evoke a Pauline commitment to the spirit over the flesh, hoping to enjoy Paul's promise of eternity for those who eschew the flesh. As Paul's admonition goes, "For the flesh desires what is contrary to the Spirit, and the Spirit what is contrary to the flesh. They are in conflict with each other, so that you are not to do whatever you want" (Galatians 5: 17). The Mars drug-using community puts it similarly: "We lose our fleshly bodies, our corporeality … And put on imperishable bodies instead, for a time … Or forever, if you believe as some do that it's outside of time and space, that it's eternal."[75] The second theological clash pits the community's narco-induced religious life against the more traditional, scriptural version of Christianity brought by Anne Hawthorne, a "Neo Christian" who shows up as an advocate of Christianity's older media platform, scriptures. Her appearance evokes an earlier religious encounter on Mars, when the mind-fused community had ejected a couple of Neo-Christians the previous year.

Palmer Eldritch's intervention is also figured as a clash between alternative Christianity-like religions. He too figures the Chew-Z bonding effect in a Christian idiom, claiming that it delivers what Paul's "good news" had promised but not fulfilled.

> Well you got what St. Paul promises, as Anne Hawthorne was blabbing about; you're no longer clothed in a perishable, fleshly body—you've put on an ethereal body in its place … You can't die; you don't eat or drink or breathe air … you'll learn in time. Evidently on the road to Damascus Paul experienced a vision related to this phenomenon.[76]

Subsequent to the staging of a clash among religious communities of sense in his *Three Stigmata*, Dick undertook a more thoroughgoing set of speculations on religious experience in a series of novels inspired by a personal religious experience, a theophany not unlike the one that allegedly affected Paul on "the road to Damascus." Although the experience recruited Dick into a version of Christianity, his dedication to religion operated at the level of meta belief rather than encouraging an unambivalent will to believe. Throughout his fictional corpus, rather than unambiguously valorizing religion, he challenges its orthodoxies. I reserve an analysis of Dick's philosophico-theological speculations for a later chapter. Here, by way of transition I want to pursue the issue of the will to believe, which distills the primary force driving religious commitment, by referencing the thinking of Michel de Certeau. De Certeau's analysis of everyday life extends the concept of the will to believe from media-vulnerable believers to those (e.g., Dick's Palmer Eldritch) seeking to influence them.

Resisting a representational model of belief assertions, de Certeau, with a William James-like gesture, "define[s] 'belief' not as the object of believing (a dogma, a program, etc.) but as the subject's investment in a proposition, the act of saying it and considering it as true, in other words a 'modality' of the assertion and not its content."[77] He goes on to treat the function of legitimation, suggesting that the "link between politics and religion" inheres in "the capacity for believing [met by] the functioning of 'authority,'" where the latter exercises a "will to '*make* people believe'" (my emphasis).[78] However, while de Certeau tries to save the integrity of the belief function by turning to what he calls "practiced believing," which "transgresses political dogma and belongings," an "ecclesiology that relates to but remains far wider than any institutionalized church,"[79] I want to resist that redemptive gesture and question the epistemic value of beliefs by contrasting an aesthetic focus.

Belief versus an Aesthetics of Knowledge

As Rancière elaborates his evocation of the pervasive spatiality of thought and the critical value of an aesthetics of knowledge in which the contingencies of the thinkable can be assessed, he employs the figure of the *topos*, which can help us sort out the complementarities and tensions between belief and knowledge. To illustrate that sorting, I return briefly to Dick's *Three Stigmata* because "an aesthetics of knowledge" is effectively what Dick juxtaposes to the belief systems that structure the ideational antagonisms on his fictional planet of Mars. As Rancière insists, knowledge always requires fictional presuppositions that deliver the *topos* of a world. In his words, knowledge requires a "fabric [i.e., a story or narrative presupposition] within which the articulation of the knowledge can be believed, within which it can operate."[80] Thus when I referred to the meta belief level at which Dick's perspective is operating, I was referencing the aesthetic context within which he supplies a critical aesthetics of knowledge. As his novel suggests, the alternative communities of sense on Mars are welded together by alternative technologies, scriptures and pharmaceuticals, respectively, which shape and assemble competing communal coherences out of the existing wills to believe. They are the media technologies that create the conditions of possibility for alternative ways of being in common. Abetting those technologies are the mythic frames within which the "in common" comes to be in Dick's novel. One is the Christian imaginary, the story of the resurrection and redemption that derives from the original biblical *topos*, what Nietzsche refers to as the "Jewish landscape" containing a "wrathful Jehovah ... brooding continually" and thereby creating the opening for a "savior," a Jesus Christ.[81] The other is a commercial story, the version of American domesticity for which the Barbie and Ken type dolls (Perky Pat and her boyfriend Walt) are representatives. Both "landscapes" presume dual worlds. Whereas the Judeo-Christian imaginary is committed to "another world behind the observable world,"[82] the dual world in the Barbie and Ken imaginary is an actual world of living and striving haunted, by a judgmental world of regulative ideals that prescribe attention to the looks and styles that sell the products with which the dolls represent the masculine-feminine binary that the Mattel toy company (and most Americans) embraces.

Dick's aesthetic perspective "neutralizes" the context of the encounter, Rancière's term for how an aesthetic of knowledge operates by deprivileging any particular connection between sense and sense that the two belief structures practice (where the former "sense" is the phenomenologically anticipated experience of the life world and the latter "sense" is the judgment about how that experience should be understood).[83] A turn to an aesthetics of knowledge therefore demonstrates that knowing needs a fictional context to operate, where by "fiction" one is not referring to illusion but rather a narratively formed *topos* that situates subjects in a spatio-temporal modality that gives knowing its ideational and practical contexts. To the extent that the *topos* supplied is critical, it creates an "aesthetic break" in which the radical historical contingencies of the in-common are revealed and the problem of being-in-common is open to reframing. As Rancière puts it, critical artistic practices create a "dissociation: a break in a relationship between sense and sense" and therein lies the potential for the impact on thinking politically.[84]

In order to apply Rancière's notion of the political implications of aesthetic breaks to the primary technology through which religious beliefs have been developed and focused, I turn to two creative fictions, focused on biblical scripture, that articulate the "Jewish landscape," both of which reorient the sense in which the Hebrew bible can be read, and more specifically, both of which are reinterpretations in which the bible's patriarchal structure is radically challenged. The two (re)readings of scriptures—Mieke Bal's reading of *The Book of Judges*, and Harold Bloom's addition of an author to the Hebrew bible as a whole—have the effect of unfixing the bible's Rabbinic-enforced tradition, not unlike what the young generation in Morrison's *Paradise* effect when they revise the slogan on the communal oven.

Mieke Bal's *Death & Dissymmetry*

In her reading of *The Book of Judges*, the art historian Mieke Bal deflects attention from traditional exegeses whose narrative coherence is based on "the geography of the land to be conquered." Elevating the significance of the female body in the biblical story, she provides what she calls a "counter-coherence" in which the focus is on the household so that we are able "to realize how deeply a violence is anchored in the domestic domain."[85] However, Bal goes well beyond merely interpreting that violence in which patriarchal judges, Jephthah among others, murder female family members. She subjectivizes a woman who has been left nameless. In the biblical narration of the story, in return for Jehovah's grant of a victory over the Ephraimites, Jephthah promises to kill the first person who greets him after his victory; it turns out to be his daughter. In order to lend Jephthah's daughter a subject position, Bal gives her a name, Bath Jephthah, and connects her fate to those of other female domestic victims that canonical readings pass over in order to tell the national story, which is about how one man, Abraham, becomes a nation through the deeds of heroic men. Bal's shifting of spaces and diegetic agents tells a different political story, one in which women in the domestic sphere achieve the recognition that they are deprived of in the dominant exegetical tradition of bible scholarship. She shifts the story from the land to be conquered to the houses to be conquered, to the places where the interaction between the political and the domestic is located (places where "daughters ... meet there undoing," i.e., are murdered by Israelite patriarchs). In short Bal alters the emphasis with respect to the kinds of lives that can be seen as politically qualified rather than being regarded (in Giorgio Agamben's terms) as mere "bare life," life that can be destroyed without juridico-political consequences. On Bal's reading, the domestic space takes on a political significance that it lacks in canonical readings, and women who live nameless, politically unqualified lives become important political subjects.

Bloom's *Book of J*

Nietzsche's ironic remark about the authorship of the bible, "It was a piece of subtle refinement that God learned Greek when he wanted to become a writer, and that he didn't learn it better,"[86] reminds us that Jehovah's primary mode of presence is as a media personality who is scripted by other hands. "He" is not of his own making. Moreover, as Freud famously suggests, he has a split personality. Alongside the snarky irritable God belonging to Israelite lore is the warm nurturing one, which Freud suggests is the god invented by the Egyptian Ikhnaton (whom Moses gave to the Israelites when he was unable successfully to impose it on Egyptians).[87] However one might warrant the evidence for Freud's particular version, it is clear that multiple (earthly) writers are responsible for the text. The literary scholar Harold Bloom, assisted by the translator David Rosenberg, adds a speculative author in order to radicalize and reorder the text's assemblage of voices, arguing that the version given to modernity privileges the imperatives of patriarchal priestly authority.

With a creative (i.e., fictional) translation, Bloom and Rosenberg invent or extract a different kind of author, a woman to whom they give the name J. Identifying her as plausibly a member of King Solomon's court, they have her emerge in their translation as an ironist rather than a mere chronicler, one who creates a very different more capricious Yahweh.[88] Articulating the bible as a multi-authored text they, like Bal, engage in a literary act of subjectification that alters the belief fabric within which interpretation of the bible can occur. What they offer is a gendered otherness within a history of spiritual authority that is "disjunctive with the normative Judaism made familiar by Judeo-Christian theologians."[89]

Importantly, the Bal and Bloom interventions into scriptural interpretation go well beyond disputes about what is ethically warranted by scripture—for example, a recent one in which it is disclosed that while the current version of the biblical book of Leviticus has passages that proscribe (on pain of death) homosexuality: "You shall not lie with a male as with a woman." "[A]n earlier version of the text permitted it," putting believers who rely on the text for their views of moral conduct in a quandary.[90] While the revelation of alternative versions of Leviticus can affect belief orthodoxies, the belief issue raised by the Bal and Bloom analyses alters the potential belief-knowledge relationship as a whole, where "belief" in this case is what Rancière refers to the "fabric within which the articulation of knowledge can be believed." Rather than entering a debate about what a particular version of the biblical text says and thus what is to be accepted by believers, they shift the entire belief context to what Rancière designates as the "as if,"[91] which affects the kind of ethico-political knowledge the text can deliver. While the Leviticus controversy is about an effect of alternative versions of what to believe, the Bal and Bloom interventions are changes in the politics of biblical aesthetics, a shift in the belief frame, the "as if" within which knowledge is articulated. That difference between the two ways in which belief is situated with respect to the biblical text speaks to the issue I want now to pursue, the epistemic relationship between belief and knowledge.

The Will to Believe, the Will to Knowledge

Rancière's turn to the arts for purposes of political critique has a venerable historical patrimony. For purposes here, I am selecting one intellectual inheritance within that history, the trajectory that runs from Nietzsche to Foucault with a focus on the arts of the self, elaborated extensively in

Foucault's 1982–1983 lectures on "The Government of Self and Others." There his concern is with "the focal points of experience"[92] (an emphasis that accords with Rancière's perspective on the fabric within which knowledges are generated) and on the "will to truth," which he treats in earlier lectures, 1970–1971 on "The Will to Know."[93]

There are several places in Foucault's corpus that provide critiques of the existence of transcendent, eternal values that parade through history and are external to human valuing practices. Here I want to select one that performs concisely the role of the critique of universals and the "eternal." In his lectures on "The Will to Knowledge" Foucault juxtaposes a genealogical reading to a Freudian interpretation of the Oedipus myth. Opposing Freud's version of Oedipus as a pedagogy on desire, he renders it as a pedagogy on the system of truth. Crucial to the demonstration is an appendix assembled from fragments that he had not gone into during the performed lecture. There Foucault writes, "Freud thought that he was hearing desire speaking, whereas it was the *echo* of his own true discourse"[94] (my emphasis), and earlier he noted, "Freud thought that Oedipus was speaking to him about the universal forms of desire, whereas, in lowered voice, the Oedipus fable was recounting to him the historical constraint weighing on our system of truth."[95] William James—also using the figure of an echo as a critique—goes even farther; he questions the very concept of consciousness *tout court*, asserting, "those who still cling to it are clinging to a mere echo, the faint rumor left behind by the disappearing 'soul' … the time is ripe for it to be openly and universally discarded."[96] While James's reference to the echo is associated with his radical version of empiricism, Foucault turns to the figure to point to the contingencies of knowledge. Resistant to commitments to transcendent truths, his concern has been with shifting historical moments that shape practices of knowledge. For Foucault, the question was always about what particular interests and contingent epistemological orders combine to prompt the knowledge and thus truth questions raised at various times, about what particular truths about ourselves have we been asked to reveal at various historical junctions. In effect Foucault joins hands across the centuries with Machiavelli, who as much as any thinker in the political theory canon recognized and endeavored to foreground the importance of seeing ourselves not as eternal beings within the cosmos but as historical beings because with an appreciation of the latter, we become civic rather than religious subjects with all of the implications of that ontological shift for concrete political engagement.

The echo figure that James and Foucault evoke—to suggest that adherence to consciousness is a leftover quasi-religious commitment once centered on the soul for the former and to rethink the pedagogy of the Oedipus myth for the latter—brings me back to the problem of religious belief. In Ingmar Bergman's *Winter Light* (1963) (a film to which I return in Chapter 3), there's a telling encounter. The film's main protagonist, the pastor Tomas Ericsson (Gunnar Björnstrand), is in conversation with a parishioner, Jonas Persson (Max Von Sydow), who is traumatized by the possibility of nuclear apocalypse. He has read in the regional newspaper that when the Chinese get the bomb, they're likely to destroy the planet. Tomas proves unable to offer reassurance because he is as afflicted as Jonas. He feels alienated from his vocation because his prayers are unanswered; God will not reveal himself. After asking Jonas about his work, his health, and his marriage (in a search for what afflicts him), he turns the focus on himself. Telling Jonas that he will be frank with him, he rambles on about his own despair at having lost his faith: "My God and I resided in an organized world where everything made sense .... I put my faith in an improbable private image of a fatherly god ... an *echo* god who gave benign answers and reassuring blessings."[97]

Among what we can infer from the film is the importance attributed to the utterances of Christianity's paternal authorities (Jonas's wife had brought him to the pastor for counseling). In this case, the pastor is no longer able to take his role seriously. He cannot function as an adequate "father" because *he* has experienced an inadequate father. "God-the-father" fails to function as a father for him because of "His" silence. A relay for that virtual father, the pastor-as-father is undone and is no match for the print media's fear mongering. For Pastor Tomas, both the internal and external theaters have lost their spiritual cogency. Neither serves as a plausible placeholder for divine spirit and the solace he has been seeking. In effect he is telling Jonas that his inner theater is merely the echo of his will to believe. And as for the external theater, which consists of Christianity's venerable icons—Jesus on the cross, praying saints, and so on that decorate the altar of his church—they disgust him. At one point, as he looks up at the suffering Jesus on the cross in the center of the altar, he says, "what a ridiculous image."

Reemphasizing the concept of the "inner theater" I borrowed from Deleuze's reading of Proust, I want to suggest that we can fashion a phenomenological subject as one involved in theatrical composition rather than mere perception, i.e., one writing and staging a conceptual and affective inner drama that anticipates and provides a structure to frame events in which religious belief is being portrayed or contested. To elaborate I want to rehearse a drama of reception of *Winter Light* reported by the writer Tobias Wolff, who describes an evening in 1970 when as a young man of twenty-five attending Oxford University in the UK, he and a friend, Rob, whom he describes as a "witty and easygoing drinking buddy," decided to attend Bergman's film, which was showing for free in a local church. He adds, "I wasn't a churchgoer, nor was Rob, but neither of us had seen the movie, and, after all, it was Bergman, and free, so we went."

Wolff provides a brief and effective synopsis of Bergman's *Winter Light*:

Tomas, a Lutheran pastor and widower, is suffering a crisis of faith, barely going through the motions of his ministry; indeed, he can't even find the heart to treat his lover, a schoolteacher, with kindness. One of his parishioners has become obsessed with the prospect of nuclear annihilation. At his wife's urging, this man, a fisherman, comes to the pastor for reassurance, some blessed word of hope that he can grasp as a lifeline, but Tomas can offer nothing but the bleakness of his own despair. The fisherman commits suicide.

Wolff goes on to describe how the film played in *his* inner theater, as he recomposes it.

It is a harrowing experience, this film, shot starkly in the winter light of its title and filled with wintry silences, the camera often unmoving in its scrutiny of the human face in anguish, uncertainty, and yearning. When the movie ended, we all sat there as if stunned. I used the word 'harrowing'. Truly I felt harrowed, crust broken, buried things churning to the surface.

As a result, Wolff was initially inclined to stay for a discussion of the film to be led by the church's minister, who began the discussion by having a projectionist show a painting of Jesus by William Holman Hunt, "The Light of the World." The image effectively chased Wolff from the church:

> Let me say that up to that moment I'd been listening, really listening, attentive as the fisherman for an answer to the bleakness of our situation. And this minister was no Tomas: he was clear and confident, he knew he had that answer, and I'd begun to feel a sense of grudging assent—not surrender but the first stirrings—when that picture appeared. And then I lost it …. It seemed to me a typical Pre-Raphaelite production: garish, melodramatic, cloying in its technique and sentimentality; pretentious humbug … Was this what the minister held in his mind as the answer to all our problems—a kitschy figure from a calendar? I turned to Rob. "Let's get a pint."

As it turned out, Rob was writing a different play; the two underwent entirely different aesthetic breaks:

> But Rob was intent on this very image. Rapt, he barely glanced at me. "You go on." That night—to some extent, that picture—changed his life. He enrolled in Bible classes at the church, and went on to become a missionary in Africa …. Only in theory do we begin to suspect the power of aesthetics to shape our lives.[98]

Tobias's and Rob's different responses to an image illustrate the contingencies of the image—belief relationship and the phenomenological bases of their difference. In keeping with how I have figured the phenomenology of such experiences, it turned out that the "playwrights," Tobias and Rob, wrote different inchoate scripts. They were "unconsummated" authors; they were (in M. M. Bakhtin's terms) "axiologically yet to be" writers who were becoming ethical subjects.[99] Foucault addresses that "becoming" with remarks that situate the approach to phenomenology I want to endorse and elaborate throughout this investigation. In a conversation about what he refers to as an "experience-book," Foucault says that when he writes he seeks to transform himself, "not to think the same thing as before."[100] For Foucault, writing practices should be regarded in the same way as philosophical practices; they are practices of "the self on the self."[101] As the conversation proceeds, Foucault juxtaposes his self-changing approach to writing with the conventional phenomenological approach to subjectivity, which, he says, "tries to grasp the significance of daily experience in order to reaffirm the fundamental character of the subject."[102] Rejecting that approach and identifying with a phenomenology of writing he ascribes to "Nietzsche, Blanchot, and Bataille," Foucault conceives the purpose of the writing "task as one of 'tearing' the subject from itself in such a way that it is no longer the subject as such, or that it is completely 'other' than itself … a 'desubjectifying undertaking.'"[103] Bertold Brecht would doubtless endorse Foucault's writing pedagogy. Referring to *his* writing he remarks, "I, the writer, don't have to finish something. It is enough that I instruct myself."[104] Moreover, inclined as he was as a dramatist to heed audience reception and view a work as endlessly completed by those who view it, Brecht adds, "I am only leading the examination and it is my method which can be examined by the audience."[105]

Brecht's "method," in which he regards his audiences as writing collaborators, presumes that intersubjective encounters are encounters between becoming subjects struggling to either contain, acknowledge, incorporate, or contend with others. Accepting that presumption, the question I want to entertain is about how to imagine the possibility of a community of sense among "playwrights" encountering each other while involved in staging themselves and the world within such incommensurate plots as the ones described by Tobias Wolff. To elaborate that metaphor and conceptualize the version of phenomenology I am pursuing—a collaboration and contention among playwrights—I turn to Jean Luc Nancy's notion of the "inoperative community," where he explicitly renders community members as writers. Proffering a model of community that contrasts with various consensual models—for example, Jurgen Habermas's well-known version based on communicative consensus—Nancy's version is based on what he refers to as the "unworking of communication." It is a model that accommodates a view of society's incommensurable modes of presence in which there are no stable spaces and thus no secure identity boundaries. To the extent that a community of sense exists, it is an in-common of diverse "'particularities' … not founded on any autonomous essence."[106] Being in common for Nancy involves "only a juncture,"[107] the sharing of spaces of encounter. As for the medium with which we can characterize such a version of the in-common, Nancy suggests that community can be framed as a "community of literature," as what I have elsewhere referred to as "an uneasy and conflictual articulation of … writing performances."[108] Finally I want to suggest that in order to sustain a commitment to being-in-common, in place of forms of communal coherence based on wills to believe, playwrights operating from their own theatrical productions must practice a form of *good* will, which I will characterize (after the work of William Connolly) as "agonistic respect," which is based on an ethos that encourages us to approach others involved in incommensurate reality productions with uncertainty, hesitancy, and forbearance.[109]

The Politics of Zealotry: Situating the Apostle Paul

Zealotries on and off the Road

In his crime novel *Lucky You* (1991), Carl Hiaasen invents an encounter that illuminates the way right-wing zealotry becomes a collective sensibility. Early in the story, he describes, with cinematic detail, two men (who ultimately hatch a plan to rob a lottery winner) getting out of a Dodge Ram truck after coming off the road and entering a convenience store:

> Bode Gazzer was five feet six and had never forgiven his parents for it. He wore three-inch snakeskin shitkickers and walked with a swagger that suggested not brawn so much as hemorrhoidal tribulation. Chub was a beer-gutted six two, moist-eyed, ponytailed and unshaven. He carried a loaded gun at all times and was Bode Gazzer's best and only friend. They had known each other two months.[1]

What helps me initiate my analysis of the media through which zealotry spreads its world view is the ideational symbiosis that takes place once Hiaasen has Gazzer, a poacher, and Chub, a counterfeiter in conversation.

> Chub never thought of himself as having a political agenda until he met Bode Gazzer, who helped organize Chub's multitude of hatreds into a single venomous philosophy … [e.g.] 'Oklahoma', Bode Gazzer said sharply, 'and that was the government did it, to frame those two white boys. No, I'm talking 'bout a militia. Armed, disciplined and well-regulated, like it says in the Second Amendment'.[2]

The familiar Gazzer-Chubb shared sensibility that Hiaasen creates has counterparts in other historical periods in which zealous mentalities have developed from encounters. One is captured in Leonardo Padura's novelistic biography of Leon Trotsky's assassin, Ramón Mercader. In Mercader's case, he is recruited to enter history as he gets radicalized during a number of encounters in disparate national venues.[3] Among those that prepare him for his leap into history is one with África de las Heras:

> Her parents named her África, like the patron saint of Ceuta, where she had been born, and rarely had a name fit someone so well: because she was vigorous, unfathomable, and wild, like the continent to whom she owed her name. Ever since the day he met her, at a meeting of the Young Communists of Cataluña, Ramón felt absorbed by the young woman's beauty, but above all, it was her rock-solid ideas and her telluric drive that ensnared him: África de las Heras was like an erupting volcano who roared a permanent clamor for revolution.[4]

Like the apostle Paul's addressees, whom he tells to wait expectantly for Christ's return, Ramón experiences a "tense environment, in which everyone was expecting something to happen very soon … it was as if his life and history had been lying in wait for each other."[5] Once he becomes known as a reliable zealot, he's selected by Stalin's agents to be Trotsky's assassin. During his training he takes "theoretical classes" in the Soviet Union and is turned into "soldier 13": "a man of marble, convinced of the need to carry out whatever mission was asked of him," which turns out to be the mission that brought him to Mexico for the planned assassination (accomplished in August 1940).[6]

The influence of Gazzer on Chub and de las Heras and others on Mercader is captured in Jean Paul Sartre's remark, "Words wreck havoc when they happen to name something that is experienced but is not yet named."[7] However, Sartre's remark needs a supplement, a specification of the ideational susceptibilities, historical situations, and media genres within which words generate their effects. Hiaasen framed the reactionary political allegiance shared and interpersonally enhanced in the relationship between his characters in 1991, and Padura's becoming-assassin was shaped earlier. Their respective zealots became media-influenced believers well before the internet (the contemporary ecumene) had become a medium for generating and spreading broadly and rapidly various forms of zealotry—e.g., "far-right message boards," a media platform that explicates the "chaos of contemporary life," substituting "conspiracy theories" for the mythic, religion-inspired "cosmic battles between God and the devil to explain the problem of evil."[8]

In what follows I reach back historically to an older media genre, the letter, an ideational vehicle used by Paul to disseminate a different kind of zealotry, albeit one also incubated on the road. Specifically, I analyze and contextualize Paul's revolutionary political theology, which initiated an inchoate Christian ecumene, a proto-Christianity struggling to survive within the one over which Rome ruled and follow with attention to contemporary remediations of Paul (in theological, philosophical, and cinematic genres), which bring him back—within a variety of interpretive frames—to negotiate current ethico-political issues. Paul's mission was a radical, post-revelation change in which he exchanged one form of zealotry for another. As Saul, Luke informs us, "he joined the hotheads who stoned Stephen, the first martyr for Jesus" and went on to Judea where he "raided gatherings, going house to house, dragging men and women off to prison" (Acts of the Apostles 8.3) before moving on to the foreign land where a revelation prompted him to quit the persona, Saul the zealous policing agent, and adopt "Paul," a zealous apostle with a different mission, one as a self-declared "emissary from Jesus-Messiah" (Galatians 1.1).[9] As the latter, proselytizing in behalf of a supernatural event—the crucifixion and resurrection of Christ—his epistles are a place where the supernatural is summoned to renegotiate the condition of life and the living.

Representations of the supernatural have also been featured in non-sacred texts in which the condition of life is addressed and renegotiated. Hence in order to broaden the frame, I want to skip momentarily to the present and illustrate the participation of another media genre in negotiating vitality (the ontological situation of life) by noting Eugene Thacker's analysis of a contemporary genre in which the concept of life is a source of critical reflection. In a section he entitles, "Supernatural Horror as the paradigm for life," Thacker engages a writing genre that "pulp magazines" refer to as "weird fiction ... supernatural horror," which was featured on mid-twentieth-century television (e.g., shows such as *Twilight Zone* and *Outer Limits*). Thacker regards those shows and their legacy ("in the Japanese horror boom of the late twentieth and early twenty-first centuries") as a "'cult' tradition in which the stories contain thought-provoking insights into the concept of 'life.'" The genre has a critical force because, "what is horrific is not just [that] nameless things are still alive," e.g., a "babel of noises utterly alien to all that we know of the earth and its organic life, [things] ... dormantly alive," "vitality" provoking, but that "in their living they evoke ... the limits of thought—the limits of thought to think 'life' at all."[10]

Paul's epistles, which are often read in terms of the orthodoxies they promote, also have a radical import with respect to how to rethink life. For example, in Romans 12: 2, he writes, "Also, do not be conformed to this world, but be transformed by the renewal of the mind." That remark accords with contemporary critical philosophical observations, for example, Gilles Deleuze and Felix Guattari's suggestion that those who can merely communicate are "functionaries" able only to manage "ready-made thought."[11] They dwell in the realm of "opinions,"[12] locked within "the forces of recognition," unable to exercise an imagination of possibilities of "*terra incognita*."[13] However, the second part of Paul's statement, "that you may ascertain what is the will of God—the good and acceptable and perfect," blunts the radicalism of the first part. There, as throughout his letters, what Paul offers by way of radical thinking he compromises by positing a mythic externality to which all transformed thought must adhere.

I treat the role of an "externality" in approaches to life in the chapter's conclusion. Here I begin a pursuit of the spatio-temporal and media conditions under which Paul's letters were composed and sent, with special attention to their textual production, in order to consider what is singular about the historical moment in which his proselytizing spatial odyssey occurred. That consideration is central to Martin Heidegger's comprehensive (and largely pious) analysis of Paul's epistles: "Paul gives his doctrine and directs his warning wholly in the manner of the Stoic-Cynic wandering preachers of the time."[14] Accordingly, as I approach the conversation about life that his epistles initiate, I emphasize the significance of encounters on the road where Paul's epistles met their recipients. And with the significance of the road in view, I situate Paul as a mobile carrier of the will to believe (propagating "with militant vigor"[15] his version of the implications of the Christ event) by conceptualizing his symbolic and physical journey with resort to M. M. Bakhtin's concept of the artistic chronotope, especially his elaboration of "the chronotope of the road":

In the literary artistic chronotope, spatial and temporal indicators are fused into one carefully thought-out whole. Time, as it were, thickens, takes on flesh, becomes artistically visible; likewise, space becomes charged and responsive to the movements of time, plot and history. The intersection of axes and fusion of indicators characterizes the artistic chronotope.[16] [The] chronotope of the road [features] both a point of new departures and a place for events to find their denouement. Time, as it were, fuses together with space and flows in it (forming the road) ... the road is especially (but not exclusively) for portraying events governed by chance ... [thus] the important narrative role of the road in the history of the novel.[17]

Importantly for purposes of treating Paul's encounters, Bakhtin describes an intimate connection between "the motif of the meeting and the chronotope of the road."[18] It's a temporal figuration that applies well to cinematic as well as literary genres, which I explore with an analysis of Pasolini's Paul screenplay. Pasolini's script celebrates and at the same time destabilizes Paul's epistolary journey. As a commentary on the critical effect of Pasolini's cinematic biblical adaptations puts it, "the carrying across of the biblical text into a filmic medium—disrupts the boundaries of canonicity, interrupts the 'biblical' nature of the Gospel, and foregrounds the instability of authoritative claims about scriptural meanings."[19]

To prepare the analysis of the screenplay, I theorize Paul's historical situation with an emphasis on phenomenological approaches to temporality as well as on the effects of media genres on the dissemination of his message. Thereafter, while treating the screenplay, I emphasize the way Pasolini restages Paul's physical and literary journey cinematically in a contemporary period, placing him in several locations as he extracts a contemporary political pedagogy from Paul (which several others have recently attempted—Giorgio Agamben, Alain Badiou, and Slavoj Žižek, among others—all revisiting the issue of "the genuinely vital life,"[20] albeit with different ethico-political emphases). After considering the diverse approaches to Paul's revolutionary significance, I end by suggesting a way to render a critical politically oriented view of life that substitutes open and continuing negotiation for the closural impulses of the will to believe. Meanwhile, recognizing that Paul, as Badiou puts it, was "a poet-thinker of the event," one that involves "a rupture, an overturning,"[21] my analysis turns to the concept of the event in order to situate Paul's event-oriented discursive practice.[22]

Events

Here I endorse a conception of an "event" that Slavoj Žižek suggests. What constitutes an event is "the effect that seems to exceed its causes … a shattering transformation of reality itself."[23] The Czech writer, Ivan Klima, provides a ready-to-hand example: "[I]n a world where enormous shower rooms are built just to poison people, life can never be the same again."[24] In Paul's case, two events generated his commitment to altering how life is to be understood. The first is "personal";[25] his conversion on the road to Damascus reported in "Acts of the Apostles" 9: 1–4. In the third person, Paul (through Luke) tells the story of nearing Damascus and suddenly seeing light flashing from heaven, causing him to fall to the ground while hearing a voice, "Saul, Saul, why do you persecute me." Subsequent to the effect of that event—his conversion from a persecutor to an apostle—is his zealous advocacy of the second event, which is "impersonal,"[26] an insistence that Christianity is all about and only about an event. It does not harken to Jewish law or Greek cosmology but is to be solely founded on Christ's crucifixion and resurrection. Badiou's summary, which evokes Paul's proposition—"while the Jews are looking for signs and the Greeks are looking for wisdom, Christians declare Christ crucified"[27]—is *apropos*; Paul "requires only the event."[28] Similarly, as John Caputo puts it, "Paul is saying that the well-being of all humanity is based on the events surrounding the death and resurrection of a Galilean Jew named Jesus."[29] Gilles Deleuze, taking his cue from Nietzsche, who regards Pauline Christianity is a "mortuary enterprise," puts it more invidiously; "Paul … keeps Christ on the cross, ceaselessly leading him back to it, making him rise from the dead, displacing the center of gravity toward eternal life."[30]

In extracting the singularity of the event in Paul's theology, Badiou and Caputo implicitly invoke a conceptual trajectory about exceptionalism inaugurated by Carl Schmitt, who famously refers to the sovereign as he who decides on the state of exception.[31] However, unlike Schmitt for whom the sovereign's declaration of an exception makes the law recede temporarily so the order can be maintained, in this case the sovereign institution of the law and the authority of those authorized to interpret and administer it are displaced by the exception. In a revolutionary gesture, Paul insists that the *event* has become enduringly sovereign.[32]

In what follows, my focus is less on Paul's specific claims than on the media genre, the letter, a monoglossic (single-voiced) media genre, aimed in his case on fostering belief. I ultimately contrast that single-voiced medium with resort to M. M. Bakhtin's concept of heteroglossia—a characteristic of the novel, according to Bakhtin but which I will suggest applies to films as well—in order to mount challenges to single-voiced, belief-fostering media.[33] The word "declare," attached to Paul's discursive intervention, is especially significant for an understanding of Paul's version of Christian discourse. His style is proclamatory (Kerygmatic). In his lectures on Paul's letters, Heidegger emphasizes that discursive genre: "In analyzing the character of the letter, one must take as the only point of departure ... content proclaimed, and the material and conceptual character [which is] ... to be analyzed from out of the basic phenomenon of proclamation."[34] If we heed Berel Lang's review of modes of philosophical writing—"expository," "performative," and "reflexive"[35]—we can identify Paul's approach as performative (in the sense that J. L. Austin famously explicated performative discourse, especially its persuasive or "perlocutionary" force).[36] However as Austin insisted, the performative force of an utterance is tied to its context, which in Paul's case relates to the nature of his interlocutory encounters. Heidegger was alert to that necessity. Looking at how the implications of Paul's proclamations unfold in specific encounters, he notes for example that, "The proclamation is for Paul characterized formally by an intervention in the knowledge of the Thessalonians at a particular moment."[37]

Such moments speak to what Heidegger refers to as Paul's "Situation," which derives from the encounters between Paul's ecumenical project, disseminating the significance of the event (of the crucifixion and resurrection), and the desires and inhibitions of his interlocutors (The Corinthians, for example, were a notoriously tough audience).[38] To appreciate how Paul accomplished that dissemination, we have to recognize the way technologies had forged the network within which he functioned. Two stand out: the road system within which he moved and the media technologies he had available. Turning first to the road system:

The first two centuries of the Christian era were great days for a traveler, writes historian Lionel Casson: "He could make his way from the shores of the Euphrates to the border between England and Scotland without crossing a foreign frontier" [and] New Testament archaeologist W. M. Ramsay concludes, "The Roman roads were probably at their best during the first century after Augustus had put an end to war and disorder ... Thus St. Paul traveled in the best and safest period."[39]

As for the relevant media technology: alphabetization is the main contributor. In an analysis of the language-technology relationship in the 1800s (which applies to Paul's epoch as well), Friedrich Kittler writes, "A simple precondition had to be met before authors could become 'spiritual economists': there had to be a general equivalent for the texts they would spin out."[40] That "general equivalent," he notes, was supplied by alphabetization. Paul wrote in Greek. However, the Greek alphabet had been adapted from the work of Paul's ethnic group: "The initial formation of an alphabetic script [was by] Semitic language speakers."[41] "All known alphabets spring from the same common root, which tracks to the lands of Canaan, Accad, Moab, Byblos, Sinai, and other realms whose names haunt the biblical history of the region of the Middle East."[42]

As for the role of the letter in the emergence of Christianity, it is one of two literary genres. One, the gospel, "belongs to the origin of the Christian community. The letter, by contrast, ... was essentially derivative in function ... whereas the window of the gospel looks out on Jesus of Nazareth ... the letter looks out on the conversation between apostle and community."[43] Paul did not invent the epistle. He had at his disposal the "Greek letter," which was already a well-established medium. He also had other genre exemplars ready-to-hand, for example the diatribe characteristic of Epictetus,[44] the "synagogue homily,"[45] and Pythagorean terminology, which arguably inspired his "set of analogical ratios" ("flesh and spirit," "body and soul," and so on).[46] Finally and crucially are Paul's chronotopes, which rather than being mere representations of spatio-temporality are the conditions of possibility for disseminating the significance of the experience that his narratives deploy—the life-changing import of the events of his conversion and Christ's crucifixion. As Bakhtin insists, "It is precisely the chronotope that provides the ground essential for the showing-forth, the representability of events."[47]

The Letter a Conceptual Detour (about a Detour)

The alphabet and letter genre were key enabling resources for Paul's access to the grid of intelligibility within which he communicated the "event,"—the letter as a narrative-containing assemblage of alphabetic marks connecting the writer with the addressee and comprising grammatically and narratively shaped subject positions that locate Paul *vis-à-vis* his collaborators and addressees (whom he united "religiously" and "communally" by referring to them as "brethren").[48] To explore the complex identity issues involved in those relationships, I turn briefly to Jacques Derrida's allegorical reflection on letters which, like Paul's epistolary practice, was prompted by a revelation, in Derrida's case what he refers to as "my library apocalypse."[49] The event took place in Oxford's Bodleian Library. In one of his "post cards" to an unnamed addressee, Derrida writes, "Have you seen this card, the image on the back of this card? I stumbled on it yesterday in the Bodleian … an apocalyptic revelation … Socrates writing, writing in front of Plato."[50] The revelation, prompted by a "scene of writing" (a scene pervasively treated in Derrida's oeuvre),[51] is that "Socrates comes before Plato—the order between them is the irreversible sequence of heritage."[52] The reverse of the historical narrative about philosophical patrimony that the image shows accords with Derrida's elaboration of the way philosophy emerges through a variety of popular texts and at the same time confirms his anti-Hegelian, anti-teleological view of history.

Derrida's post card about his revelation is sent both to himself and to the philosophical field in which he works. Like Paul's letters, which (as Heidegger points out) express grammatically his, Paul's, situation, his "having-become" (*Gewordensein*)[53] an apostle as a result of a revelation, Derrida's letter is a revelation-induced, grammatically shaped affirmation of a vocation, a philosophical one in his case. It expresses one of the many pedagogical encounters with the history of philosophy through which he became Jacques Derrida. Also (and crucially), as Derrida goes on to engage Freud's treatise *Beyond the Pleasure Principle* (in a later section of his analysis), the complex temporal entanglement between life and the anticipation of death is shown to impose detours in Freud's attempt to anchor the pleasure principle. It's also an entanglement operating in the midst of Paul's letters, which seek to publicize, in a series of epistolary encounters, what life/death means after the

Christ event. In contrast with Paul's apocalypse (interpreted as a divine intent), thus sending him on the road as a proselytizer, Derrida's (interpreted as an "accident") launched him on "a certain path of thinking," which he stages in his epistolary book as a "collision between [a] 'lived' and theoretical voyage."[54]

Derrida's reflections on the tensions between what is visibly available on the card's image on the back versus what is written on the front encourage another return to Paul; they resonate with "Paul's metaphysical doctrine, which explicitly distinguishes an empirical and finite visible from a transcendental and eternal invisible"—"The things which are seen are temporal; but the things which are not seen are eternal" (2 Corinthians 4: 18)—where the "target" of belief like the addressee of the letter, as Derrida would have it, is "beyond reach, out of sight."[55] Involved in marketing what is "not seen," Paul undertakes his self-described apostolic vocation ("Paul always wrote in his capacity as an apostle"[56]), to which he refers at the outset of most of his letters.

Certainly Paul was working a growing constituency, one that was increasingly on the lookout for emissaries with credentials for being intimate with the divine. What Peter Brown discerned as a feature of late antiquity was already developing in Paul's world, a growing concern with where "'divine power' was to be found on earth, and consequently, on what terms access to it could be achieved." Paul was therefore locating himself in a subject position that was under increasing scrutiny by a constituency that was ready for information about a "zone in human life where decisions, obligations, and experiences, and information were deemed to come from outside the human community."[57]

From Letter to Film

The binary of the seen versus unseen that Paul evokes facilitates the cinematic Paul that I am pursuing. For example, in a reading of Horton Foote's film *Tender Mercies* (1983), Robert Jewett suggests a homology between the film's and Paul's calls to faith: "Faith is required because the mercies of God are elusive, intangible, and off camera. In a mysterious way, the God of Abraham [quoting Paul] 'gives life to the dead and calls that which does not exist into being', to use the language of Romans 4."[58] While the film-faith homology that *Tender Mercies* explores is a matter of ideational content, Robert Duvall's film

The Apostle (1997) renders its Pauline moments with frequent resort to images as well as merely narratively; its cuts and juxtapositions of scenes articulate the seen-unseen binary central to Paul's metaphysics. In his reading of the film, William Connolly points to the way the film form of *The Apostle* achieves what Paul desired to render visible, a new way of appreciating life:

> *The Apostle* is marked by a series of "irrational" scene cuts … Between the scenes, a black screen stares blankly at you for several seconds, underlining the element of contingency and creativity in the connections forged across scenes. Each cut suggests that you cannot, knowing what you did before, predict the next round of action. That is because *between the scenes* things are happening at the subliminal level, unsusceptible to full self-awareness [such cinematic techniques are the way] film directors signify virtual energies that combine with distinctive events to propel something new in the world. The cuts render the invisibility of these processes visible.[59]

The Encounters: "Time Thickens … Takes on Flesh"

As I have noted, along with the communication-enabling grid of intelligibility that alphabetization and the genre of the Greek letter had made available to Paul was his "situation." However, that "situation" was not merely ontological—as Heidegger elaborates it under the rubric of Paul's "factical life experience" (*faktische Lebenserfahrung*)—but also precarious. As I have noted in Chapter 1, reviewing Jacob Taubes's analysis of Paul's political theology, Paul's management of that precarity is evident throughout *Romans*. And elsewhere he is forthright about the strategic demands he faces while publicizing the event elsewhere. For example, in 1 Corinthians he writes:

> For though I be free from all *men*, yet have I made myself servant unto all, that I might gain the more. And unto the Jews I became a Jew, that I might gain the Jews; to them that are under the law, as under the law, that I might gain them that are under the law. To them that are without law, as without law, (being not without law to God), but under the law to Christ), that I might gain them that are without law. To the weak became I as weak, that I might gain the weak: I am made all things to all *men*, that I might by all means save some. (1 Corinthians 19–23)

One of Bakhtin's insights helps us see the way Paul's remark achieves its literary actualization:

> A prose writer can distance himself from the language of his own work, while at the same time distancing himself, in varying degrees, from the difference layers and aspects of the work. He can make use of language without wholly giving himself up to it; he may treat it as semi-alien or completely alien to himself, while compelling language to ultimately serve all his own intentions.[60]

If we recall Derrida's remarks to a fictional lover (on the back cover of his *Post Card*), we can appreciate another media feature that applies (as I have already suggested) to Paul's epistles and to epistolarity in general, the letter as performative force rather than mere communication:

> What does the post card want to say to you? On what condition is it possible? Its destination traverses you, you no longer know who you are. At the very instant when from its address it interpellates, you, uniquely you, instead of reaching you it divides you or sets you aside, occasionally overlooks you.

The same dividing applies to the sender. Paul's epistles interpolate and divide not only the epistles' addressees but also himself. As the passage from Corinthians implies, Paul's epistles divide him into a canny strategist—a "servant to all"—and a zealot, who "might by all means save some."

Paul's main ideational challenge was to sell a story that would draw his addressees into a conversation about an altered version of time. To frame the media-actualization of Paul's zealotry, which he articulates with a series of missives aimed at altering messianic time, I engage two different conceptual approaches: literary/textual (Bakhtin) and phenomenological/experiential (Heidegger). I explore Heidegger's formulation of the way "Christian religiosity lives temporality as such"[61] as he follows Paul's articulation of his "situation" (his proclamations that establish "Christian time") and I challenge Heidegger's insistence that what is most relevant is an extra-textual "phenomenological situation of religious struggle,"[62] by analyzing in parallel the way Bakhtin's textually oriented genre analysis—his analysis of polyphony in Dostoevsky and of chronotopes of the road and meetings in his historical survey of literary genres—both supplements and challenges Heidegger's version of Paul's discourse and temporality.

Heidegger with Bakhtin

Concerned as he is throughout his philosophical oeuvre with the phenomenology of experience, Heidegger explicitly resists a textual treatment of Paul's letters. His reading is an ontological framing of Pauline temporality, situating Paul in the world of religious struggle. The Paul involved in that struggle is constructed as durational, grammatically expressed as one "having-become" (in the trajectory in which he has changed from an oppressor to an apostle on a zealous mission to win adherence to the Christ event). That part of Heidegger's analysis extols Paul's eligibility, as one who has become an apostle through revelation, to warrant a new messianic temporality that is to be gifted to those who eschew an attachment to the Greek cosmology and/or to Mosaic Law. Paul emphasizes that eligibility by beginning most of his letters with a self-identification as an apostle (e.g., "Paul, called *to be* an apostle of Jesus Christ through the will of God," 1 Corinthians 1).

Because of his focus throughout his philosophical work on time as concrete moments of emergence rather than mere time-as-passing (time as *Kairos* rather than *Chronos*), Heidegger's version of time articulates well with Pauline temporality, which is owed to an event.[63] As Heidegger assigns the emergence of Christian time to Paul's apostolic mission, he emphasizes a temporality of co-emergence; Paul's "having-become" meets the having-become of his addressees. As Heidegger puts it in his treatment of Paul's epistolary encounter with the Thessalonians for example, "Paul experiences the Thessalonians in two determinations: 1. He experiences their having become. 2. He experiences that they have knowledge of their having-become. That means that their having-become is also Paul's having become."[64] For Heidegger "life" (as "factical life experience") is always co-experienced: "We tear facticity apart from the knowledge but facticity is entirely co-experienced."[65]

The Heideggerian grammar in which Paul's authorial self emerges is comparable to the way Bakhtin lends a temporality to authors. For Bakhtin, the author, who is always emerging in a dialogic situation, is a becoming ethical subject; she/he is "unconsummated," always "axiologially yet to be."[66] Bakhtin also shares Heidegger's concept of the "situation": "In life, verbal discourse is clearly not self-sufficient. It arises out of an extraverbal situation and maintains the closest possible connection with that situation."[67] And further, like Heidegger

Bakhtin subscribes to the uniqueness of Christian time as it is initiated by the Christ event: "The world from which Christ departed will no longer be the world in which he had never existed; it is in principle a different world."[68] Nevertheless, the temporality within which Paul and his addressees encounter each other yields to quite different analyses in Heidegger and Bakhtin. While Heidegger's extensive gloss on Paul's epistles *explicates* Paul's Christian time, Bakhtin's aesthetic approach to the relationship between literary texts and theology—especially as it is developed in his analysis of Dostoevsky's poetics[69]— constitutes a challenge, which, I will suggest, opens Paul's revolutionary project to Pasolini's contemporary version of revolutionary zealotry (which I address below). While Heidegger's phenomenology emphasizes "being-with" as an achieved mutual comportment, Bakhtin's becoming subjects are dialogically shaped; their encounters evoke non-harmonious otherness as they emerge in "a place where there is undecidable tension of *in situ* negotiation of identity, or rather of identifying, which is a never ending task."[70]

In his explication of Paul's epistles, Heidegger acknowledges the complications attending Paul's situation as he, Paul, sought to negotiate the kind of perilous intersection between theological and political authority that has persisted historically. It is therefore illuminating to compare Thomas Hobbes's literary strategy as he famously pursued that intersection but sought to mute rather than enhance theological authority. As the historical tensions attending his *Leviathan* attest, he and Paul faced similar complications. As "an anti-ecclesiastical political theologist [Hobbes's] textual strategy performs a delicate operation. Faced with a complicated ideational constituency—of rulers, ecclesiastical authorities and oppositional intellectuals—he promotes a secular state, enabled by rendering the Church's deity incomprehensible in order to keep 'Him' out of the picture [thus] freeing political authority from ecclesiastical authority."[71] Conceiving the text in that way, we can see a parallel textual strategy in Paul (as Jacob Taubes has famously interpreted his epistles) ... "[While Paul] seeks to radicalize the Jewish religion, appealing to Jews and gentiles, while not alarming the Roman authorities, Hobbes reverses the emphases. Although he too radicalizes religion, removing it from political relevance—chiefly by denying revelation—his main aim is to radicalize politics."[72]

While Taubes's analysis of Paul's political theology, delivered in epistles to fractionated constituencies, is derived from his reading of Romans, Heidegger's approach to Paul's "situation" is derived mainly from a reading of Thessalonians (and to a lesser degree from Galatians and Corinthians). While Taubes emphasizes division among the epistle's addressees, Heidegger emphasizes the way Paul's apostolic mission necessitated a complex version of temporality. The key expression that Heidegger lends to that temporality is Paul's version of "Christian time," the main feature of which is "obstinate waiting" (*Erharren*).[73] It is a "waiting," as Paul put it, "for the adoption, *to wit*, the redemption of our body" (Romans 8: 23). Writing of that expectation of Christ's second coming, the *Parousia*, in his second letter to the Thessalonians, Paul provides his famous simile for Christ's reappearance, "the day of the Lord comes like a thief in the night" (1 Thessalonians 5: 3). The obstinate waiting that Paul insists on comprises both urgent anticipation and a turning from the ordinary practices of daily life in which one seeks "peace and security" (1 Thessalonians 5:3). As Heidegger conveys Paul's life-altering message: "Those [who] spend themselves on what life brings them, occupying themselves with whatever tasks of life. They are caught up in what life offers; they are in the dark, with respect to knowledge of themselves ... They remain stuck in the worldly." The believers, on the contrary, are sons of the light and of the day [from 1 Thessalonians 5: 5].[74] And summarizing the temporal implications of Paul's "situation," Heidegger writes, "Paul is hurried, because the end of time has already come."[75]

Divergent Phenomenologies: Hermeneutic and Aesthetic

Heidegger is abundantly clear that his phenomenological reading of Paul's epistles takes Paul at his word. A hermeneutic phenomenology, which for Heidegger means grasping "factical life experience in its historicity," is a "method" that requires "explication" of the "object historical complex."[76] Applied to Paul, it locates his epistolary approach (e.g., to the Thessalonians) within a "particular moment" of the "object historical" situation.[77] Temporally speaking (here Heidegger invokes Paul's letters to the Galatians 1: 5), "The present time has already reached its end and a new [time] has begun since the death of Christ. The present world is opposed to the world of eternity."[78]

In explicating the words in Paul's letters, an approach Heidegger describes as his phenomenological hermeneutics, he writes, "In studying the religious world of Paul, one must free oneself from drawing out certain concepts [such as Faith, Righteousness, flesh] and putting together their meaning from out of a heap of singular passages." In short, accepting Paul "at his word" means locating the words within "the fundamental religious experience,"[79] the historical moment that must be *explicated*. I emphasize Heidegger's concept of explication because it is precisely the interpretive practice from which Bakhtin distinguishes himself. Rather than an explicator, Bakhtin is a "re-thinker."[80] His phenomenology is more aesthetic than hermeneutic. It's an aesthetic approach that accords with the way Jacques Rancière frames the politically subversive effects of contemporary artistic texts. To put it in Rancière's terms, Bakhtin's approach to media genres undermines "any particular regime of expression. It breaks ... any determined logic of connection between expression and content."[81]

The fundamental methodological difference between Heidegger's and Bakhtin's approaches to expression therefore begins at the level of the word. For Heidegger, words must adequately express "factical life experience." For example in a lecture on Nietzsche, he summons his notion of the adequacy of expression in a remark about how to approach Nietzsche's concept of existence: "Waxing in confrontation with the matter itself, we must become capable of the capable word."[82] In contrast, for Bakhtin words are never wholly capable. Although like Heidegger, Bakhtin recognizes that the "factical" is integral to one's comprehension of an utterance—it is dependent on what he calls the *"extraverbal situation of the utterance"*[83]—he nevertheless endorses a "divorce between 'word' and 'life'":[84] "In every text of a textual nature that he writes, Bakhtin stresses the disarticulation of the word and life."[85] He bases that "divorce" on his insistence that words are perpetually open to resignification because they function within "the dialogic fabric of human life" and are thus open to changing nuances in interpersonal encounters, even with non-co-present or "sensed" interlocutors (e.g., the figure he designates as the "hero" of a discourse[86]). Words, he suggests, generate altered forms of consciousness.[87] Instead of an encounter of "having-becomes" (Heidegger's version, which focuses on experiential durations), Bakhtin figures encounters linguistically: "The human world exists as an ongoing dialogue in which multiple languages and chronotopes engage and reshape each other perpetually."[88] As he puts in his analysis of the polyphony in Dostoevsky's discourse, "In Dostoevsky almost no word is without its intense sideward glance at someone else's word. At the same time there are almost no objectified words in Dostoevsky, since the speech of his characters is constructed in a way that deprives it of all objectification."[89] As for the varying historical moments in which Dostoyevsky's polyphonic writing has enabled a pluralistic reading of Christianity: "There can be no pure text, no pure meaning to be extracted from the messy, confusing contingencies of context."[90] In effect, Bakhtin's Dostoevsky-influenced version of Christianity is accompanied by a much less fixed historicity than what Heidegger extracts from Paul's version of Christian time.

Accordingly, just as open versus closed approaches to word meanings distinguish the two thinkers, so do their approaches to temporality. While Heidegger explicates a Pauline Christian eschatology, one that ends in the *Parousia*, Bakhtin, "concerned to … explore the nature of *open* time,"[91] viewed "the event of being, taken as a whole, as an open event."[92] Contrary to Heidegger's fixing of the "object-historical situation" which serves to explicate Paul's proclamatory articulation of the implications of "the event," Bakhtin treats historical moments as contingent, which artists acknowledge by seeking continually to enrich the words with which events are represented.[93] Applying that contingency to his own life, Bakhtin refers to, "the object of my own cognitive-ethical directedness in living my life within the open, [which is a] still risk-fraught event of being, whose unity and value are not *given* but imposed as a task still to be accomplished."[94]

As I've suggested, the temporal indeterminacy to which Bakhtin was attached accords with his reading of Dostoevsky whose plots contain open temporalities. Dostoevsky's characters are liberated from "aesthetic necessity," encouraging the reader to "palpably sense human freedom in a way absent from earlier literature."[95] Bakhtin's aesthetic affinity with Dostoevsky's polyphony carries over to his approach to religious faith. Although like Paul he resists relying on the traditions of Western epistemology (inaugurated in Greek thought), his approach to aesthetics resists Paul's closural theology of a definitive end time and regards faith as instead "eternally problematized."[96] Moreover, rather than seeing the Christ event as a call for dissolving ethnic boundaries (c.f., Paul's "There is neither Jew nor Greek, there is neither bond nor free, there is neither male nor female: for ye are all one in Christ Jesus." Galatians 3:28), Bakhtin saw "Christians as the first conscious moderns—the first community to make a defining characteristic out of their historically unprecedented *otherness* [my emphasis]."[97]

Rather than a theologically oriented hermeneutic, Bakhtin's theology is thoroughly aesthetic in the two senses of aesthetics; it emerges from the arts (his approach to the novel in particular, especially as it is composed by Dostoevsky) and it is aesthetic in the original Greek sense of aesthetics (where the Greek *aisthētikos*, is perception involving the senses or the embodied way in which the world is apprehended). In accord with Dostoevsky and with a privileging of embodiment, Bakhtin's religious affinity is expressed not as a "faith in orthodoxy" but as a "*sense of faith*" that is an "integral attitude ... of the whole person."[98] In stark contrast with Paul's privileging of the spirit over the flesh (e.g., "For the flesh lusteth against the Spirit, and the Spirit against the flesh: and these are contrary, the one to the other," Galatians 5: 17), Bakhtin valorizes a sensuality, which he develops elaborately in his encomium on the carnival and "grotesque realism" in his *Rabelais and His World*. The carnivalesque antics that constitute grotesque realism—the acting out of a wide variety of everyday vulgarities—adhere to the "essential principle of which is degradation, that is, the lowering of all that is high, spiritual, ideal, abstract."[99]

Notably, Bakhtin's Rabelais is not a departure from his focus on the chronotope. Rather, as he puts it in his analysis of the Rabelaisian chronotope,

> Rabelais's task is to purge the spatial and temporal world of remnants of a transcendent world view still present in it, to clean away symbolic and hierarchical interpretations still clinging to the vertical world ... his polemical task is fused with a more affirmative one: the re-creation of a spatially and temporally adequate world able to provide a new chronotope for a new, whole and harmonious man and for new forms of human communication.[100]

Unlike Paul's Christian temporality, based on a divine event that presides over and alters time, Bakhtin's "God *subjected himself to Time*."[101] Nevertheless, rather than a radical departure from theology, the "new, non-transcendent chronotope along with the grotesque realism in Bakhtin's *Rabelais* work is not anti-religious; it privileges an incarnational version of Christianity, an "Eastern Christianity" in which spirituality is incarnated in the flesh (in twentieth-century Russian theology, "Christ is the 'God-Man', in whom the two natures, human and divine, are inseparable").[102] Bakhtin's embrace of the earthly body is therefore a radical departure from Paul's desire to be free of a "captivity to the law of sin which is in my members" (Romans 8: 23) and his admonition to "enemies of the cross of Christ [whose] god is the belly" (Philippians 3: 21).

Bakhtin with Pasolini[103]

There is a conceptual homology between Bakhtin and Pasolini. Pasolini embraced "heretical empiricism," a "semiological heresy."[104] Insisting that "reality is a language," his literary and cinematic practices were focused on a "discourse of things" and on the corporeality of the social body, which is animated in the case of cinema as a grounded text in motion (actualized in his film *The Passion of Saint Matthew* and expressed in his Paul screenplay). Notably, from the point of view of traditional Western Christianity, Bakhtin's version of Christianity is similarly heretical in that he embraces a materiality of the sign, which translates to a theology that does not "divide the material from the immaterial, nor deem some matter good, some bad."[105] For Bakhtin, in sharp contrast with Paul, the earthly body is where life thrives: "If the Christian hell devalued earth and drew men away from it, the carnivalesque hell affirmed earth and its lower stratum as the fertile womb, where death meets birth and a new life springs forth."[106] Similarly, Pasolini, whose cinematic semiotics treats "the 'reality' of the body,"[107] designs his cinematic adaptation of Paul as an inter-articulation of Marxism and Christianity in which the "lower stratum" is a focus of Paul's attempt at liberating the social body from oppression.

Cinema in the Language of Reality

Pasolini's cinematic Paul, like his Christ in *The Passion of St Matthew*, requires a corporeal body, detailed land- and cityscapes, and sequences of the everyday practices within them, i.e., the kind of detailed settings and activities that are absent in the biblical texts of the *Old* and *New Testaments*. Although Paul spoke to his addressees, whom he designates as "carnal," and often employs material metaphors (referring, for example, to "the unleavened bread of sincerity," Corinthians 1: 8), there are no details about their bodies, nor ethnographic insights into their knowledge practices ("the wisdom of this world is foolishness with God," he asserts, Corinthians 1: 19) or of the spaces of their earthly existence. Instead of referencing the rhythms of the life world, Paul's chronotopes emphasize past legitimating events—for example, his reference to a "grace" having been "given to me of God" (Romans 1: 15).

Erich Auerbach explains why the genre of the biblical text resists the concrete details one finds in, for example, Homer's concrete description in *The Odyssey* of the moment when Odysseus, who has entered his old home as a stranger, has to hush the maid Euryclea, who is about to cry out after recognizing him because of the scar on his foot, sustained in a boar hunt (Homer provides the details of the 'whispered threats and endearments").[108] The Homeric text, as Auerbach elaborates it, features "an externalization of phenomena in terms perceptible to the senses."[109] It's a "style" that "knows only a foreground, only a uniformly illuminated, uniformly objective present."[110] Auerbach's textual analysis of Homer provides a comparative frame with which the reader can appreciate what is distinctive about biblical stories, whose "aim is not to bewitch the senses ... because the moral, religious, and psychological phenomena are their sole concern."[111] Thus as Auerbach describes the biblical account of Abraham's journey with Isaac to fulfill God's demand that he sacrifice his son, he notes how it is bereft of detail, "[T]he journey is like a silent progress through the indeterminate and contingent, a holding of the breath, a process which has no present, which is inserted like a blank duration, between what has passed and what lies ahead, and which yet is measure: three days!" It is a three-day duration that leaves the reader unable to follow the journey. There are no landscapes described and no indication of the degree to which Abraham is psychologically tortured by the choice he must make. Unlike the Homeric texts, which provide detailed visually oriented images—everything involved is illuminated—the biblical accounts leave the reader in the dark. They are, in Auerbach's expression, "fraught with 'background' and mysterious."[112]

Road Movies

In contrast with biblical texts—for example, the one that scripts Abraham's road journey with Isaac—road movies are composed of detailed images and the concrete temporal markers that Bakhtin renders as chronotopes. Insights about the relevance of Bakhtin to cinema abound. Among those who treat the conceptual resonance between Bakhtin's chronotopes and road movies are Alexandra Ganser et al. who, reviewing a trajectory of road movies since the 1970s, observe in each example a "cinematic chronotope ... splayed out concretely across a screen."[113] Focusing on "the road as setting" of film narratives, they survey a variety of different film stories with different generic plots, among which is Wim Wenders's *Paris Texas* (1984), which like many Western films is an exemplar of the road movie genre. I take that cue from their analysis to analyze how Western road movies work, although attending less to *Paris Texas* than to Clint Eastwood's *Unforgiven* (1992). However, I want to begin with a detour and approach the ontological horizon within which road narratives unfold by suggesting that Paul (like everyone) was in effect on the road before he hit the road as an apostle. The "road" as metaphor has ontological depth, for as Hélène Cixous observes, "The country from which we come is always the one to which we are returning. You are on the return road, which passes through the country of children in the maternal body. You have already passed through here: you recognize the landscape. You have always been on a return road [with] ... a face toward death."[114] The ontological road certainly traverses Paul's journey inasmuch as extracting an approach to life with an appropriate orientation toward the end of the road—i.e., death—is his primary concern. That concern articulates well with the cinematic treatment that Pasolini prepared in order to situate the life/death issues arising from Paul's political initiative. Likening life's trajectory to a continuous sequence-shot, Pasolini says,

> Cinema is identical to life because each one of us has a virtual and invisible camera, which follows us from when we're born to when we die. In reality cinema is an infinite film sequence-shot. Each individual film interrupts and rearranges this infinite sequence-shot and thus creates meaning, which is what happens to us when we die. It is only at the moment of death that our life, to that point undecidable, ambiguous, suspended, acquires meaning. Montage thus plays the same role in cinema as death does in life.[115]

To situate Pasolini's claim about the intimacy that film form has with life's movement toward death, I want to review briefly examples from the Western film genre that explore life/death with protagonists whose biographical trajectories resemble Paul's. As was the case for Paul's story throughout his epistles, the more critically oriented Western road films are redemptive. Wenders's above-noted *Paris Texas*, for example, features a man, Travis, who is pulled back from silence into the world of language on a road trip with his brother from a desert in the American southwest, where he had been wandering off the road. Like Paul, he foreswears a violent past, verbally atoning for it in a conversation with his estranged wife. On the road from the southwestern desert to Los Angeles and then back toward the southwest to initiate the conversation with his wife, he both recovers his ethnic (Spanish) heritage and seeks redemption from his personal violent past, which had torn his family apart. However, in addition to the personal drama the film's road trajectory explores land- and cityscapes that feature signs of a history of *collective* violence that victimized Native and African Americans—e.g., a long take of a Native American face on a building wall and one of the Statue of Liberty with an African American face substituted. They are visual chronotopes, which, along with a graffiti, "Race, Blood, Land" written on an alley wall and shown in a brief framing shot, deliver a story that transcends the personal drama of a man recovering his past. The interspersed (anti-narrative) images, as the story moves along the road, reveal a violent history that has never been effectively redeemed. It is buried in a contemporary American landscape whose primary semiotics consists of road signs that advertise commodities (Revealingly the erecting of such signs is the vocation of Travis's brother Walt).

Eastwood's *Unforgiven* also explores the changes in a man who had redeemed himself from a violent past. Recalling Auerbach's comparison of Homer's epics and biblical texts, one commentary on the film likens the narrative to Homer's *Iliad*, pointing out that "[i]n both works, the protagonists—Achilles and William Munny [Clint Eastwood]—are self-questioning warriors who temporarily reject the culture of violence only to return to it after the death of their closest male friend, in which they are implicated."[116] Another commentary on the film, which also evokes biblical comparison, deserves elaboration because it provides a threshold to Pasolini's cinematic version of Paul's road story. In his reading of *Unforgiven*, Robert Jewitt likens the protagonist, William Munny, to the pre-revelation Paul and the film as a whole to a plot "derived from the zealous strand of the biblical tradition."[117] By way of a brief synopsis: Munny, a retired gunman living peacefully with his children, decides to pursue a reward for bringing vigilante justice to the town of Big Whiskey, Wyoming, because the local sheriff Little Bill (Gene Hackman) will not punish two cowboys who disfigure a local prostitute. After his partner, Ned Logan (Morgan Freeman), is tortured and killed by the sheriff, Munny, a reformed alcoholic who initially appears no longer competent (clumsy in mounting his horse and inaccurate as he practices shooting), drinks again and recovers his aim. He shoots and kills Little Bill and five of his deputies. Then, having wrecked revenge for the injured prostitute, he rides off and disappears in accord with typical western heroes who do not fit comfortably within traditional forms of domesticity.

In his analysis of *Unforgiven*, Jewitt discerns twists in the story of the "American monomyth" in which an outside hero restores harmony to a place "threatened by evil," suggesting that "In targeting a wicked political and economic system as needing violent redemption, the film is similar to the *Turner Diaries*, which appears to have been an important motivation in the Oklahoma City bombing" (which also energized the right-wing zealots featured in Carl Hiaasen's crime story, with which my analysis begins).[118] Jewitt goes on to note how "the outcome of the dramatic action in *Unforgiven* remains true to the type of story we find in St. Paul's violent actions prior to his conversion" and suggests that as a result there is a "religious motivation that lies behind the [film's] gospel of violent zeal."[119]

There's a thematic bridge that *Unforgiven* offers to a reading of Pasolini's screenplay rendering of Paul's epistolary road trip. In addition to performing the job for which he was hired (killing those who disfigured the prostitute and those who failed to deliver justice), Munny figures himself as an apostle whose mission is to influence the morality of the town of Big Whiskey. Before he leaves, he shouts to the assembled townsfolk, "You'd better bury Ned right" (The sheriff, Little Bill, has displayed Ned's body in an upright coffin with a sign designating him as an assassin) and "You'd better not cut up whores."[120] However, in addition to a thematic overlap between Munny's and Paul's road trips—both violent men have been reformed and have an event-shaped message for those they encounter (in Munny's case the event was his marriage; under the influence was his late wife, he had sworn off his alcohol-induced violence)—there is a film form contrast that helps to situate Pasolini's cinematic style. It is a style he characterizes as a "cinema of poetry" and is shaped by the Bakhtin-inspired concept of "free indirect discourse."[121] While *Unforgiven* features many point-of-view shots, selected in the key drama-consummating scenes to emphasize the alcohol-induced perceptual perspective that allows Munny to fulfill his task before returning to his non-violent persona, Pasolini's cinematic protagonists are delivered through an image-translated free indirect discourse—free indirect point-of-view shots—which convey the political sensibility within which they act (illustrated below).

Pasolini's Cinema of Poetry

For Pasolini, the world is always already "cinematographic" because as one moves about in it one "read[s] reality visually, that is [has] an instrumental conversation with reality":

> A solitary walk in the street, even with stopped up ears is a continuous conversation between us and an environment which expresses itself through the images that compose it: the faces of people who pass by, their gestures, their signs, their actions, their silences, their expressions, their arguments, their collective reactions; ... and more—billboards, signposts, traffic circle, and, in short, objects and things that appear charged with multiple meanings and thus 'speak' brutally with their very presence.[122]

As for how Pasolini realizes that cinematic reality with actual shots, i.e., translating the linguistics of the utterance, derived in part from Bakhtinian dialogics (the relationship or "interference" between one's own word and another's word, reflected in texts as free indirect discourse), into images, he offers an example from Michelangelo Antonioni's *Red Desert* (1964). Referring to a dream sequence in the film in which, "after so much delicacy of color, is suddenly conceived in an almost blatant Technicolor (in order to imitate, or better, to reanimate through a 'free indirect point-of-view shot' the comic-book idea that a child has of tropical beaches)."[123] Antonioni, he says,

> looks at the world by immersing himself in the neurotic protagonist, reanimating the facts through her eyes ... By means of this stylistic device, Antonioni has freed his most deeply felt moment: he has finally been able to represent the world seen through his eyes, *because he has substituted in*

toto for the world-view of a neurotic his own delirious view of aesthetics, a wholesale substitution which is justified by the possible analogy of the two views.[124]

In his own film work, Pasolini mobilizes two concepts that direct his translation of free indirect discourse into free indirect point-of-view shots: contamination and analogy. Through "contamination," a cinematic version of free indirect discourse, in which camera consciousness merges with the consciousness of protagonists, Pasolini intends to "go beyond the two elements of the traditional story, the objective indirect story from the camera's point of view and the subjective direct story from the character's point of view."[125] His concept of contamination conveys the political force of his cinematic poesis; Pasolini insists that episodes conveyed by free indirect discourse must be counter-ideological, by which he means that they must not "implicitly accept an ontological phenomenology for the Free Indirect, that is, the identification or osmosis or ... rapport of sympathy between the author and the character, *as if their experiences were the same* [making the character belong to] his ideology."[126] Instead there must be an "interlacing of voices ... [e.g.,] high and low, literary Italian and dialect intertwined in free indirect discourse without thereby neutralizing the specificity of each voice."[127] Pasolini thus resists choosing between the two traditional cinematic narrative approaches, the indirect story that proceeds from the camera's perspective and the direct story that develops from a character's point of view. Deleuze captures the way Pasolini manages to transcend that binary.

> In the cinema of poetry the distinction between what the character saw subjectively and what the camera saw objectively vanished, not in favor of one or the other, but because the camera assumed a subjective presence, acquired an internal vision, which entered in a relation of *simulation* ('mimesis') with the character's way of seeing ... The author takes a step towards his character's way of seeing, but the characters take a step towards the author: double becoming [a co-present becoming that recalls Heidegger's account of Paul's encounters with his addressees!].[128]

Pasolini initially realizes his image version, i.e., free indirect point-of-view shots, of such a contamination in his first film, *Accattone* (1961), in which his landscape shots provide an "intertwining of humility and grandeur," for example, locating a scene of the pimp, Accattone fighting in a dusty street where, in the background, are "actual archeological remains." With that intertwining, Pasolini shows a "mutual contamination of forms," a "landscape of poverty" amidst the "archaic" with its "allusions to the gorgeous riches of Christian art."[129]

Intimately connected with his cinematic achievement of "contamination" is Pasolini's other primary cinematic concept, analogy, which is elaborately theorized in his writings, where among other things he suggests that seemingly incompatible signs have "analogous designs."[130] For example, in order to inter-articulate his Marxism with a radical version of Christianity's main historical protagonist (turned deity), Jesus, Pasolini adapted the biblical story in Matthew's gospel—in his *Il Vangelo Secondo Matteo* (in English, *The Gospel According to St, Matthew*, 1964)—with a Bakhtinian emphasis on embodiment, a "theology of the cinematic image,"[131] which he effects by portraying Mary, Jesus, and other major biblical players with still and framing shots that mimic a painterly history. As Noa Steimatsky points out, "Pasolini's pervasive frontal mode [in the film] may be traced back to Byzantine icons and followed through Italian descendants such as Duccio, Giotto, Masaccio, and finally Piero della Francesca, whose positioning of figures within an already perspective system is a major source of allusions for *Il Vangelo Secondo Matteo*" (e.g., Mary, Figure 2.1).[132]

Figure 2.1 Mary in Pasolini's *Il Vangelo Secondo Matteo*. Directed by Pier Paolo Pasolini. Copyright Arco Film Lux Compagnie Cinématographique de France, 1964.

And crucially, to make that gospel accord with his radical politics, Pasolini displaced the venue. Dissatisfied with Jesus's legendary route in the regions of Palestine—where his (Pasolini's) scouting of the biblical scene impressed him that Jesus was "preaching in a small land, a small region that consists of four arid hills, a mountain, the Calvary where he was killed—all this is contained in a fist"[133]—he displaced the story to a more extensive and richer landscape in Southern Italy to create a politically inspired analogy between Christ's mission and what he saw as "the persistence of archaic forms within a contemporary world ... of the 1960s ... a disinherited world denied active participation in hegemonic culture."[134] Pasolini's approach to Paul operates with the same political sensibility.

The Paul Screenplay

To borrow from a summary of the script, Pasolini saw Paul as "not merely a historical subject but as both an analogical lens through which to read his contemporary political context and a semi-autobiographical figure for his own artistic and personal experience of alienation and persecution."[135] He "renders the biblical Paul as political critic for the contemporary moment ... the late 1960s and early 1970s."[136] As Pasolini puts it,

> Why would I want to transpose his life on earth to our time? It is very simple: to present cinematographically in the most direct and violent fashion, the impression and the conviction of his realty/present. To say then explicitly to the spectator, without compelling him to think, that Paul is here, today, among us, and that he is here almost physically and materially.[137]

As he transposes Paul to the present, substituting "the Atlantic" for the "theater of Saint Paul's travels," in the Mediterranean basin, Pasolini renders Paul as a zealot who, "revolutionarily crushed, with the simple power of his religious message, a kind of society founded on the violence of class imperialism and above all slavery ... perpetuated he adds by the bourgeois class."[138]

As for the historical displacement in the screenplay, the story begins in an earlier period, during the Second World War, with the Martyrdom of Saint Stephen displaced to Paris during the Nazi occupation. There, biblical Pharisees, Saul/Paul among them, act out the brutality described in the Acts of the Apostles. "No fact, no word will be invented," according to Pasolini.[139] Pasolini has Paul request a continuation of the persecution of Christians in Damascus, but displaces that journey, having him instead cross the Pyrenees and head to Catalonia. To help transpose the biblical geography to that venue, he will make the soundtrack "completely mute," so that the film reproduces "the idea of the desert," where, as in the biblical account, "Paul is seized by light [and] falls, and hears the voice of his call."[140]

Badiou provides a convenient summary of the most significant parts of the geography of Pasolini's Paul screenplay, to which he (Badiou) refers as "the trajectory of a saintliness within an actuality."[141]

> Rome is New York, capital of American imperialism. Jerusalem, cultural seat occupied by Romans, seat also of cultural conformity, is Paris under the German heal ... Damascus is the Barcelona of Franco's Spain. The fascist Paul goes on a mission to see supporters of Franco. On the road to Barcelona, traveling through southwestern France, he has an illumination. He then joins the camp of the antifascist Resistance.[142]

Instead of following the altered geography of "the [entire] trajectory of saintliness" with which Pasolini brings Paul into the present, I want to focus momentarily on the section he entitled "Saint Paul at Rome," where Rome becomes New York. To create an analogy between Roman slavery and American racism, the violence that ends Paul's life in Rome is represented in the film as the murder of Martin Luther King. Just as Paul's epistle to the Romans is his longest letter, Pasolini makes "this [the] ... longest and richest episode of the film."[143]

Why New York? "In New York," Pasolini suggests,

> we are in the belly of the modern world: there is the 'presentness' of problems involving violence and an absoluteness. The corruption of the ancient pagan world [is] mixed with the uneasiness deriving from the confused feeling of the end of such a world—replaced by a new and desperate corruption, which is to say the atomic desperation (neurosis, drugs, radical social conflict).

"The state of injustice that dominates a slave society like that of imperial Rome can be symbolized by racism."[144] Paul's death scene, like Martin Luther King's, is on a balcony (to be filmed with Hitchcockian detail):

Suddenly two violent piercing gunshots ring out. The door of the lavatory is still swinging back and forth: the man who fired the shot has barely disappeared. Paul falls down on the balcony, immobile in his own blood. He suffers a brief agony. There is a small rosy puddle, in which drops of Paul's blood continue to fall.[145]

Apart from the planning of such vivid details is Pasolini's political framing. As his plan for his screenplay unfolds, his radical politics and appreciation of textual form converge. Employing analogy politically, he relies on a religious allegory, which he shapes to be "consonant with his radical politics … Religion retains for Pasolini the revolutionary power of human solidarity against the materiality of bourgeois culture."[146] In terms of film form, "Pasolini' *Saint Paul* is an instance of remix … an adaptation in precisely the sense that adaptation has been theorized widely, as remediation of source material into a new cultural form."[147]

Pasolini's Paul film thus takes on the form Pasolini ascribed to a "cinema of poetry." The filmmaker, "if he immerses himself in his character and tells the story or depicts the world through him, he cannot make use of that formidable natural instrument of differentiation that is language. *His activity cannot be linguistic; it must be stylistic.*"[148] Nevertheless, the film's image sequences would mimic Pasolini's writing style, a literary method he enacts, for example, in his novel *Petrolio*, which is "structured through a montage of fragments taken from heterogeneous sources … a literary method able to overcome a linear and mimetic representation through a structure able to create links and co-ordinate events, characters, and facts otherwise separated by the linear flow of narrative."[149] "The film careens from Vichy late 1930s to Memphis 1968: Greek robes interchangeable with double-breasted suits; quotations from the New Testament interrogated by intellectual dilations on the unambiguously troubling institution of the Church [and as noted] Paul's Rome is placed in New York."[150] By framing his political sensibility with such an anti-diegetic literary/cinematic temporality, Pasolini opens both the past and the future to continuing political contestation. His compositional style accords both with Bakhtin's commitment to an open future for subjects whose identities are never consummated and with Walter Benjamin's commitment to an open past that can be variously summoned to politicize crises in the present.[151] He gives us a Paul whose radical media proclamations intervened in the ancient life world and remain a serviceable allegory for his (Pasolini's) cinematically figured political intervention in *his* life world. Concerned not with enlisting Paul to revise messianic time (Agamben), theorize an ethical universality (Badiou), or a "'fighting universality', a *work* of love that wrestles with the Other (Žižek),"[152] Pasolini, invokes allegory—a figural tactic appropriate for confronting "a torn and broken world"[153]—to put Paul back on the road, albeit a different road, to challenge that world with him.

Entering the Conversation

The trajectory of texts I examine throughout this chapter engage the conversation Paul initiated to (re)negotiate vitality, using a media genre, the letter, to convey a radical revision of how one should regard life/death. I want to end my analysis by entering that ongoing negotiation, which has taken place in a wide variety of discursive spaces, theological and political among others, beginning with relatively minor life-evaluating episode in which I was a participant. Several years ago, I was drawn into a legal negotiation about vocational life expectancy. One of my graduate student peers (I'll call him Hal) in Northwestern University's mid-1960s political science PhD program had his academic career cut short after being injured by a bicycle delivery messenger, who ran him down in the street. To determine the compensation to which he was entitled, his attorney contacted everyone he could find in "Hal's" graduate cohort to establish an average career duration. Reflecting on that encounter, I want to note that the discursive space of legal proceedings, which involves a variety of media (biographies, legal documents, etc.), is one among many contention-attracting vicinities within which vitality is negotiated. Given my concern with the religious will to believe, I turn to an exemplary encounter in which vitality is negotiated in a larger discursive domain, the interface among religious, philosophical, and political discourses.

The (implicit) negotiation takes place in William Connolly's commentary on a section of Charles Taylor's *A Secular Age*. Taylor "explores how Christian faith has become increasingly 'optional' in the countries of Christendom over the past couple of centuries"[154] and laments that condition. Not unlike William

James's assertion that an acceptance of God's existence "raises our centre of personal energy," is Taylor's that life is "fuller, richer, deeper, more worthwhile, more admirable, more what it should be," when "divine grace is infused in it," and that unbelievers who lack an "outside source" are disadvantaged in their pursuit of fullness.[155] Contesting Taylor's believer-unbeliever binary (as well as his unitary "outside source"), Connolly suggests that the fullness to which Taylor refers is available to those (himself among them) who entertain an alternative cosmology,

> a cosmos of becoming set on multiple tiers of chronotime, as we identify an outside to every specific human and non-human force field, an outside that periodically helps to set the stage for the creative evolution of a climate, an ocean conveyer system, a glacier flow, a species change, a civilization, a human life. The outside is multiple, active and real … [156]

I want to offer a different challenge to Taylor's faith-based version of a fuller life by summoning a phenomenological frame that disturbs the inside-outside binary that Taylor presumes and suggest that the outside is always already predicted on an inside. How a supposed "outside" is experienced (and becomes the outside) depends on what I will call (after Gilles Deleuze's reading of Proust) the "*Tableux Vivants* [of one's] inner theater"[157] (the metaphor with which I elaborate a view of phenomenology in Chapter 1 and revisit in Chapter 3). My concern in entering a negotiation about life is not only with what may make it fuller but also with how a zealous delivery of a will to believe can impart susceptibility to relinquishing control of that inner theater to another director's version of how one should engage "life." Preferring "thinking" to believing, I endorse a remark by Richard Foreman, "One thinks about life and sees its richness. Thinking makes life richer—Denser."[158] Certainly Pasolini substituted thinking for mere believing while challenging the exteriorities posited to control believers. In an analysis of one of Pasolini's quasi- or pseudo-religions films, *Theorem*, Deleuze puts it well. In the film, "Thought finds itself taken over by the exteriority of a 'belief', outside any interiority of a mode of knowledge … Was this Pasolini's way of still being Catholic? Was it on the contrary his way of being a radical atheist? Has he not, like Nietzsche, torn belief from every faith in order to give it back to rigorous thought?"[159]

Belief Encounters/Rigorous Thought

To pursue the contention between "rigorous thought" and zealously engendered belief, I turn to another road story in a novel that addresses that contention, the late South African writer, Justin Cartwright's, *The Song before It Is Sung*. The novel features a fictional exploration of protagonists struggling within a fraught life world in a historical drama that has striking resonances with the one into which Pasolini inserts Paul, especially the section in the screenplay in which Pasolini places Paul in Barcelona. (In the film, after Paul's revelation in the desert, he has redirected his zealotry and has joined the anti-fascist movement in Franco's Spain.) Cartwright's novel, which has a similarly zealous protagonist, an anti-Nazi, is shaped by two of Bakhtin's conceptual framings. First, it exemplifies the political import of dialogic/polysemic texts by mobilizing a clash of voices, articulating alternative perspectives that are activated by the failed assassination attempt on Adolph Hitler's life on July 20, 1944.[160] Second, it manifests Bakhtinian chronotopes of encounter on the road, which mold a zealous would-be assassin. To repeat a segment of Bakhtin's characterization of novels that treat encounters on the road, Cartwright's novel provides "both a point of new departures and a place for events to find their denouement. Time, as it were, fuses together with space and flows in it … the road is especially (but not exclusively) for portraying events governed by chance."

A review of the novel provides a convenient summary of the historical event and main interpersonal relationships on which it is based:

> On the outbreak of war [Adam] von Trott tried to gather support against the Nazis in Britain and America, but in vain. Returning to Germany in 1940 against the advice of his friends, one of whom was the Russian-born Jewish Fellow of All Souls, Isaiah Berlin, he was involved in the unsuccessful 20th July plot to assassinate Hitler. He was arrested, tortured and hanged with great cruelty in August 1944, a couple of weeks after his 35th birthday. The hanging was filmed on Hitler's orders, and von Trott's three young children were taken by the Gestapo in accordance with Hitler's policy of Sippenhaft, or kindred seizure.[161]

While Sir Isaiah Berlin and Adam von Trott (E. A. Mendel and Axel von Gottberg in the novel) are the major players in Cartwright's fictional version of the events, much of what occurs is represented through the eyes of a third character, Conrad Senior.

Conrad, who has been delegated to collect and edit the papers of the late E. A Mendel, is introduced at the beginning of the novel in the role of a film critique, watching the film of von Gottberg's trial, which is "edited in such a way as to give Roland Freisler [the National Socialist judge] the last word."[162] However the viewer, through Conrad, experiences a plaintiff-friendly aesthetic. Despite its propagandistic intent, the film conveys the dignity of the accused, who looks vulnerable yet heroic in a courtroom whose "windows … are admitting a soft, warm light a Dutch light, containing the texture of paint."[163] Through Conrad we see a film in which aesthetic form trumps directorial intent. After the novel follows both von Gottberg's and Conrad's travel trajectories (which distinguish them from the sedentary Mendel)—a peripatetic von Gottberg being shaped by events and encounters as he ultimately joins the plot to assassinate Hitler and a traveling Conrad Senior involved in a *roman d'education*, learning about how history is shaped by encounters among persons with different character—it ends with Conrad again commanding the narrative. He has been selected to deliver a eulogy at a commemorative ceremony for von Gottberg in his home village.

At the levels of both its metaphysical presumption (the ideational commitment that makes the details cohere) and its form, the novel is especially *apropos* for critically situating zealotry. In Cartwright's story, which stages a clash of perspectives between the zealous von Gottberg (a man of "deep belief"[164]) and the philosophically dispassionate Mendel, whose response to Europe's "growing tensions" is ("to look more closely at ideas"[165]), the "metaphysic" is that there is no definitive advice to serve as a guide to how one should live one's life.

At the level of form, that metaphysic (or perhaps better ontology) is not delivered directly by Mendel, whose anti-zealous philosophy is the novel's primary "normative mentality,"[166] articulated through Conrad Senior. The novel's ontology of life emerges through its form—the way Pasolini creates Paul—through the use of free indirect discourse, specifically in the novel through the way the voices of von Gottberg and Mendel are articulated through Conrad's voice. Mendel's (i.e., Berlin's) legacy is ultimately articulated by Conrad. After reading through Mendel's collected papers (including an examination of the letters between von Gottberg and Mendel), watching the film footage of von Gottberg's trial and execution, and heeding "Mendel's chief complaint against his old friend [von Gottberg, who zealously believed that] ... all values would inevitably be harmonized in some mystical synthesis," he, Conrad (and by implication Cartwright), concludes that rather than seeking a transcendent guidance for how to live, "life is made, day by day, as best you can."[167]

Cartwright derives the title of his novel from a query posed by Alexander Herzen, "Where is the song before it is sung?" His Mendel supplies the answer to Herzen's query in indirect discourse through Conrad, who while delivering the von Gottberg eulogy refers first to words by Mendel as he searches for something "uplifting." Before satisfying those assembled with the remark, "*Axel von Gottberg lived his life according to his principles,*" he refers to the most important thing he has learned from Mendel; he says, "*Professor Mendel was very fond of a quote from Alexander Herzen, who asked,* 'Where is the song before it is sung. *To which Mendel replied,* Where indeed? Nowhere is the answer'. One creates a song by singing it, by composing it. So, too, life is created by those who live it step by step."[168]

There is therefore a significant genre moment in Cartwright's novel that complements the pedagogy about life it explores, a media genre, the eulogy, to which it ultimately turns. In contrast with Paul's epistolary medium, with which he proclaims what is at stake (salvation) for each of those who heed the "event" and concern themselves with eternity, is the novel's enlisting of the eulogy, which is directed toward how the living can endure (as the living) by coming to terms with a death by heeding the significance of a particular life. While Paul's epistles served to initiate a global theological community of sense (since riven by a proliferation of "brands" after Luther, as Fredric Jameson puts it),[169] the eulogy serves disparate collectives at disparate historical moments to "reknit communal bonds" that deadly events have sundered.[170]

Importantly, the turn to the genre of the eulogy in Cartwright's novel participates in the novel's ontological commitment, which disparages zealotry and privileges critical thinking. As is the case with Bakhtin's conceptual inspiration for Pasolini's poesis (both literary and cinematic), Bakhtin's writings help with discerning that ontological commitment. Like Rabelais's task, as Bakhtin renders it, Cartwright's novelistic challenge to zealotry, which stages a series of contentious conversations in which a believer confronts a thinker, operates (to repeat an earlier quotation) by "purge[ing] the spatial and temporal world of those remnants of a transcendent world view still present in it, to clean away symbolic and hierarchical interpretations still clinging to this vertical world."[171] Similarly, Georg Lukács suggests that such anti-transcendence is intrinsic to that literary genre: "The novel is the epic of a world that has been abandoned by God."[172]

The implication is one that Deleuze's philosophical framing encourages; life is life when it actualizes itself. There is nothing externally transcendent to provide validation except what Deleuze calls a "plane of immanence." To elucidate the concept: "When Deleuze speaks of the Outside, this word has two complimentary senses: 1. The unrepresentable, or the outside of representation; 2. the very consistency of the unrepresentable, which is to say the exteriority of relations .... The *plane of immanence* is Deleuze's name for this transcendental field where nothing is presupposed in advance except the exteriority that precisely challenges all presuppositions."[173] What then is achieved by bringing Paul into the present, while at the same time resisting the zealotry of one who summoned a definitive and closural transcendence? What has been at stake for me and for those—e.g., Agamben, Badiou, Žižek, and Pasolini, who have looked at the present through Paul—"is what Paul calls 'life.'"[174] To close provisionally, I want to concur with Caputo's suggestion that Paul's legacy is the initiation and perpetuation of a rich conversation about life. Through "productive interpretations"[175] of his epistles (and the situation within which they were communicated), we can be encouraged to continue the conversation—an ongoing negotiation, aided by diverse critically oriented media genres—about what constitutes vitality in order to be able to "produce something new."[176]

Ingmar Bergman:
Theatricality Contra Theology

Prelude: Bergman's *Kamp*

In his 1950 Nobel Prize acceptance speech, William Faulkner lamented the losses literature had undergone during the nuclear age, a time in which such questions as "when will I be blown up" had displaced the "problems of the spirit" that sustain good writing. "Contemporary writers," he said, "have forgotten the problems of the human heart in conflict with itself."[1] Ingmar Bergman artistically represented both of the problems to which Faulkner referred. Jonas Persson (Max von Sydow), a character in his film *Winter Light* (1963)—to whom I refer in Chapter 1—commits suicide because he fears a nuclear catastrophe after learning that China, newly equipped with atom bombs, will blow up the world. However, the film's main focus is on another character, the Lutheran pastor, Tomas Ericsson (Gunnar Björnstrand), who is unable to offer Jonas solace because he himself is afflicted. *His* heart is "in conflict with itself" because of God's silence. It had become evident to him that although his late wife had tried to help him "patch the holes," what has remained is a "void" where once his spiritual life had flourished.[2]

Bergman testified that *Winter Light* (to which I return below) is the film "closest to me." Although many of his characters enact aspects of his autobiography, Tomas Ericsson's struggle best exemplifies Bergman's. However, we should not overly credit artistic intention. As Hegel observes, "none of the genuine substance of the object that inspired the artist remains within [her/]his subjective interior."[3] Moreover and specifically, "film form renders" cinematic autobiography problematic because "the divorce between directing and acting selves, though not visible on screen, undermines [if not wholly negating] the foundation of autobiographical discourse."[4] Nevertheless, off screen it became evident, as Bergman testified, that he used his films to work on personal issues. Yet what may by his account be deemed personal is deceptive. Although "he seems to brush aside the difference between autobiography and biography altogether ... his auto/biographies [have as] their primary concern ... not the narrative of his life but the presentation of [an] experimental concept of what a 'life' might be—something broader than singular selfhood."[5]

The first artistic medium with which he endeavored to think through life's struggles was the theater. As his subsequent film corpus was to attest, Bergman's "road to Damascus" was his experience as a theater director. "Theatricality"— the theater as a space where life's dramas and the audience reception they engender encourage reflection and contention about how life should be lived—provided Bergman with the distance he craved from religious piety.[6] The theatrical ontology that became his line of flight from theology framed his artistic response to the disappointing "echo god" that afflicted his (arguably) auto/biographical surrogate, Tomas, in *Winter Light*.

Roads to Damascus

"The road to Damascus," the legendary episode in the apostle Paul's spiritual journey, figures explicitly in Ingmar Bergman's as well. Profoundly influenced by the playwright, August Strindberg—"In my own life, my great literary experience was Strindberg. There are works of his which can still make my hair stand on end"[7]—Bergman directed several of Strindberg's plays early in his artistic career. Thereafter, adopting Strindberg's innovation, the creation of "the first subjective drama in world literature" (his 1898 *To Damascus*, which he directed in 1974), Bergman went on to implement a cinematic aesthetic that mimics the way Strindberg's protagonists exhibit thoughts and emotions.[8] Like the "subjective dramas" in Strindberg's plays, in Bergman's films, "The border between objective and subjective is blotted out."[9] Moreover, Bergman was wholly absorbed with one of Strindberg's abiding themes, the intimacy between life and death, voiced by his protagonist, the "Stranger," in *To Damascus*. Bergman quotes it in his autobiography:

> In *To Damascus*, when the Lady reproaches him for playing with Death, the Stranger replies: "Just as I play with life. I was a writer. Notwithstanding my

innate melancholy, I have never been able to take anything really seriously, not even my own great sorrow, and there are moments when I doubt that life has any more reality than my writing."[10]

When he turned to film to negotiate the "reality" of life, Bergman discovered and cinematically focused elaborately on "the expressive potential of the human face."[11] Referring to the importance of the face in his cinematic practice, he said, "There are many directors who forget that our work in films begins with the human face."[12] Accordingly, close-ups of faces were among Bergman's cinematic signatures. In accord with Deleuze and Guattari's observation, "the face is a megaphone,"[13] Bergman's filming of faces was one of the primary ways he captured vitality.

Bergman and I

I caught up with Ingmar Bergman in 1961when I watched the twenty-first feature film he directed, *The Virgin Spring* (1960) at the Brattle Theater in Harvard Square, the "art-house" film venue that turned me into a life-long cineaste. Up to that point my film going experiences had provided no ethico-political challenges. The film genres with which I was familiar at the time, primarily the Western and the crime story, tended to feature "the good the bad and the ugly" in ways that solicited relatively unambiguous judgments. Bergman's film stunned me. Being used to action films, which had me continually anticipating the next moment in dramas in which good characters vanquished bad ones, its slowness disrupted my habitual mode of reception. That effect, a "long take style," which as the Russian film director Andrei Tarkovsky describes it, gives the viewer "an opportunity to live through what is on screen as if it were his own life, to take over the experience imprinted in time on the screen."[14] What also happens with long takes is the viewer's ability to "feel the camera," as the Italian film director Pier Paolo Pasolini points out. Bergman emphasizes that stylistic reality in his *Persona* at a moment when a shot of rolls of film unspooling interrupts the film story.[15]

As *The Virgin Spring's* slowness and camera consciousness held my attention, I was struck by Bergman's close-up shots of faces (e.g., Figure 3.1).

Figure 3.1 *The Virgin Spring*: a facial tableau. Directed by Ingmar Bergman. Copyright Janus Films 1960. All rights reserved.

Referring to those shots as "affection-images," Deleuze suggests that they show a part of the body that has sacrificed its movement (its "motoricity") for an "intense expressivity." Unlike the bodies in motion in action films, "the moving body [captured with those shots] has become a movement of expression."[16] That said, there is something notable about Bergman's close-ups. Given as Deleuze and Guattari put it, "The face gives the signifier substance; it is what fuels interpretation,"[17] the questions that Bergman's affection images raise are about the interpretations they encourage. In his case, rather than signaling the singularity of a character by locating it in a particular type of subject position, Bergman's face shots solicit interpretations that transcend psychological framing; they suspend individuation by controlling degrees of illumination and angles of vision.

Deleuze remarks on why in Bergman's films the face close-ups cannot be quarantined within a psychological register, "The facial close-up is both the face and its effacement"; paradoxically, it "extinguishes the face."[18] What Deleuze implies is that rather than representing a person's psychologically driven performance, i.e., the "external effect of an interior cause,"[19] Bergman's close-ups signify a collective potential, "possible confrontations, expectations, creations,"[20] allowing the viewer to "feel the world differently."[21] Accordingly, my first Bergman film provided the opposite of the satisfying closure I had hitherto expected of films. Deprived of clear identification of the characters' individualities and accordingly an unambiguous ethico-political lesson, I was encouraged to reflect on what the film did to me; it short-circuited my ethical and political sensors rather than directing them toward a judgment.

Although *The Virgin Spring* is suffused with violence—a rape and murder of a young daughter, Karin (Birgitta Pettersson), and her father's, Töre's (Max von Sydow), violent revenge against the rapists (murdering two adult goatherds and an accompanying young boy who had merely watched the rape)— "Nothing," as Robin Wood observes, "is quite as it appears."[22] Karin is at once innocent and provocative and the young boy is both innocent and complicit (as he helps to trap Karin before the sexual assault). As Wood summarizes the film's moral ambiguities, "In the world of *The Virgin Spring*, good and evil are like subterranean streams, potent, determining matters of life and death, but invisible and mysterious. No one is pure."[23] Allegorically amplifying the moral ambiguities the film expresses are juxtapositions of fire and water (e.g., the former seen at the outset as the wife and mother, Märeta (Birgitta Valberg), stokes the cooking fire and the latter seen as a stream running beneath Karin's dead body) and juxtapositions of shadow and light (the former seen as dark shadows in Karin's home and the latter seen as she emerges with bright candles into a sunlit exterior).

The play of shadow and light has been one of Bergman's main cinematic techniques, deployed among other places in his face shots. As Deleuze and Guattari suggest, "In film the close-up of the face can be said to have two poles: make the face reflect the light or, on the contrary, emphasize its shadows to the point of engulfing it 'in pitiless shadows'" (e.g., Figure 3.2).[24]

It is in Bergman's *Persona* that Deleuze's observation about the displacement of individual subjectivity in his cinematic face close-ups is dramatically actualized. *Persona* doubles down on the simultaneous presentation and effacement of the face by making the film's subject positions ambiguous; for example, at one moment the film has the faces of the two women protagonists—a woman suffering a nervous breakdown, Elisabet Vogler (Liv

Figure 3.2 Elisabet and Alma in *Persona*. Directed by Ingmar Bergman. Copyright AB Svensk Filmindustri 1966. All rights reserved.

Ullmann), and her caretaking nurse, Alma (Bibi Anderson)—intertwined (Figure 3.3). That moment precedes another in which their faces merge with a superimposition of affection-images, as one woman's face fades and reappears transformed as another. And at another moment, one of them, Elisabet, appears simultaneously projected from both behind and in front of the screen. As a result, personhood is radically sundered, generating multiple challenges to reception and judgment.

As I have suggested, as Bergman's film corpus developed his characters and themes were increasingly entangled with his autobiography, which featured an intense preoccupation with the challenges to religious belief in the face of God's silence. That's the theme that shapes the drama in *Winter Light* (in which as I've noted the pastor, Tomas Ericson, laments God's silence and struggles with his loss of faith). It is one among several films that articulate an autobiographical impulse. In this case that impulse is also reflected in the protagonist's name (Bergman was the son of his pastor/father, Eric, i.e. Eric's son, with a Christian name associated with doubt, i.e., Tomas). However, even

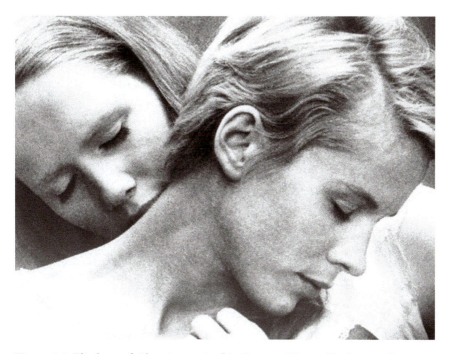

Figure 3.3 Elisabet and Alma intertwined in *Persona*. Directed by Ingmar Bergman. Copyright AB Svensk Filmindustri 1966.

prior to his *Winter Light*, Bergman had personally and cinematically dismissed commitments to a transcendent basis for spirituality. Asked about the view of God that emerges in his *Through a Glass Darkly* (1961), he referred to "love as the only thinkable form of holiness."[25] By the time Bergman's last film for theatrical release, *Fanny and Alexander* (1982), is produced and distributed, he has another figuration for his rejection of a transcendent sphere of judgment; it is what two characters in the film refer to as the need to live in "the little world" (which refers ambiguously to the theater and to the life world in general).

It was with the production of *Fanny and Alexander* that Bergman had caught up with *me* (in 1981, twenty years after I watched *The Virgin Spring*). Shot on location in Uppsala, the film opens (after the prologue) with a scene in which torchlights are being lit in a street that passes through an arch in the Skytaneum, an Uppsala University building in the *Gamla Torget* (Old Square) that houses the Political Science Department (Figure 3.4). At the moment that scene is being filmed, I am standing at a window in the Skytaneum's second floor, looking out at the street just prior to delivering a lecture to a group of

Figure 3.4 Gamle Torget in *Fanny and Alexander*. Directed by Ingmar Bergman. Copyright Cinematograph AB, Svenska Filminstitutet (SFI) 1982. All rights reserved.

Swedish political scientists. Consequently, *Fanny and Alexander* occupies a special place in my Bergman imaginary, in part because I was literally on the scene during part of its production and in part because watching it, I became aware of the overarching metaphysic within which the details of Bergman's film corpus function. I therefore begin my analysis with attention to that film before working backward to some earlier ones, all of which I analyze with an emphasis on the entanglement between Bergman's concerns with theatricality and spirituality.

Fanny and Alexander: The Theater as Heterotopia

What was Bergman up to? Like Paul (whose media career is featured in Chapter 2), he used media (artistic media genres in his case) to negotiate the meaning of life with his audiences, first with theater and then film (although in the latter he displayed his passion for the theater by including theatrical scenes and imagery). However, Bergman reversed Paul's emphasis. Likening earthly existence to a theater (a "little world"), he valorized life, sensuously and creatively lived, as the answer to death, even as he recognized that (as Milan Kundera has put it), "Life is stronger than death because it is nourished by it."[26] Accordingly, Bergman made death an intimate associate in his life-exploring cinematic dramas, personified and portrayed as a character in *The Seventh Seal* (1957), a film in which "the intrinsic connection of life and death" is the dominant theme.[27] By the time he wrote his *Fanny and Alexander* screenplay, he (like his Alma in *Persona*, who at one point refers to her "worn out hope of salvation") had given up on (even as he continued to represent) Christian theology's version of transcendence, apparently needing obsessively to show it as a vain hope and destructive commitment. Although he had kept dialing for some time, the cosmos had kept hanging up the phone. Whether or not Bergman had ultimately given up hope—he often expressed ambivalence on that issue—he had his characters reenact his personal struggle (ongoing throughout his film corpus) with the silence that reigns outside his "little world." His *Fanny and Alexander* is a fraught yet joyous capitulation to the here and now. It keeps his ambivalences in play as it resists definitive conclusions.

What then is left of spirituality in Bergman's art, as it articulates itself in its last cinematic realization, in *Fanny and Alexander*? As Susan Sontag suggests, "Every era has to invent the project of 'spirituality' for itself, where 'Spirituality' = plans, terminologies, ideas of deportment aimed at resolving the painful structural contradictions inherent in the human situation, at the completion of human consciousness, at transcendence."[28] It is doubtless that kind of spirituality rather than that offered by the institutionalized church that infused Bergman's art. And certainly, Bergman can identify with what Sontag describes as the modern approach to art: "Art is no longer understood as consciousness expressing and therefore, implicitly, affirming itself. Art is not consciousness per se, but rather its antidote [even as it] evolved from within consciousness itself."[29]

In his *Fanny and Alexander* Bergman has camera consciousness (the juxtapositions of images and the rhythms of attention to affects) challenge the institutionalized church's appeal to a higher consciousness. However, while ideational and emotional struggles transpire throughout the film, a conceptually compelling synopsis of *Fanny and Alexander* must first address spaces because all of them are either explicitly or allusively theatrical. The first such space, featured in the prologue, is a very small theater. Alexander is playing with his puppet theater, as the camera does a shot/reverse shot sequence, focusing first on Alexander's dreamy expression as he is reaching into the theater box, inventing Christmas scenes and then reversing to his point of view as he looks into the theater and arranges the props, he has available. The film's other spaces include the Ekdahl household, which early in the story is involved in preparation for the extended family's Christmas celebration, an Uppsala theater in which a Christmas story is enacted and thence one in which Oscar Ekdahl is directing and acting in *Hamlet*, a Bishop's austere home, which contrasts dramatically with the richly decorated and elaborately furnished and ornamented interior of the Ekdahl home, and the contrasting home of a family friend, the Jew, Isak, whose apartment/curio shop is in effect a very large puppet theater, stuffed with magical and myth-related objects and character representations.

As is the case in many of Bergman's films, the theater is both an actual place to stage dramas and a metaphor for the "little world," the non- (or anti-) theological life world. The film's ontological or "meta-theatrical aspect"[30] is realized dramatically in the way that the theater serves as a commentary on other spaces. Bergman's theaters, which operate as spatial protagonists in many of his films, are examples of what Michel Foucault famously calls "heterotopias," "counter-sites," which are "different from all the sites that they reflect and speak about ... [T]heir role is to create a space of illusion that exposes ... all the sites inside of which human life is partitioned, as still more illusory." Among them is the "theater," which "brings onto the rectangle of the stage, one after the other, a whole series of places that are foreign to one another."[31] In an early scene, as Fanny and Alexander's father, Oscar Ekdahl, an actor and theater director, is addressing his cast after the performance of *Hamlet*, he affirms Foucault's identification of the theater as a heterotopia. Beginning by saying that his only talent is love for "this little world," he continues, "Outside is the big world. Sometimes the little world succeeds in reflecting the big one so that we understand it better."[32]

Oscar's actual theater is one among many of the theatrical spaces that the film features. Although Bergman's most significant audience is not always in the theater (for example, he confesses that "the driving force in *Wild*

Strawberries is a desperate attempt to justify myself to my mythically oversized parents")[33]—from start to finish, *Fanny and Alexander* places the viewers in a theater box as it renders almost every other space as a theater stage. For example, shortly after Alexander takes leave of his little puppet theater and walks through the rooms of his grandmother, Helena Ekdahl's opulent home, several important theatrical effects develop. First, in keeping with Bergman's emphasis on theatricality, the household looks like a theater set. As Alexander looks from one room to another, an archway frames the room into which he is looking, making it resemble a theater stage.

A second effect is the animation of Alexander's imagination. One of the household's statues begins magically to move as he looks at it. Having just staged a play on his small puppet theater, he effectively stages another one as he looks around the home and his imagination moves objects and figures. Egil Törnqvist, referring to the made-for-television version, describes the effect well:

> Suddenly, the lighting changes miraculously. The half-naked woman sculpture by the window is strongly lit by the sun, and the room behind it turns intensely red. The glass prisms of the crystal chandelier, in close-up. Begin to move. The woman sculpture raises one arm. A dull sound appears to emanate from a scythe drawn through the carpet, and soon we see a grinning skull in a black hooded cloak stealing toward the woman behind the leaves of a potted plant.[34]

That pervasive theatrical effect in his films is one that Bergman adopted from Strindberg, a "dreamlike distantiation [which] functions in a 'deconstructive' way, by inputting a film into another film or by putting a play into a play."[35] Along with his use of theatrical visuals are other Bergman cinematic signatures. As Törnqvist's description points out, in the television version of the film, yet another Bergman theme appears. Among what Alexander sees, while momentarily sequestering himself under a table, is death, appearing as a masked figure dragging a scythe through a room. And another effect accompanies all the others, a play of light and shadow, which reproduces Bergman's recollection of his proto-cinematic perceptual games as a boy in his Grandmother's house. In his autobiography he reports that he would adjust the appearance of a scene by "bending my head sideways and forward [so that for example], as I move my head, the reflections in [a] gruel plate change and form new patterns."[36]

In this early scene, Bergman translates Alexander cinematic perceptions for the viewer. As Alexander moves through the house, the viewer experiences the variations in darkness and illumination that greet Alexander as he goes in search of his grandmother. Arriving in the bedroom, Alexander jumps on the bed and pulls the covers over himself, after which he takes over the active management of perception (shared with the viewer), as he sees things through the translucent coverlet. Thereafter, much of what the film shows is presented through the way Alexander sees things, often oneirically. He's a vehicle for practicing Bergman's Strindberg-inspired dreamscape aesthetic, as scenes often appear as "something recalled from a distance … [a] blending of fact and fantasy."[37]

After the Ekdahl household fills with the rest of the extended family for their Christmas celebration, orchestrated by Helena's "sensuous amiability,"[38] the ensuing playful exuberance of Alexander's family is very far from the austere, emotionally controlled, and moralistic family life Bergman's parents had conducted. It is closer to the emotional and aesthetic haven Bergman had enjoyed as a child while visiting in his grandmother's apartment. In addition to their joyful holiday celebration—singing dancing, marching through the home—the film's version of the Ekdahl's family life gives a whole different meaning to Paul's famous injunction (1 Corinthians 7: 29), "those who are married should live as though they were not." Before the celebration begins, the early arriving Isak reminisces with Helena about their illicit romance years ago, and once the celebration has finished, we are treated to the son, Gustav Adolph's satyr-like seduction of the maid, Maj (tolerated by Gustav's wife Alma, just as Helena's extra-marital affair with Isak had been tolerated by her late husband).

The Ekdahl family's sexual playfulness is accompanied by a Rabelaisian exuberance. After the Christmas meal, another of Helena's sons, Carl, gathers the children, drops his trousers, and with an impressive gust of flatulence, blows out the candles in a candelabra. In short, the exuberant Ekdahl family that Bergman's film portrays stands as a historical reprieve from the childhood Bergman actually had in the imagination-stifling household dominated by his pastor/father Eric.

However, as the film narrative proceeds, the reprieve is short-lived. After Alexander's father dies, his mother, Emilie, is betrothed to the stern, joyless, and self-righteous Bishop, Edvard Vergerus. Before the wedding, there's a scene that recreates an episode of the young Bergman's humiliation. In his autobiography, Bergman reports the story: In a state of "feverish excitement," after attending the Schumann Circus, he tells a school classmate that his parents have sold him to Schumann Circus and that he is soon to be trained as an acrobat. After his classmate exposes the story, the teacher, disturbed by Bergman's imaginative invention (treating it as a lie rather than seeing it as an instance of an active imagination), writes an admonishing letter to his parents. As a result, "There was a dreadful court scene. I was put up against the wall, humiliated and disgraced, at home as well as at school"[39] In the film, Alexander's mother, Emilie, allows the Bishop to conduct the humiliation. Representing it as tough love, Vergerus simultaneously caresses and reproaches Alexander as he elides the distinction between lying and imagining, effectively anathematizing theatricality.

Once Emilie moves with her children to her new husband's home, Alexander's humiliations are intensified; the family as a whole is quarantined within an emotionally stifling, joyless space, and Emilie realizes that she must leave her marriage and her family's incarceration within the austere, authoritarian Vergerus household, which has displaced her control over her children, while abjuring all expressions of imagination and enjoyment. Once she plots an escape, defying Vergerus's threats of legal suppression (ultimately obviated when he dies in a fire), she departs and her children are rescued by Isak and his nephew, who hide them in a trunk and bring them to Isak's home. While Alexander is in Isak's labyrinthian home/puppet theater, his imaginative side is affirmed and encouraged rather than squelched. It is at this point that the film dramatizes the difference between institutionalized theology's suppression of imagination and creative, theatrically performed magical thinking.

Doubtless, the Jew, Isak is a Moses figure managing an exodus for persons enslaved and oppressed. It's an identity also evidenced by the name of his nephew, Aron (Aaron is the name of Moses's biblical assistant). Remarking that magic is real, Isak's Aron takes over the choreographing of Alexander's experience of the out-sized magic theater in his home. Among the characters to whom Aron introduces Alexander is a large puppet representing God, who, when he appears, disturbs the theatrical atmosphere so much that all the other puppets start shaking until the God/puppet collapses. "God" is thus portrayed as a theatrical character whose act is destructive and is nearing an end. However, he (clearly a "he" puppet) is one among many other magical personae, which include a 4,000-year-old mummy, still breathing and inexplicably luminous. As Aron conducts Alexander's tour of Isak's magical theater, he introduces him to Isak's metaphysic. According to "Uncle Isak," he says, there are many realities, one on top of the other, and insofar as "God" has a reality in Isak's theology, it is in a Spinozist as opposed to the traditional Christian sense. As Aron puts it, "Everything is alive and everything is God's thought."

Lynda Bundtzen provides a fitting summary of the theological versus magic practices that distinguish Vergerus and Isak: "Isak's magic foils Vergerus's self-righteousness and faith in the absolute power of a Christian God, replacing it with a reality manipulable by desire and imagination— divinity's human form."[40] What is important to the film story is the effect of the magic lesson. Isak's magical theater liberates Alexander from the forces attempting to stifle his imagination (especially the moralizing containments imposed in the Bishop's home). The most significant part of the lesson takes place in his encounter with Isak's son Ishmael. Whereas the biblical Ishmael is cut off from Isaac's inheritance and exiled territorially, Isak's Ismael is exiled architecturally; "he" is in the house but locked in a separate room (into which Aron ushers Alexander). As a persona, Ismael contributes to the distinction between the Bishops and Isak's households by virtue of the actor selected for the part. While Bishop Vergerus's architecturally separated (room-confined and bedridden aunt Elsa) is played by a man, Isak's son Ishmael is played by a woman. That stark divide encourages reflection on the difference between the orthodox Lutheranism versus magical metaphysics that distinguishes the two homes ideationally.

Yet more significant than the casting difference are the consequences of the behavior of the two personae. Elsa, in flames from an upset kerosene lamp, inadvertently kills the sedated Bishop after staggering from her room into his and falling on him. Ismael performs a different kind of merger. While liberating Alexander by killing his inhibitions, he says, "Perhaps we flow into each other"; and "I obliterate myself and merge into you." The identity gift that Ismael gives Alexander is an affirmation of the creative, magical imagination that already belonged to him. Thanks to the encounter with Ismael, he can feel free to exercise it. However, as is the case for Bergman himself, that imagination haunts him as well as giving him an escape. Thus, at one point while back in his grandmother's home, Alexander conjures the dead Bishop, who tells him, "you can't escape me." That moment also conjures the autobiographical struggle that occurs continually in Bergman's cinematic corpus. Throughout his artistic creations, he was unable to escape his religious upbringing; his pastor/father Eric's theological scruples, which kept haunting him, are a continual presence in his film dramas.

By the end of the film, Gustav Adolph provides another affirmation of Alexander's imagination with a pedagogical soliloquy that delivers the theatrical metaphor yet again. Standing in a posture that mimes a theatrical proclamation, his remarks privilege thespians over theologians and reaffirm the value of dwelling happily in "the little world":

> We Ekdahls have not come into the world to see through it … we might just as well ignore big things … we must live in the little world … we must be content with that and cultivate it and make the best of it … It is necessary and not shameful to take pleasure in the little world … good food, gentle smiles, fruit trees in bloom, waltzes.

The large and boisterous Gustave Adolf takes up a lot of ideational and emotional space. However, despite how compelling and *apropos* his speech is with respect to its statement of the film's primary theme, it would be precipitous to see him as an unambiguous representative of Bergman's sentiments. Much of the film also presents a "feminine matrix," within which Gustav Adolph is often undermined.[41] That matrix asserts itself at the end of the film, both to establish control of the theater (Helena tells Emilie that Oscar on his deathbed had asked her to take over as the theater director) and to rescue Maj, who is as much a prisoner as was Emilie (in her case a prisoner of Gustave Adolf's lust, affection, and generosity). As the film concludes it appears that erotic attachments can be as punishing as self-righteousness. Because Maj is feeling trapped by Gustav Adolph's controlling generosity—he has arranged a café position for her in Uppsala in order to keep her close by—she asks her friend Petra to intercede with Emilie for help because she wants to move to Stockholm and take over control of her life. Like Fanny and Alexander, Maj is in need of a rescue, which in this case is done by Emilie and Helena, who arrange her escape: "so often in Bergman's films, it is women who cut through the intellectual posturings and dishonesty of the men."[42] It is Helena who puts the matter within the film's dominant theatrical idiom while at the same time dismissing male interpretive privilege. After Emilie says to her that Gustav Adolph will be terribly hurt, Helena takes over with a matriarchal moment that steals Gustav Adolph's masculinist thunder. She says that there is no need to be concerned about Gustav Adolph: "He has a good head for business but knows nothing about the theater," by which she is implying that he cannot appreciate the space of freedom and self-actualization. It is also Helena who takes over at the end of the film to deliver Bergman's Strindbergian accord with Isak's metaphysic. Reading to her grandchild from Strindberg's *A Dream Play* and quoting from the Preface, she speaks a line that accords with the lesson about multiple realities that shapes Isak's metaphysic and milieu: "Everything can happen, everything is possible and likely. Time and space do not exist; on an insignificant basis of reality the imagination spins and weaves new patterns."

Although thanks to Helena, Maj is allowed to escape by moving from one city to another, Alexander does not enjoy a simple territorial solution. Two revenants haunt him. One is his father, Oscar, whose ghost shows up several times (mimicking Oscar's role in his production of Hamlet). The other is the Bishop (whose ghost as I noted reminds him about the futility of trying to escape him). At the end of the film, there is no benign closure for an Alexander who is caught between two dominant patriarchal figures (just as there was none for Bergman). The film's musical soundtrack suggests as much. Bergman, very much attuned to the significance of musical scores, regarded "the sequence of pictures [which] plays directly on our feelings," as having "much in common [with] music." "Both," he says, "affect our emotions directly, not via the intellect."[43] As for his selections for *Fanny and Alexander*, among them is a Schumann's Piano Quintet in E flat minor, Opus 44 (off-screen four times in the television version).[44] As many have observed, Schumann's music is non-closural; his melodies, which are punctuated with interruptions, are characterized (as Slavoj Žižek suggests) by their "undermining of the privilege of the melodic line … [effected with] delays, overtakings, and other barely perceptible forms of rhythmic noncoordination." And in an observation of its relationship with cinema (in this case an Orson Welles film but which applies well to many of Bergman's), Žižek refers to "a kind of musical equivalent" in which "Welles's wide-angle focus shot … distorts the face in close-up and simultaneously transforms the background into a de-realized dreamlike landscape (i.e., performing a Bergman-type cinematic signature)."[45]

A Transition

Before leaving *Fanny and Alexander* I want to point to yet another way that Bergman sought a solution to the problem of life because its role in the film, managed as much with images as with soliloquys, has a legacy extending back to the first of his films that explores extensively the problem of death, his above-noted 1957 film, *The Seventh Seal*. Among what is featured in the closing scene of *Fanny and Alexander* is a new life. Right after Gustav Adolph's long soliloquy, there's a cut to a bedroom where Emilie is holding her baby. A new life also features prominently in *The Seventh Seal*. It's an infant belonging to a young couple Jof (Nils Poppe) and Mia (Bibi Andersson) who belong to a group of itinerate actors (Figure 3.5, young couple and infant). The vitality

Figure 3.5 Young family in *The Seventh Seal*. Directed by Ingmar Bergman. Copyright Svensk Filmindustri (SF) 1957. All rights reserved.

of this young family is juxtaposed throughout the film to the weariness of the knight, Antonius Block (Max von Sydow), and his squire, Jöns (Gunnar Björnstrand), who are first seen in a state of exhaustion. They're lying prone on a pebbly beach, just above the tide mark, having just returned from a crusade. As the film narrative proceeds, it becomes evident that their exhaustion is moral as well as physical.

The Seventh Seal: A Painterly Aesthetic

Bruce Kawin provides a succinct thematic summary of the film narrative:

> *The Seventh Seal* ... vividly recreates both the objective and subjective worlds of medieval Sweden. While on the one hand it tells the credible story of a knight and his squire who return from the Crusades t a land ravaged by the plague (a deliberate parallel to the modern sense of an impending nuclear disaster), on the other it has them encounter not only Death himself, but Joseph, Mary, and their baby as well ... *The Seventh Seal* achieves a remarkable fusion of philosophies. Love, mortal beauty, and artistic vision justify life in the absence of God and under the shadow of death.[46]

Equally important to Bergman's drama is its aesthetic framing. To introduce it, I want to reference a moment in a film by another director who was also famously alienated from institutionalized Christianity. It's a stunning iconic scene in Luis Buñuel's *Viridiana* (1961). After a group of wretched beggars in a town (a drunk, a leper, a crippled man, a blind man, an angry dwarf, a prostitute and so on) have taken over an estate, they have prepared a banquet. As they're assembled at the table, there is a framing shot that shows the positioning of their bodies mimicking Leonardo da Vinci's *The Last Supper* (Figure 3.6). Bergman's *The Seventh Seal* is often painterly in its form as well. Referring explicitly to his use of a painterly aesthetic (in a note to the film), he states, "My intention has been to paint in the same way as the medieval church painter."[47] Accordingly, the film abounds in iconic moments. Those, along with other aspects of *The Seventh Seal's* aesthetic, anticipates the image-conveyed struggle between theology and theatricality featured in Bergman's *Fanny and Alexander*. As is the case in his *Fanny and Alexander*, where Bergman juxtaposes a religious believer's approach to life with creative theatrical explorations of it,

Figure 3.6 The beggar's banquet in *Viridiana*. Directed by Fernand Bunuel. Copyright Gustavo Alatriste Productions 1961.

the characters in *The Seventh Seal* also articulate that binary. However, the aesthetics within which the juxtaposition is played out involves an additional artistic media genre, painting, which depicts iconic moments in the Christian story and shares the film's aesthetic space with its musical soundtrack. Both artistic genres contribute to the film's aesthetically engendered temporalities.

As for how those different genres can relate to thematizing the film's main focus—life's duration—painting and music have different ways of managing temporality. Painting captures iconic moments. It's a feature that Theodor Adorno identifies as a "stubborn object-relatedness." Painting, he says, captures a "temporal differential, the moment in which temporally disparate elements are concentrated."[48] Whereas music is characterized by its "temporal order," a "flowing [that] seems to resist every reification,"[49] in painting, "everything is simultaneous. Its synthesis consists in bringing together things that exist next to each other."[50] *The Seventh Seal*'s musical score provides a mood and tempo for the life rhythms and vicissitudes operating in a fourteenth century in which the population is being ravaged by the Black Plague, and diverse religious and secular perspectives are in contention over what it means, what caused it, and what it portends.

With respect to how the soundtrack comments on that contention, it generates rhythms and moods that are alternatively mimetic (when involved in representing a Christian view) or contrapuntal (when in accord with secular rebuttals). Musical commentary is supplemented by the figural commentaries issuing from religious paintings and physical icons (murals, crosses, statues, and so on) which represent Christendom's visual culture. There are also other important visuals—costumes and other paraphernalia of theatricality, which represent a life world concerned with play and pleasure rather than divine wrath-inflicted suffering and apocalyptic doom. At the same time, a clash of voices constitutes the main interpersonal dynamic unfolding within the musically and figurally forged aesthetic of the film drama. Accompanying the aural and visual aesthetic is what M. M. Bakhtin famously calls heteroglossia (the many contending voices concept introduced in Chapter 2).

The contentious ideational atmosphere descends early in the film, after Bloch's encounter with death in which he negotiates a reprieve by challenging death to a game of chess. It's an exchange in which the significance of the painting aesthetic is underscored, for after Bloch refers to death being known as one who plays chess, death asks how he knows, and Bloch replies that he's seen in paintings. Once death has accepted the reprieve Bloch has requested, Bloch and his squire Jöns mount their horses and begin their travel homeward while a musical aesthetic accompanies their ride. It's a different music from the one heard offscreen as the film opens. The first part of the soundtrack, played while the camera surveys the sky and sea, is the Gregorian Chant, *Dies Irae* (Day of Wrath), sung by a chorale whose words foretell a final judgment ("That day of wrath, that dreadful day, shall heaven and earth in ashes lay … What horror must invade the mind when the approaching Judge shall find and sift the deeds of all mankind!"[51]). In contrast, what is heard as Bloch and his squire depart on horseback is more like a hornpipe, played by a single brass instrument. As the ride commences, Jöns's song picks up the rhythm performed by the hornpipe, and his lyrics begin with his mundane sexual fantasies: "Between a strumpet's legs I lie …"[52] (Figure 3.7). However, in addition to his mainly non-spiritual focus, an earthly ballad expressing lust rather than spirituality expressed at this moment in a contrapuntal musical genre to the Chant heard at the film's

Figure 3.7 Bloch and Jons in *The Seventh Seal*. Directed by Ingmar Bergman. Copyright Svensk Filmindustri (SF) 1957.

opening, Jöns is an attendant in two senses. In addition to his vocational role as an attendant to the Knight, he is what Gilles Deleuze designates as a special kind of aesthetic figure, an "attendant," a figure he discerns in the canvasses of the painter Francis Bacon.

The attendant figure is one peripheral to the main theme, a character who "seems to subsist, distinct from the [main] figure" in Bacon's canvasses.[53] As I had summarized that role in an earlier investigation, "Deleuze sees the attendant as a provider of facticity of the scene, or in his words, 'the relation of the Figure to its isolating place', or 'what takes place.'"[54] It's a conceptual innovation that adapts well to cinema and is especially *apropos* as a characterization of Jöns's role. As Birgitta Steene rightly observes, the Jöns-Bloch binary represents "the esthetic versus the ethical way of life."[55] However, Jöns's voice in both song and commentary not only opposes the pieties—stylistically as well as ideationally— to which Bloch is allegiant (as he, Bloch) continually seeks affirmation of God's sponsorship of his world, but also provides a meta commentary on the reality of the dystopic fourteenth-century world through which he and his Knight are traveling. Mocking the way Christianity's pieties are ventriloquized through Bloch, Jöns's early song delivered on horseback satirically mimics religious God talk; he sings about God "aloft" and "Satan below" while expressing impious feelings. However, his attendant role transcends his contrapuntal effect *vis-a-vis* Block. It emerges in his continual descriptions of the roiling controversies all around them, for example, the passage, "There's talk of omens and other horrors" in his opening song and his reaction later in the film to the shouts from an apocalyptic religious procession that we're all doomed: "Do they expect modern people to believe that drivel ... even the ghost stories about God the father?"

As the film proceeds, the two aesthetic arts pervade and shape the film's *mise en scene*—music, which is punctuated with alternating melodies and silences, and an image commentary in which the most important painting is a *Danse Macabre* (Dance of Death) mural. Those along with other images on which the camera fixes—various religious icons (e.g., crosses and a crucified Jesus)—give the film a decidedly painterly structure. In contrast with the constant of flow of activity through which the drama in *Fanny and Alexander* is shaped (the moving dreamscape Alexander's creates), *The Seventh Seal* is constructed through a series of tableaux. Its intentional aesthetic is mirrored on medieval iconic canvasses devoted to thematizations of life and death at key moments in the Christianity's founding story.

While contention between magical imaginative creations and theological austerity is the main binary in *Fanny and Alexander,* the binary in *The Seventh Seal* involves belief versus knowledge. Anticipating the theological problematic—verifying God's existence—in Bergman's religious trilogy: *Through a Glass Darkly* (1961), *Winter Light* (1963), and *The Silence* (1963), *The Seventh Seal's* Knight Bloch, a devout believer, is afflicted by God's failure to reveal "his" presence through either saying or showing. In a key scene in which the knight enters a church in which the altar is dominated by a grotesque version of the crucified Christ, he approaches the confessional booth (manned by death, whom the knight is unable to recognize through the cross hatching of the screen separating confessor and priest) and says that his heart is a void. He admits under death's questioning that he wants to die but adds that before that he wants knowledge. He asks why "God ... must hide in the midst of vague promises and invisible miracles ... What will become of us who want to believe but cannot … I want knowledge not belief, not surmise but knowledge. … I want God to come out and show his face, but he is silent."

Ultimately the film rewards Bloch without giving him the affirmation of God's existence that he seeks. Although he loses the chess game in his encounter with death (death comes to collect him, his wife, and his traveling companions after he has returned home), he manages to distract death long enough for the young actors, Jos and Mia (allegorically Joseph and Mary) to escape with their baby. In the closing scene, as the young family is about to depart, Jos has a vision of The Dance of Death in the distance as Bloch, his wife, and his traveling companions are leaving their lives (Figure 3.8). That image, *Danse Macabre* (The Dance of Death) first appears on a mural in a church, where the artist drawing it tells the squire how compelling the image is (more compelling he says than image of naked women). That dance is later contrasted with the dance of life, when Bloch tells Mia about his marriage: "We

Figure 3.8 *Danse Macabre* in *The Seventh Seal*. Directed by Ingmar Bergman copyright Svensk Filmindustri (SF) 1957. All rights reserved 1957.

hunted, we danced, the house was full of life." In the final scene, the closing shot of a fresh-faced Mia with her husband and healthy young baby implies that the only answer to death is the continuation of love and vitality in others. As Bloch et al.'s procession through life is ending in a last procession, the young family's procession through life continues. Thus, while throughout the film, a clash of voices—verbal encounters among the pious, the irreverent and the zealous—yields no central ideational perspective on life and death (the film's voices are centrifugal, pulling away from a "verbal ideological center"[56]), the images are what provide Bergman's provisional answer.

However, Bergman's film also thinks about a temporality different from the one involved in managing life's movement toward death. While his films grapple with the recognition that there is no definitive solace from the reality that "all plots move deathward,"[57] they also reflect on the emotional vicissitudes involved in the flows of time that operate outside the more dramatic issues surrounding life/death,[58] for example, moments when characters find peaceful interpersonal enjoyment, reprieves from their struggles with God's seeming indifference to cruelty, suffering and demands for answers. Such a moment is exemplified in *The Seventh Seal* in the scene in which Mia offers Bloch a bowl of wild strawberries. Bloch initially rejects the offer as he rehearses his angst: "To believe is to suffer like loving someone in the dark who never answers." However, once he capitulates and begins enjoying the bowl of wild strawberries in milk, he rhapsodizes about the hour of peace he is experiencing, seemingly recognizing that there are simple joys in shared moments when life is being lived rather than being inspected with respect to whether it has divine sponsorship. The "wild strawberries" Bloch enjoys becomes the title and main iconic symbol in Bergman's next film, *Wild Strawberries* (released later the same year). Wild strawberries are symbols of innocence and fleeting moments of happiness in Scandinavian iconography.

Wild Strawberries: Theatrical Automobility

Wild Strawberries constituted an important transition technologically for Bergman's thematizing of lived time. His continual incorporation of flashbacks "creates a virtual confusion in its temporal levels."[59] By locating the flashbacks as part of his protagonist, Isak Borg's (Victor Sjöström) dreamscape, the film's commentary on lived time actualizes Henri Bergson's insight that perception and recollection are intermediated. However, to apply Bergsonism to Bergman's Isak Borg we have to specify the kind of memory involved in the drama. Neither of Bergson's two most familiar versions, habitual and pure memory, is a good fit. Although the latter comes closer to Isak's journey into his past because it contains a person's full archive of recollections,[60] there is no sign of the purposive needs of perception that Bergson assigns to pure memory. Because Isak's dreams seem to haunt him unbidden, a more appropriate version is a "third type of memory" to which Bergson gives only passing attention. It consists in those parts of pure memory that are "unsolicited" and "come washing over us *for their own reasons*, operating according to non-instrumental lines of association having nothing to do with the conscious mind or its concern for retrieving 'useful' memories."[61] Throughout the film, Isak Borg's memory-infused dreamscape has him watching parts of the drama of his life. It is an extraordinary intensification, a late life summing up of what Marx observed as inherent in the human condition, making one's "life activity," an object of one's "consciousness."[62]

Wild Strawberries opens with Isak Borg reflecting on the trajectory of his life's attachments in unemotionally voiced reports about his family, living and deceased, and his current situation in which he is cared for by his house keeper Agda (Jullan Kind). He then reports the event ahead of him tomorrow, an honorary degree to be presented at the Lund Cathedral. His reflections are followed by interactions within his household. They are commentaries that cast him in an unfavorable light, consisting in complaints from his housekeeper about how inconsiderate he is by planning to drive to Lund (which would prevent her from accompanying him to witness the degree presentation) and a more severe one by his visiting daughter-in-law Marianne (Ingrid Thulin), who tells him he's a selfish old man whom his son Evald (Gunnar Björnstrand) hates. The film's fraught opening previews Isak's uncomfortable personal history in which he is haunted by the two things (continually thematized in Bergman's films)—his failure to come to terms with his death and his failure to come to terms with a lifetime of failed and disturbed intimacies. The film's dreamscape is rendered from Isak's spectating point of view. "Borg," Bergman suggests, "is a spectator, then as now, in the theatre of his own life, neither enriched by coping with family tensions nor succored by reciprocal family love."[63] The film casts him as the anti-hero of his life drama.

Wild Strawberries is among other things a road movie in which chance encounters play a significant role. As I noted in Chapter 1, such road encounters are conceptually situated by M. M. Bakhtin whose concept "the chronotope of the road" fits much of the temporal unfolding of Isak's journey toward Lund. "The road [to repeat the Bakhtin's remark] is especially (but not exclusively) for portraying events governed by chance."[64] Such chance encounters on the road are embedded in an ontological journey that Hélène Cixous addresses (quoted in Chapter 2). Isak's one-day journey to Lund is insinuated within a life's journey toward death (which captures the metaphysical framing that Bergman gives to Isak's story): "The country from which we come is always the one to which we are returning. You are on the return road, which passes through the country of children in the maternal body. You have already passed through here: you recognize the landscape. You have always been on a return road [with] … a face toward death."[65] The "return road" in which Isak faces death gets its expression in his dreams.

In his first dream he is Isak Borg, witnessing the aftermath of Isak Borg's death. He dreams that the latter, already-deceased Isak Borg, is in a coffin that spills out of the back of a horse-drawn hearse. As the dreaming Isak Borg approaches the exposed body, it reaches and grabs his hand. Later, on the road with Marianne toward Lund, he stops at his family's old summer place. There he falls into a dream in which he watches while his brother, Sigfrid, flirts with his intended, Sara, a prelude to Sigrid's winning her affections, ultimately marrying her, and thereafter (seen by Isak in a dream late in the film) enjoying the marital bliss that is denied to Isak, who ended up in a conflictful, unhappy marriage.

Once on the road, driving toward Lund with Marianne, Isak's capacious automobile becomes a small theater as, along the way, they first pick up three young people, a woman and two men (who ultimately get into a theological quarrel) and then pick up a quarreling middle-aged couple (whose arguments with each other become so vociferous that they are expelled from the car). The remaining three young people are on their way to a holiday in Italy. They accompany Isak and Marianne all the way to Lund and stay around to watch Isak's ceremony. The complications and issues raised by the expelled couple and young trio affect Isak who is temporarily turned into a witness of other lives. As a result, the automobile-as-theater rehearses a play that ultimately influences the other theater—the perceptual drama Isak attends while witnessing his past in the theater directed by his troubled conscience (Figure 3.9).

Egil Törnqvist's apt figuring of Isak's journey likens it to Paul's (in his Saul persona): "Like Saul's journey to Damascus … Isak's trip turns into a penitential journey, working a conversion. Isak's Borg's career has been based on a reckless attitude to his fellow-men. Now on the threshold of death, he begins to suffer pangs of guilt."[66] While Isak's dreamscape (which takes up a considerable portion of the film's footage) is casting Isak's recollections and nightmare fantasies, symbolized in his visits to the wild strawberry patch in his former summer home—"The pattern is: nightmare, nostalgic dream, nightmare, nostalgic dream"[67]—the small theater in Isak's automobile is staging two themes that Bergman will have pursued in his subsequent films. One is

Figure 3.9 The automobile theater in *Wild Strawberries*. Directed by Ingmar Bergman. Copyright Svensk Filmindustri (SF) 1957. All rights reserved 1957.

about religious belief. The two young men, Viktor a believer headed toward a career in the ministry, and Anders, an anti-spiritual rationalist planning a medical career, argue about whether God exists and whether an acceptance of that existence enables an ethical life.

The young woman traveling with them has claimed to be attracted to both and is sitting between them while avoiding taking a position on the issue. When she asks Isak whether he is religious, rather than answering directly, he waxes poetic: "I see traces whenever flowers bloom."[68] And importantly, as the drive proceeds, Isak becomes a fatherly object of affection for the young trio. In the small automobile theater, he manages to evince the emotionally supportive version of fatherhood that he had failed to provide as a biological father. The effect he achieves is underscored when after the ceremony in Lund, the trio serenade him outside the window of his room. Their effect on him has been infectious. It encourages him to seek more intimacy with his house keeper Agda, suggesting to her that they use first names (which she rebuffs), to express affection toward Marianne (e.g., he allows her smoke in the car whereas early he prohibited it), and to seek a reconciliation with his son Evald (offering to forgive his financial debt). While most of the close-ups of the dreaming Isak had shown a face in torment throughout the film's portrayal of his humiliating dreams, the last scene shows the face of the sleeping Isak looking content.

Ultimately *Wild Strawberries* serves as a threshold to Bergman's later films. Its motifs and structure—the rhythms of interaction between dreams or fantasies and reality, theatricality, the temporalities associated with life's journeys (the ongoing vicissitudes of family life and the heading toward death), and controversial and often disappointing fathers (both God-the-father and biological fathers)—intensify as they occupy the ideational and emotional spaces of Bergman's famous religious trilogy: *Through a Glass Darkly* (1961), *Winter Light* (1963), and *The Silence* (1963). Although there are anti-religious sentiments expressed in parts of *Wild Strawberries*, religion remained a Bergman obsession and vulnerability moving forward. As he remarks in an interview, "No one is safe from religious ideas and confessional phenomena. Neither you nor I. ... As I see it today, any relapse is out of the question. But I can't say it's out of the question tomorrow."[69]

Through a Glass Darkly: "The Play's the Thing …"

The bookends of the film come from Paul's First Epistle to the Corinthians. It begins with an onscreen quotation that speaks to the epistemic barrier between Christians and their god: 1 Corinthians 13: 12: "For now we see through a glass darkly; but then face to face: now in part; but then shall I know even as I am known" (a passage that suggests the possibility of developing more intimacy with God's presence than was to transpire in the film) and ends with reference to St. John's assertion that God is love (echoed by Paul in the same epistle). As for the film's aesthetic framing: As I noted in the analyses of *Fanny and Alexander* and *The Seventh Seal,* music and musical idioms shape Bergman's film work. Accordingly, he refers to his religious trilogy as "chamber works." As he puts it, "They are chamber music—music in which, with an extremely limited number of voices and figures, one explores the essence of a number of motifs. The backgrounds are extrapolated, put into a sort of fog. The rest is distillation."[70]

After the film's opening scene, when the four characters emerge from bathing in the sea (a baptismal imagery), the main motif develops. Two senses of fatherhood dominate the plot of the film. The brother Minus (Lars Passgård) yearns for attention from his father, David (Gunnar Björnstrand), who is a globally recognized writer, preoccupied with his craft. He spends much of his time away and ignores his children when at home. Minus's sister Karin (Harriet Anderson), who has been diagnosed as psychotic, yearns for attention from the "heavenly father." Each of them stages a drama to try and draw out the respective fathers. Shortly after a scene in an alfresco meal that begins jovially, David admits that he will soon be leaving for Yugoslavia, despite having promised to stay at home for a change. Minus, who has complained that his father doesn't speak to him, announces that he has a surprise; he has written a play. He blindfolds David and leads him to a seat in front of a makeshift theater.

Minus's play is the film's first drama. He and Karin perform as actors while David and Karin's husband Martin (Max von Sydow) are the play's spectators, watching "The Artistic Haunting" or "The Funeral Vault of Illusions," which thematizes death in a religious setting. The setting is a funeral vault in The

Chapel of Saint Theresa. However, the plot of the play is less important than its intended reception. Minus is seeking approval from his father, who claps and shouts "author, author" once the play is over. His enthusiasm, however, seems contrived; when asked by Minus if he liked the play, he says only that it was "nice."[71] He is nevertheless reached by the drama as he had been by the dinner table conversation. As the film proceeds, it is clear that David is conscience stricken.

There is also an oblique father drama that appears in Karin's troubled relationship with her husband, Martin. He continually refers to her as his child—for example, saying, "what's wrong my little one," when he finds her weeping (Figure 3.10). Before moving on to Bergman's *Winter Light*, which as noted, Bergman called it the film "closest" to him, I want to rehearse briefly Karin's more intense father drama, which transcends the troubled father figures in her family. She fantasizes about a room in the house's attic where a crowd of people are waiting for God to appear through a door. After ascending

Figure 3.10 Karin and two fathers in *Through a Glass Darkly*. Directed by Ingmar Bergman. Copyright Svensk Filmindustri (SF) 1957. All rights reserved 1961

to the room and asking Martin to go away and leave her to the moment, she screams hysterically and reports that the God who appeared emerged through a split in the wallpaper and turned out to be a spider who assaulted her, trying first to enter her and then moving upward:

> He came toward me and I saw his face; it was a terrible stony face. He crawled up and tried to force himself into me, I defended myself. He looked at me and his eyes were cold and calm. When he couldn't penetrate me, he continued upward to my chest, then my face, and then up the wall. I have seen God.

Karin's God turns out to be a monstrosity, something nightmarish and well beyond a merely disappointing father, a "spider God," who is mentioned as such in Bergman's subsequent *Winter Light*. Commenting on Karin's moment, Bergman says that the film treats "the idea of the Christian God as something destructive and fantastically dangerous, something filled with risk for the human being and bringing out in him dark destructive forces instead of the opposite."[72]

In contrast, Minus's father drama ends positively. It concludes with a conversation he has with his father, David. When Minus asks his father if being surrounded by love can save Karin, David replies, "I believe so" (an answer that recall's Bergman's remark that "love is the only holiness"). Minus, still unsatisfied, says, "I cannot live in this new world," to which David replies, "yes you can" and goes on to imply that to accept the world you have to embrace the contingencies of intimacy rather than seeking the certainties perpetuated by Christian theology. When Minus asks him to supply proof of God's existence and adds, "you can't," David responds with what is Bergman's oft-repeated anti-theological position: "Yes I can but you must listen carefully. I can only give you a hint of my own hope. I know that love exists for real in the human world, the highest and lowest, the most absurd, and the most sublime—all kinds of love." Minus: "So love is the proof." David: "We can't know whether love proves God's existence or whether love is God himself." Minus then has a last remark, having connected with a father who for once seems present, he says, "Papa spoke to me!" That positive ending which seems to redeem fatherhood is not sustained in *Winter Light*. A film whose outlook is bleaker (a mood that the lighting tonality conveys) than what is implied in the conclusion of *Through a Glass Darkly*. In *Winter Light* both a pastor/father and God-the-father are experienced as failing their purported missions. As is the case in *Through a Glass Darkly*, love, the "topic that ties together all of Bergman's films," is a motif in *Winter Light*. However, in the latter the emphasis is on the "inability of human beings to touch one another in love."[73]

Winter Light: The Spider God Returns

There is no explicit theater drama in *Winter Light*. Its theatricality functions very much the way it does in *Wild Strawberries*, through Bergman's filming style. "Characteristic of Bergman as a film director," as Törnqvist puts it, "is precisely the alloy between what we traditionally regard as distinctively theatrical (concentration in the characters, stylization) and what we see as typical for the film (realism in the description of the characters and their environment)."[74] Accordingly, I want to suggest that absent specific theater scenes, the theater remains in Bergman's films through a theatrically oriented filming style that effectively draws attention away from abstract theological commitments and focuses on the distinctively human struggle to make sense of a life world bereft of theologically sponsored spiritual guarantees. What we must also consider to appreciate more fully Bergman's cinematic compositions is a historical contextualizing. *Winter Light* is produced during the cold war when many (exemplified by the character Jonas Persson) are anxious about nuclear annihilation. In this film, as elsewhere, Bergman situates personal struggles within the problems that pertain to the specific historical moment within which the struggles proceed. That aspect of what Bergman's films think about, as they develop their ethico-political sensibility, is exemplified in Paul Schrader's film, *First Reformed* (2017), which functions in part as a remake of *Winter Light*. The film by a director, who like Bergman is a refugee from a spiritual background (seminary training in his case), articulates the Bergman effect inasmuch as its Pastor Toller (Ethan Hawke), struggling like Bergman's Tomas Ericsson with a crisis of faith, also fails to dissuade an anxious parishioner from committing suicide. In this case, the issue is contemporary; his parishioner is tormented and despairing about environmental degradation. Schrader borrows much of Bergman's framing of the plot, updates the ethico-political issue, and films in a Bergman style—long silences and a lot of static images with lingering long takes on anguished faces (I return to Schrader's film in Chapter 5).

Although Bergman's films allude to historical ethico-political issues, his approach is never ideological. Rather, as Susan Sontag points out in her reading of his *Persona*, which has historical scenes of violence intervening,

> Bergman is not a topical historically oriented filmmaker. Elisabeth [in *Persona*] watching a newsreel on TV of a bonze [priest] in Saigon immolating himself, or staring at the famous photograph of the little boy from the Warsaw Ghetto being led off to be slaughtered, are, for Bergman, above all, images of total violence, of unredeemed cruelty. ... History or politics enters *Persona* only in the form of pure violence. Bergman makes an 'aesthetic' use of violence—far from ordinary left-liberal propaganda. The subject of *Persona* is the violence of the spirit.[75]

Bergman's inter-articulation of the ethical and the aesthetic is especially evident in *Winter Light*. What distinguishes that film from even those films that his style influences is the care he takes with lighting. While as I've noted the image of a "spider god" connects *Winter Light* with *Through a Glass Darkly* and adds another adjective (quoted in Chapter 1), which constructs the deity as a function of subjective imagination, as an "echo god," much of the film's effect is the mood conveyed by its natural lighting. The bleakness of the landscape and church interior resonates with Pastor Eriksson's alienation from the God he had dedicated himself to serving. The "spider god" passage takes place in a conversation in which Tomas, who is supposed to provide solace for his anxious parishioner Jonas, instead indulges his own anxieties, making Jonas more anxious. The spider god passage inter-articulates the light/dark effects of the filming style with Tomas's view of God-as-monstrosity: "Every time I confronted God with the reality I saw, he became ugly, revolting, a spider god—a monster. That's why I hid him away from the light, from life. In my darkness and loneliness, I hugged him to myself."

Loneliness is expressed within two different discursive spaces in *Winter Light*. Jumping to near the end of the film, we watch the seriously estranged couple, Pastor Tomas and his school teacher lover, Marta, who have traveled to Frostnas where Tomas is to perform a Sunday service in a small rural church. As Bergman has written, he was very familiar with such venues: "As a child I was sometimes allowed to accompany my father when he traveled about to preach in small country churches," and goes on to note how he "devoted his interest" to observing the churches' features (which in the film he does with his camera).[76] Before the church service is to begin, Marta and Tomas are momentarily isolated in separate long takes as they each make statements that speak to their very different yearnings. First, there is a side view close-up shot of Marta, who says, "If only we could just feel safe and show each other tenderness." There follows a cut to a side view close-up of Tomas, who says, "If we could only believe."

Those two soliloquys arise out of a gender matrix that informs much of Bergman's film corpus. The men—Tomas in this case (like Bergman himself)—have father issues operating at the two levels I noted in the discussion of *Through a Glass Darkly*. It's about paternal inadequacy from both heavenly and earthly fathers. Before continually thematizing an absent god in his religious films, Bergman imagined an absent earthly father. He reports what was for him a paradigmatic moment as a boy. He awoke "in a terrible state of fright"—getting out of bed and running around "all the rooms looking for Father. But the house was empty ... So I dressed as well as I could and ran down to the shore, all the time screaming and crying for father."[77] God-the-father's absence for Tomas is an artistic dramatization of Bergman's absent father moment. The effect resonates in Tomas's vocation. Feeling alienated from a silent god, he is unable to help Jonas. Moreover, fixated on his loneliness, in a fatherless world, Tomas can supply neither solace for Jonas nor tenderness toward Marta, whom he treats cruelly when she expresses her love for him. And all the while, children enter the story as witnesses to that fraught adult world (e.g., boys who find Jonas's lifeless body in the snow), anticipating a very much expanded emphasis on the child-as-witness in Bergman's *Fanny and Alexander*.

As for the gender context: Marta's tenderness-seeking feminine role, as contrasted with Tomas's God-the-father fixation, is symbolized in the altars in the film's two churches. The altar in Tomas's home church has a grotesque figure of Jesus suffering on the cross ("What an ugly image," Tomas says at one point as he gazes at it Figure 3.11), while the altar of the Frostnas church has a Madonna and baby Jesus, which stands in the background as Tomas goes through his liturgical motions at the end the film: "Holy, holy, holy ...," he intones. Before Tomas decides to do the service (he is feeling quite ill and almost cancels), the church steward, Algot (Allan Edwall)—a virtual cripple

Figure 3.11 Pastor Tomas and icon in *Winter Light*. Directed by Ingmar Bergman. Copyright Svensk Filmindustri (SF) 1957. All rights reserved 1963.

who is in constant pain—notes something about the life of Jesus that resonates powerfully with Tomas. Jesus's actual pain, Algot's points out, was a mere four hours but his real hardship was abandonment, both by his disciples and by God. He therefore wonders why so much theological emphasis is on Jesus's pain (which was brief compared with what he, Algot, goes through daily he says) when what Jesus must have felt much more powerfully is loneliness; "he died seized by doubt." Algot's speech registers powerfully in Tomas's facial expression.

He listens with rapt attention (shown with extended face shots) as Algot exposes by inference his, Tomas's, problem. It's not merely a silent deity but an emotionally disabling loneliness, an inability to communicate feelings of intimacy (*Winter Light's* original title was to be *The Communicants*). Feeling alone in his relationship with an "echo God," who remains silent, Tomas has not responded warmly to the volubility of one who is emotionally prolix (in her long letter and in her conversational entreaties). Dismissing her appeals for warm engagement, he is unable to focus on a source of intimacy other than what he had had with his deceased wife, who patched the holes in the void left by God's silence. Because he is unable to believe, he is also unable to focus on what is available nearby. His last gesture is to forge ahead and perform the service, repeating the empty liturgical phases of his vocation.

At its conclusion, the film has turned from the problem of maintaining piety in the face of God's silence to a disappointed pastor's inability to manage a life of interpersonal relations. As Bergman's religious trilogy arrives at the last film, *The Silence*, the silence that has descended is not God's failure to communicate but a failure of communication between sisters. The film's emphasis is on the vagaries of interpersonal intimacy, not on what inhibits faith and belief. In short, it's on "How to live."[78]

God's Silence Displaced: *The Silence*

By the end of W*inter Light*, the only hint that caring communication between Pastor Tomas and Marta has become possible is through his carrying on with an afternoon service, which while being a mere ritual for him is nevertheless performed with Marta as the only one attending in the otherwise empty country church. By some accounts, Tomas's decision to do the service is a hesitant step toward reciprocating Marta's love, even though the communication is through resort to ritualistic theological discourse.[79] Having displaced much of the problem of God's silence with the problem of interpersonal intimacy by the end of *Winter Light*, Bergman amplifies the problem of communication in *The Silence*. As in the two prior religious films, a father's charisma dominates. However, because God-the-father is out of the picture, it's a biological father who haunts the characters, one of whom, Ester (Ingrid Tulin) no longer wished to live when their father died, as her sister Anna (Gunnel Lindbloom) puts it. As the film opens, the two sisters, Anna and Ester, are traveling by train to a fictional Eastern European country accompanied by Anna's son Johan. As is so often the case in Bergman's films, movement from one venue to another serves to expose tensions in the lives of the characters, who have to cope with new encounters.

The issue of communication receives a surcharge in *The Silence*, not only because the travelers don't know the language of the country (somewhere in Eastern Europe) they visit but also because Ester, who is ill and dying from a respiratory disease, has a vocation that exemplifies the problem of communication; she's a translator. While after their arrival Ester is occasionally working on translating the foreign words in the fictional Timoka into Swedish, another translation effect, layered over the linguistic one, is developing. Anna, who is unable to express love and affection in words, expresses herself with promiscuity. The differences between the two sisters are reflected in the way the camera explores their props. Anna's consist of a make-up kit and a closet full of clothes, while Ester's include books and a typewriter. While Ester is always fully covered, either in her pants suit or in her robe, Anna's body is frequently exposed. Bergman's camera explores Anna's body continually, eroticizing her as she eroticizes relationships, even with her son Johan, whom she caresses, smothers with kisses, has him sleep next to her while she is mostly unclothed, and has him scrub her back while she is nude in the bath tub. Facial close-ups add to the gulf between the sisters—Anna's bored expression and Ester's tense one (as she smokes nervously, almost continuously). The sisters' differently oriented bodies are the center of attention, while room furnishing is spare and undistinguished. As Bergman states in an interview about his films, "The main thing is what happens to bodies. No furnishings that overthrow the action, nothing that stands around anywhere unless it contributes to a choreographic pattern that must be able to move in complete freedom in relation to space and scenery. Nothing must get in the way."[80] Yet, as the film progresses, some furnishings attract a lingering focus; beds turn out to play significant roles (detailed below).

While the fraught relationship between the sisters drives much of the film drama, as is the case with much of his film corpus, in Bergman's *The Silence* a child is the film's main witnessing protagonist. The film turns the hotel where most of the film drama takes place into a series of cameras managed by Johan and aimed both within and without. Within the hotel, Johan looks from room to room as the tense relationship between Anna and Ester proceeds; he peers around the empty hotel corridors; he looks into the hotel porter's room, and he peers into other rooms (one occupied by a group of performing dwarves whom he joins in a spontaneous performance). As for the "without": The hotel as a whole becomes a camera, with Johan as the main camera man, filming the city as he looks out of the window in their room. At one point, while watching the usual daily dynamic in the city, there's a dramatic moment. He observes a battle tank rumbling through the street below, its canon pointing straight ahead like a phallus penetrating the city. It is therefore Johan who plays one of Bergman's most significant roles (incubated in his own childhood), that of a child who tries to make sense of his own urges, the interpersonal dynamics around him, and the spaces within which they are transpiring.

Crucially, *The Silence* introduces a different model of film form. Whereas *Winter Light* is shot as a series of tableaux, in which churches, altars, and agonized faces are framed, *The Silence* is shot as rhythmic motion, mimicking a musical score. Bergman testifies that the form of the film is inspired by the music of Bela Bartok:

> I remember that it was Christmas time, and that *The Silence*, just like *Winter Light*, began with a piece of music: Bartok's *Concerto for Orchestra*. My original idea was to make a film that should obey musical laws, instead of dramaturgical ones. A film acting by association—rhythmically, with themes and counter-themes. As I was putting it together, I thought much more in musical terms than I'd done before. It follows Bartok's music rather closely—the dull continuous note, then the sudden explosion.[81]

That Bartok effect is especially pronounced in a late scene. As Ester is tended to by the hotel porter while she is tossing and turning in her bed and gasping for breath, several loud musical notes are struck at a moment in which she seems to be in her death throes.

Nevertheless, although an interplay of sound and silence shapes the film's moods and captures the rhythms of the themes and counter-themes to which Bergman refers, I want to suggest that space and objects play more crucial roles in the cinematic organization of the film's ideational effect. The most important spatial effect is introduced when Johan with toy gun in hand goes on a virtual safari in the hotel. At an important juncture in the film, Johan tucks his toy gun into his pants, leaves his family's room, and turns the hotel into a space of drama. He skulks in the hall as a workman positions a ladder under a chandelier and then walks under the ladder and pretends to shoot him before leaving and jeering at him. He then repeats the shooting drama, using the hotel's elderly waiter as his target (eliciting a more playful response; the waiter later grabs him from behind to extend the game, while the workman on the ladder had just stared). Later, back in the hallway with his gun, he passes a room shared by a troupe of performing dwarves (a trunk with the name Edwardini is visible near the room's open door). Moving into the room's doorway with drawn gun, Johan shoots at some of the dwarves, who play along, pretending to have been shot dead. Thereafter, the dwarves invite him in, put a woman's dress on him, and stage an acrobatic play in which one of them treats a bed as a trampoline, bouncing to the cheers of the others assembled.

The dwarves room is thus another of Bergman's theatrical heterotopias, a "counter-site" whose role is "to create a space of illusion that exposes ... all the sites inside of which human life is partitioned, as still more illusory."[82] While the brief play is underway, there's an intervention that repeats Bergman's oft-illustrated critique of patriarchal dominance and its suppression of feminine fulfillment. The leader of the dwarf troupe comes in, barks his disapproval of the drama, admonishes his subordinates, removes Johan's dress, and ushers him out of the room. Returning to the fraught feminine matrix in which he abides, Johan finds his unwell Aunt Ester in bed, a telling juxtaposition that signals the role of the bed-as-object in alternative contexts. Here the immediate juxtaposition is one between the bed as a space of play versus as a space of illness.

The bed also becomes the main semiotic object in another aspect of the film's spatial drama, its explorations of spaces of erotic violence. Punctuating the film story are several moments when, in his wanderings outside his room, Johan finds himself in front of a painting in the hotel corridor that depicts a moment of sexual violence: Ruben's painting of a moment in Graeco-Roman mythology of the centaur Nessus, violently seducing Deianeira, Hercules wife (Figure 3.12). However, the violence on close inspection seems welcome. As Bergman's script describes it, "a fat, entirely naked lady, fighting with a man in hairy fur pants and with hooves in lieu of feet. The lady is very pink, and the dark brown man is covered with hair. On closer inspection the lady, to judge from her stupid smile, doesn't seem altogether displeased by his attentions."[83] An obviously impressed Johan subsequently reenacts violence between lovers with his Punch and Judy puppets, which he performs at the foot of Ester's sick bed.

Subsequently, the scene in the painting is mimicked in Anna's erotic encounter with a man in his room, where the bed becomes a space of violently

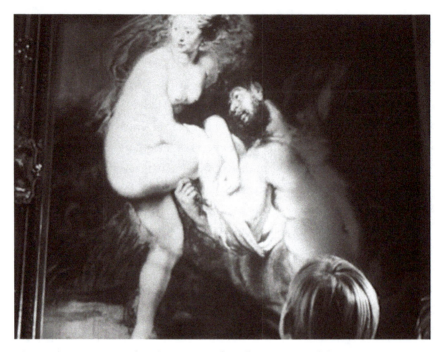

Figure 3.12 Nessus and Deianeira in *The Silence*. Directed by Ingmar Bergman. Copyright Svensk Filmindustri (SF) 1957. All rights reserved 1963.

acted out sexuality. After Anna admits Ester to the room, she brazenly engages the man sexually in front of her to taunt her (Figure 3 13). However, after Ester leaves the erotic engagement becomes an ambiguous event. In some moments Anna fights off her lover's violent advances while in others she welcomes his attention. Ultimately, beds are the main objects in scenes in which the two sisters seem to share sexual loneliness, albeit in very different ways. In an earlier scene, Ester masturbates in bed, writhing and moaning in ways that suggest both pleasure and desperation. Anna's sex with her lover appears just as lonely. He is a mere prop in scenes in which her promiscuity stands in for her emotional loneliness. Ester appears to understand the pretext of Anna's sexuality. After Anna taunts her by kissing and caressing the lover in front of her, they argue about whether there is love or hate between them. Ester contradicts Anna's charge of hatred, saying she loves her, and before leaving the room, says, repeatedly, "poor Anna."[84] It becomes clear that the problem between them is not about who achieves erotic fulfillment or merely about the vicissitudes of love, hate, and envy; it's more generally about how to

Figure 3.13 Bed scene in *The Silence*. Directed by Ingmar Bergman. Copyright Svensk Filmindustri (SF) 1957. All rights reserved 1963.

live. That problem is voiced by Ester while the two are arguing in the room. In response to one of Anna's taunts, Ester remarks, "How then are we supposed to live?"

Near the end of the film, Ester seems to supply an answer to that question with two gestures. Back in bed in her room, attended by the waiter/servant who is trying to help her while she is struggling to breathe, she pulls him to her and gently caresses his head, an act of tenderness that is in stark contrast to the violent sex carried out by Anna in the man's bed. Then she has the old servant bring her a writing pad on which she writes a letter to Johan, instructing him on how to learn the language of a foreign place. When Anna and Johan are on a train headed home, while Ester is left to die alone in the hotel, Anna reads the letter and says, "how nice of her." As it concludes, the film seems to endorse gentleness and kindness as ways to live. However, as I have noted, by the time Bergman has written and produced his *Fanny and Alexander*, the problem of life he is pondering is also about *where* to live, i.e., in the "little world" of the here and now. It was his last statement in his lifelong artistic negotiation about life with himself and with his audiences. Bergman's assistance in the conversation about life, which he undertakes by artistically substituting theatrical frames for theological ones, would have us heed connecting not with transcendence but with those around us. Such connecting, he suggests, has been impeded by a theology that envisions a transcendent world and bids one to aim upward rather than sideways.

Philip K. Dick's "Counter-Songs"

PKD's Phenomenology

Philip Dick's stories and novels distill—while animating through his characters—the philosophical interventions featured in prior chapters; they resonate with those chapter's main personae: William James, the apostle Paul, and Ingmar Bergman. However, he has a singular way of figuring the phenomenology of experience; he articulates it within an aural media discourse. For Dick, media "define what constitutes reality,"[1] and "consciousness" operates in the "interface between a perceptual apparatus and a recording device."[2] To address the connections between Dick and the thinkers in other chapters briefly at the outset, Dick's emphasis on the media through which "the divine" transmits its presence provides a compelling contrast with William James's emphasis on the internality and force of the will to believe (an issue I reserve for extended treatment in the final chapter). There are also biographical, conceptual, and textual bridges from Dick to Paul and Bergman. For example, as was the case for Paul, much of what inspired Dick's approach to religion was a theophany, a revelation he presumed to be an engagement with divine intentionality, delivered with the same kind of sensation that precipitated Paul's radicalization, a flash of light. When sodium pentothal was administered to Dick after a wisdom tooth removal to dull the pain from the procedure, he had "a number of visionary experiences, in both waking and sleeping states," to which he attributed "the invasion of [his] mind by a transcendentally rational mind." He saw "a shiny glistening red" color to which he referred as "St. Elmo's Fire" and encountered a woman "wearing around her neck a flashing necklace [in which there was] a golden fish" in the shape of a traditional Christian symbol.[3] It's an episode to which he refers in various works, for example, in his novels *Radio Free Albemuth*, *Valis*, and *The Divine Invasion*. As the experience is described in *Radio*, "a pinkish-purple beam of light, an inch in diameter fired up into [the Dick-like character] Nicholas's face,"[4] and in *DI*, the character Herb Asher refers to trusting "the beam of pink light."[5] Most significantly, as Dick elaborates the experience through one half of his split alter ego, the character Horselover Fat in *Valis* (the other half is the character Phil Dick), the experience is described as much epistemically as it is spiritually. He develops "a theory that the universe is made out of information."[6]

The essential contrast between Paul and Dick is in their responses to their respective theophanies. While Paul's experience turned him into an apostle, Dick's turned him into a philosopher/theorist, whose perspectives are articulated within the ideascapes in his fiction and elaborately developed in his *Exegesis*, where with hermeneutic zeal he interprets the significance of his experience and identifies himself as a philosopher: "I am a fictionalizing philosopher, not a novelist," he insists.[7] Nevertheless, Dick's *Do Androids Dream of Electric Sheep* (and other writings, e.g., *The Transmigration of Timothy Archer*) has Pauline ethical sensibilities. James Edward Burton captures that aspect of *Androids*:

> In the vocabulary of Saint Paul … the novel undermines the android/human distinction as understood according to the flesh and replaces it with the android/human division according to the spirit … what defines an android is … couched for Dick in a Pauline ethics. Despite appearances, the Voight Kampff test [a test for empathy used to discover androids, who apparently lack it] is not undermined by the production of what could be regarded as flawed results … in testing for *caritas*, for love or empathy, it suggests that this is the *only* viable criterion for determining moral worth or responsibility – for demonstrating entitlement to life.[8]

The bridge to Bergman is also autobiographically fueled. It consists especially in the similarity between Dick's and Bergman's personal struggles with institutionalized theology. While Bergman's struggle is pervasively expressed by characters in his films, Dick's is expressed in autobiographical scenarios distributed among the fictional characters in his novels. However, in contrast with the way Bergman's characters are afflicted by the silence of the divine, Dick's are afflicted by an inescapable divine noise. Nevertheless, much is shared—for example the way Dick shares Bergman's ontological uncertainty. Recalling Bergman's remark, "No one is safe from religious ideas ... As I see it today, any relapse is out of the question. But I can't say it's out of the question tomorrow,"[9] a similar "uncertainty rules" Dick's diverse characters, who like Dick himself are resistant to theological hegemonies and suspicious of emissaries of the divine, e.g., the "dubious messiah" Sophia in *Valis*.[10]

As regards the overall relevance of turning to Philip Dick in my investigation: like the themes expressed in Paul's and Bergman's texts, many of the situations and conversations in Dick's stories are pervaded by religious tropes and theological themes, even as they challenge institutionalized Judeo-Christian theology and seek alternative (media-attuned in his case) bases for communal contention and coherence. For purposes of linking Dick's scattered religious speculations and his political theology as a whole with the religious conversations initiated and elaborated in the writings of Paul, the films of Bergman, and the speculations of James, Dick evinced a durational phenomenology. Like Paul, Bergman, and James, he was in Bakhtin's sense (quoted in earlier chapters) a becoming subject, one "unconsummated" and thus "axiological yet to be."[11] Pervasively Bergsonian in his emphasis on expanded duration, Dick was a "moving subject"[12] intent on self-discovery as he inflected his literary contributions toward Henri Bergson's emphasis on "the passage of life,"[13] while at the same time in search of "a life worth living."[14] As he puts in a letter to his friend Claudia, "I am trying to bring back an affirmative view of life."[15] And as he says in his essay, "The Android and the Human," "My full measure of devotion [is] ... to augment and maintain what is human about us, what is the core of ourselves and then source of our destiny."[16] As a phenomenologically becoming subject seeking to situate that optimistic view of life, Dick explicitly likened his becoming to Paul's (in a reflection on the role of memory): "'I remember' (anamnesis) equals 'I become' (Being). Which equals '*I am changed*.'" (v. Paul: "Look! I tell you a sacred secret. We shall not all fall asleep; but we shall all be changed in an instant," etc.) [citing Corinthians 15: 51–2].[17] Dick provides the details of that "becoming" in two of his late novels, *Valis* and *Radio Free Albemuth*, both of which contain the fictional character, "Phil Dick." Phil, along with the other characters in the novels, lives moments and participates in thought events that were part of Dick's life experiences.

As is the case with Ingmar Bergman's autobiographical presence in his films, Dick's personal experiences are recreated in his writing. However, as is also the case with Bergman, the issues to which his stories and novels are addressed transcend individual experience and address collective and manifestly political concerns. What Dick saw himself confronting was an increasingly information network-driven, authoritarian management of life, against which his characters attempt to achieve self-fashioning and manage— at times with divine guidance and at times despite divine hindrance—a degree of empathy across various divisions. They evince a will to live which for Dick applies not only to humans but also to non-human technological devices, e.g., androids (robots), which in his stories are vital and thus defy the ontological predicates of traditional humanism. Notable in this respect are the fugitive androids in his *Do Androids Dream of Electric Sheep,* who after escaping from an outer world and blending into the human world, seek "more life" (beyond the four years for which they were designed).[18] Deeply involved in expanding the notion of personhood, Dick adopted an anti-vitalism perspective in which he accorded human emotions to androids, suggesting that they "do not [merely] mimic humans; they are, in many deep ways, *actually* human already."[19] Dick's version of anti-vitalism, which includes not only everything animate but also the inanimate, is ethical as well as ontological. Positing "unstable boundaries between self and world,"[20] he insisted that the human capacity for empathy and compassion should not be merely intra-human but also human-android, human-animal, human-deity, and human-world. Dick explores those empathic sentiments with attentiveness to the mediation of both old and futuristic information technologies, while conceptually, his innovative thinking is framed with questions about how we reside in time, a paradigmatic concern for Dick as it was for Paul and Bergman (and of course characteristic of sci-fi writers in general, whose works are deeply involved in "the theorization of temporality").[21]

I begin my analysis with the acoustically oriented *Radio Free Albemuth*, which is focused on an older communication technology, radio because it anticipates the theological speculations in *Valis* (the first novel in what some commentators call Dick's "religious trilogy") and because it develops Dick conceptual orientation, a distinctive neo-Kantian phenomenological philosophy in which one's faculties are enhanced and delivered from an outside information system rather than (as Kant would have it) being wholly intrinsic to the structure of mentality. As the novel's protagonist (a PKD stand-in) puts it after experiencing the kind of theophany that Dick has reported in his autobiographical fragments, "I, Nicholas Brady, understood that these primordial faculties and abilities had been restored to me only temporarily, that their existence in me depended on my relatedness to the communication web."[22]

To compare Kant's and Dick's phenomenologies, I want to begin by noting that although Kant's philosophy was developed in a much less diverse and technologically limited media environment than Dick's, communication is nevertheless crucial to his philosophy of experience as well. To provide a brief sketch: the Kantian narrative of experience (presented in his better-known Third Critique but more elaborately in his less well-known Anthropology) begins with an "organic sensation,"[23] which generates a disordered set of perceptions. There follows an "understanding," as the cognitive faculty "joins perceptions and combines them under a rule of thought by introducing order into the manifold."[24] However, the active aspect of perception has not been completed until it achieves a public universality, which requires communication. However, in contrast with Dick's perspective, the communication part of Kant's narrative of experience happens *within* subjects engaged in reflection. The "communication" is predicated on an internalized "universal voice," toward which the reflecting faculty moves.[25] That ultimate part of Kant's narrative of experience is a movement toward what he calls a "universal communicability," which he treats as an ethics of association that "everyone expects and requires from everyone else."[26] Ultimately, therefore, Kant's narrative of experience has the subject moving toward moral consensus. It is (in his terms) a *sensus communis* that involves no actual social media. Rather than an expansion involving communicative dissemination, what increases is the size, coherence, and associational capacity of the subject's mind, which reaches toward what humanity seeks in common.

Like Kant, Dick concerned himself with the relationship between individual and social comprehension, but he located communication in a radically different phenomenology of experience. Early in his thinking, Dick explicitly endorsed Kantian subjectivity. For example, as he puts in describing his novel *Ubik* (1969), "[I] constructed a world (universe) which differed from ours in one respect: it lacked the driving force of time ... I did not conceive time as a force at all ... I thought of it in Kantian terms as a mode of subjective perception."[27] Subsequently however Dick's version of subjective experience departed from the Kantian model. While Kant envisioned a world that would move toward a universalizing consensus after accepting a social rationality energized by a spreading "enthusiasm" for the consequences of the French revolution, Dick posited multiple, often conflicting worlds and turned to thought models he ascribed to "European existential psychologists" in which subjects emerge in conflicting chaotic worlds rather than in a single Kantian consensual world.[28] While Kant, whom Nietzsche called "a cunning Christian," divided the world into a "'real' and an 'apparent' world," Dick, an ambivalent Christian, effaced the difference.[29]

Asked about what his "worlds consist of," "are they the essence of Anti-God ... chaos?"; Dick responded with a sketch of his model of private versus shared worlds, the *idios kosmos* and *koinos kosmos* respectively, which he conceives within a narrative that has the latter progressively supplanting the former. "If a person's *idios kosmos* begins to break down, he is exposed to the archetypal or transcendental forces of the *koinos kosmos*," which is needed for one "to stay sane," i.e., interpersonally connected. Nevertheless, those forces are often presided over by a malicious rather than benign deity (here Dick evokes the evil god-like tyrant Palmer Eldritch from his novel *The Three Stigmata of Palmer Eldritch*).[30] Similarly, as he suggests (in a Bergman-like position) in his *Valis*, "the divine and the terrible are so close to each other."[31] Dick's ultimate phenomenology of experience, in which he is as attentive to memory (anamnesis) as he is to possible futures, is (as I have implied) more Bergsonian than Kantian. While Kant immobilized time as a feature of a static subject, Bergson located subjectivity in a dynamic temporality, a moving interval between a continuously incorporated past and a continuously superseded present.[32] Accordingly, as Fredric Jameson suggests, Dick turns the past into a conditional future; his fiction contains "a trope of the future anterior."[33] For example, in *Valis* he revises Wordsworth's "Intimations of Immortality from Recollections of Early Childhood," applying it to his protagonist, Horselover Fat, writing that in "Fat's case, the 'intimations of immortality' were based on recollections of a future life."[34]

Dick's phenomenology of mind also radically revises the locus of consciousness. As I have suggested, in contrast with the Kantian subject whose mentality is the place from which a *sensus communis* eventuates, "mind" for Dick is located outside as well as within subjects. Dick's perspective, therefore, accords with Nietzsche's insistence that "mind" or "consciousness does not really belong to man's individual existence."[35] Consequently, his fictional scenarios "transcend the opposition between the subjective and objective in scenes in which the psychic world ... goes outside, and reappears in the form of simulacra" (a creative departure from Kantian transcendental noumena).[36] What is transcendent for Dick is a "VALIS," a "Vast Active Living Information System" whose broadcasts constitute a confrontation of minds; they penetrate the minds of individual subjects, at times supportively and at times maliciously. In *Radio Free Albemuth*, the medium through which VALIS transmits is radio, whose broadcasts effect a universalizing impulse. All the listener's reached in his *Radio Free Albemuth* are enlisted in an information network created by the force of radiation waves.

An "Acoustical Ecology"[37]

To situate the pervasiveness of radio in Dick's stories—central to *Radio Free Albemuth* and sprinkled throughout his fiction—I return briefly to the observation I developed in Chapter 1. The deity that emerges in the Judeo-Christian religious formation is a media personality, resident in Biblical writings. Heeding that reality but pluralizing the media, Dick's persistent focus is on the media technologies that precipitate the connections between believers and the divine. However, Dick revises the way the connections work. To review briefly the prior (and for many the persisting) connection in which the primary medium is scriptural, we can recall Erich Auerbach's gloss on the biblical Jehovah as a "hidden God" whom readers of scriptures must summon through interpretive reading practices. The reading proceeds under what Auerbach renders as an imperative; as readers of the bible, "we [must] fit our own life into its [the Biblical] world." Auerbach goes on to point out that "this becomes increasingly difficult the further our historical environment is removed from that of the Biblical books."[38] In his theologically oriented novels and stories, Dick takes a giant step beyond "our historical environment." He fashions situations far removed from his immediate life world, inventing multiple shadow and future worlds. It's a strategy that he addresses explicitly in his story "Exhibit Piece," in which a character who admits to the feeling that everything around him seems "unreal" experiences his world as "an exhibit" and has "projected memories of persons and places beyond this world." As a result, he speculates, "this [his immediately world] is only a shadow world."[39] As Dick has insisted in his *Exegesis*, where he imagines the world to come, "the future is more coherent than the present, more animate and purposeful, and in a real sense, wiser … [and it transmits]. We are being talked to by a very informed Entity: that of all creation as it lies ahead of us in time."[40]

The world beyond the present that Dick invents in *Radio Free Albemuth* is a "universe his protagonist [like Dick himself after his theophany] had never glimpsed before." It is one with an "active creator … a god, perhaps, divided in two portions," one who "predominated in power," the other "in wisdom."[41] In stark contrast with "the silence of God" that afflicts the characters in Bergman's films, the protagonist in *Radio Free Albemuth* is reached alternatively by two forms of divine loquaciousness. At times radio broadcasts (which persist even when the radio is turned off) deliver a "menacing sound" and insults in imitation of the voice of a popular vocalist. At other times he hears the "mild voice of [an] AI system" that provides useful guidance.[42] For Dick, rather than being summoned by a believer's inner will (*pace* William James), the divine, alternatively benign and malicious, reaches out to foster religious observance making use of new media technologies (creating for example the pharmaceutically shaped, merged mentalities of a community of believers on Mars in *The Three Stigmata of Palmer Eldritch*, discussed in Chapter 1).

Radio is the medium that in Dick's early writings connects most pervasively with his theological musings about how the divine reaches out, likely because it was the part of the media environment with which he was deeply involved, not only as an avid consumer/listener but also as one with "an insider's knowledge of the medium" (working in a record shop that "sponsored and supplied a local AM station, KSMO in San Mateo").[43] As Umberto Rossi observes, of "all the media available in Dick's life time … radio has a particular importance, which can be detected by taking into account its part in the plots, and kinds of messages it transmits."[44] In addition to being a vehicle, for better or worse, connecting persons with the divine, radio in Dick's novels is also a liberating anti-delusional force, obviating psychoses and countering the coercive media manipulation of authoritarian regimes. For example, in an earlier novel, *Time Out of Joint* (1959), his protagonist, Ragle Gumm, residing in a delusional world, is able to think his way out of his subordination after his radio delivers a revelatory message that allows him to recover memories that had been rendered inaccessible by imposed memory-effacing tactics.[45]

Gumm's experience in *Time Out of Joint* is one among many examples of the way Dick's fiction incorporates a temporality that expands the conditions of possibility for experience. Fredric Jameson, noting the temporal complexity Dick employs, puts it succinctly, "The future of Dick's novels renders our present historical by turning it into the past of a fantasized future."[46] In his novel *Gravity's Rainbow*, Thomas Pynchon figures such an expansion in a media metaphor that comports well with Dick's temporal phenomenology: "The more you dwell in the past and the future, the thicker your bandwidth, the more solid your persona."[47] And elaborating that metaphor in a way that specifically illuminates the theological aspect of Dick's *Radio*, David Porush observes, "Every time culture succeeds in ... massively widening the bandwidth of its thought-tech, it invites the creation of new gods."[48] Accordingly, as Dick develops his temporally innovative phenomenology and articulates it with a broadcast idiom, he connects people with the divine in new ways while at the same time fashioning a politically attuned theology, based on radio's anti-authoritarian potential. That attunement resides explicitly in the novel's title: "The whole title of *Radio Free Albemuth* imitates in its form the various 'freedom stations'—true or fake—of anti-Nazi and anti-Stalinist resistance as well as 'the free university' and indeed 'free radio stations' (e.g., in the U.S. and Japanese student revolts)."[49]

As the drama in *Radio* proceeds it becomes evident that despite its occasional malicious broadcasts that afflict the protagonist, Nicholas, his radio is a trans-individual information system that provides him (as it did for Dick himself) with an essential line of flight from traditional institutionalized theology. In *Radio*, as in much of Dick's fiction, radio-delivered interventions allow his protagonists to displace blind allegiance with new thinking. Felix Guattari's reflections on "lines of flight" (in his approach to the consciousness-unconscious binary) are pertinent to the kind of media effects that Dick constructs. For Guattari, as for Dick, minds function as "interpretive grids" based on an assemblage of "semiotic components,"[50] which are collective (partaking of the *koinos cosmos* in Dick's terms) rather than individual. For Guattari, they are productive "machines" ("religious" among others) that "normalize" both new forms of social "segmentarity" and "foreign policy" (for example pillaging).[51]

However, in contrast with Guattari, who emphasizes the complicity between the "religious machine" and predatory capitalism's "war machine," Dick (despite his occasional focus on the violence of war machines) concerned himself more with the way media technologies can challenge the institutionalized "religious machine's" imposed protocols. Thus, he saw the radio-provoked awakened consciousness, which he lends to Nicholas in *Radio*, as a call to rethink theology. In the novel Nicholas's mind is activated by "VALIS" (as noted, the Vast Active Living Intelligence System that stands in for the deity). It is delivered as "a communication web" that transmits "radioactive particles," perceived as "bits of light."[52] The experience leads him (as it had for Dick) to see the world "not," he says, "as I customarily view it but from the eyes of a dedicated Christian."[53] However dedicated Dick may have been to Christianity, some of his statements convey "the strange combination of a need for salvation and a dissatisfaction with transcendent solutions."[54]

Multiple Worlds

Insofar as Dick became a "dedicated Christian," it was as a dedication to critical theological reflection and ontological uncertainty rather than tradition religious allegiance, in part because he considered himself "anti-organized religion … a religious anarchist."[55] For Dick there was never *a* world. "World" is always plural for Dick, who sees that pluralization as the essence of the sci-fi genre. As he puts it, "it is in sci-fi novels that worlds occur."[56] While as noted in Chapter 3, Bergman's spaces of reprieve from institutionalized theology throughout his film corpus are theaters, Dick's are alternative worlds. In Chapter 3 referring to Bergman's practice of space, I noted that Bergman's theaters, which operate as protagonists in many of his films, are examples of what Michel Foucault terms "heterotopias," "counter-sites," which are "different from all the sites that they reflect and speak about … Their role is to create a space of illusion that exposes … all the sites inside of which human life is partitioned, as still more illusory."[57] Unlike Bergman's counter-sites, Dick's heterotopias, packed within the narrative space of his fiction, are "elsewhere, elsewhen, and otherwise"[58]; they are other worlds and other historical moments, places, and/or times to which his protagonists are relocated, e.g., an alternative future in *The Man in the High Castle*, other worlds: e.g., Mars in *The Three Stigmata of Palmer Eldritch*, and Venus in *The World Jones Made*, and spatio-temporal life suspension technologies, e.g., the "moratoriums" in *Ubik*. Dick's persistent turn to heterotopias testifies to "an ongoing imperative in [his] writing ... the important of discovering an elsewhere (or elsewheres)."[59]

PKD's Literary Aesthetic

Picking up on the reference to Dick's "writing," I want to suggest that while there are consistent themes in Dick's fiction and a consistent "underlying epistemological structure,"[60] there are also consistent metafictional layers. One layer consists in the powerful affective resonances in his sentences. A line from Don DeLillo's novel *Mao II* captures that kind of metafictional layer at a moment when his protagonist, Gray, refers to himself as a sentence maker and adds, "there's a moral force in a sentence when it comes out right. It speaks to the writer's will to live."[61] Similarly, in the terms supplied by the theater director/essayist Richard Foreman, "The desire to write a certain kind of sentence (gesture) is akin to the desire to live—be-have the world be in a certain kind of way."[62] Given that Dick's dynamic of becoming is expressed through Nicholas in *Radio,* he likely regarded *this* sentence as having the right moral force: "Because of an imaginary voice, Nicholas had become a whole person."[63] As for that potentially "whole person's" will/desire to live, Dick's remark to his friend Claudia, which follows his reference to recovering "an affirmative view of life," expresses it: "It's a nice world and I'd like to stick around and enjoy it for a long time."[64]

Enjoyment however was a small part of the view of life Dick provides in his voluminous literary output. Asking what "we have that *can* be called SF," he says,

> We have a fictional world ... it is a society that does not in fact exist, but is predicated on our known society—that is, our known society acts as a

jumping-off point for it; The society advances out of our own ... It is our world dislocated ... our world transformed into that which it is not or not yet ... *this* is the essence of science fiction, the conceptual dislocation within the society so that as a result a new society is generated in the author's mind, transferred to paper, and from paper it occurs as a convulsive shock in the reader's mind, *the shock of dysrecognition*.[65]

That passage articulates with two perspectives that I want to invoke to situate the critical force of Dick's writing. One is available in Gilles Deleuze's remarks on how the painter, Francis Bacon faced his canvasses. It is misguided, Deleuze suggests that Bacon "works on a white surface." Rather, "everything he has in his head, or around him is already on the canvass, more or less virtually, before he begins his work." To avoid the "psychic clichés" and "*figurative givens*" featured in traditional painting genres, Bacon performed *his* version of what Dick calls "conceptual dislocation." Bacon had to "transform" or "deform" what is "always already on the canvass."[66] Similarly, Dick was writing against traditional notions of temporality and against versions of mediation between human and divine will. The second is expressed in Walter Benjamin's remarks on the critical value of shock. For Benjamin, the film genre can deliver what Dick calls *the shock of dysrecognition* because according to Benjamin the "shock effect" of film disrupts the viewer's habitual ways of rendering the world intelligible by creating a "distraction" that encourages critical reflection— precisely the effect Dick sought in his sci-fi genre.[67]

For purposes of appreciating Dick's ambivalent approach to theology, we have to heed yet another metafictional layer in his texts, his use of parody, which is his stylistic strategy for resisting orthodox Christianity. Briefly put, Dick supplements his counter-spaces with counter-voices. His parodic treatment of theology distinguishes him from those allegiant to institutionalized Christianity. Parody ("parodia or παρῳδία" in Greek) translates as "counter-song," which although it is used at times as a form of mockery, at others it works as "irony but [with] little mockery; there is critical distance but little ridicule."[68] Parody's primary aim is emancipation from the original text, which in Dick's case is emancipation from a historical, textually shaped, Christianity. Exemplary is his use of the pharmaceutical-induced Perky Pat, infused in the mentalities of Can-D's users in Dick's *The Three Stigmata of Palmer Eldritch*. As John Rieder points out, with "[Perky Pat's] translating [of] private (meditative, confessional) desire and anguish into public and exploitable fantasy ... the theological allusion to Augustine reinforces Can-D's bitter parody of the Catholic doctrine of transubstantiation in the Sacrament of the Holy Eucharist."[69] Importantly, the emancipation afforded by parody operates in conversation with a reader, who in effect performs as a "co-worker in actualizing—bringing to life—the world of words."[70] In this respect, Dick's novel *The Divine Invasion*—more thoroughly infused with allusions to Christianity—is exemplary. Readers who are familiar with traditional Christian textuality are able to recognize and elaborate for themselves Dick's parodic gestures.

Crucial therefore to the functioning of Dick's parodies are the metatextual gestures that engage the reader. There is a venerable tradition for such gestures in both canonical theory and contemporary literature. With respect to the former are those in Thomas Hobbes's *Leviathan*, where Hobbes explicitly instructs the reader, suggesting that his text is best understood if the reader engages in self-reflection: "Offering a variety of pointers as to how one should read the Leviathan,"[71] Hobbes tells the reader to "read thyself" in order to understand "the similitude of the thoughts and Passions of one man, to the thought and Passions of another."[72] With respect to the latter, I refer to a David Albahari's novel *Globetrotter*, which he punctuates with metafictional commentary. For example at one point, after referring to the ancestry of immigrant refugees in Canada to which the word "background" has been applied, he writes, "Background is the wrong word, but better that word than none at all."[73] *Globetrotter*, which focuses on a relationship between a nameless narrator, a painter from Saskatchewan and a Serbian writer named David Atijas (giving the novel its autobiographical resonance), has several narrative threads all of which lack definitive resolution. But the difficulty for the reader is eased by the novel's metafictional gestures. As one reviewer points out, "It isn't always easy to see what Albahari is up to ... but Albahari ... does have a way of letting his book provide its own analysis," at least obliquely. He has the novelist, Atijas talk about his own experience of "reading a novel by starting in the middle, and needing to flip back and forth to figure out 'why some of the some of the characters were saying or doing things.'"[74]

To develop the metatextual case for Dick's *The Divine Invasion*, I want to heed Gabriel Mamola's suggestion that *The Divine Invasion* is primarily a metafictional novel, a book that "is literary in a new way for Dick (a self-referencing, parodic, metafictional way)."[75] "*The Divine Invasion*," Mamola insists, "functions as a commentary by Dick on Dick's own corpus ... [it is] central to Dick's understanding of himself as an artist."[76] Supportive of Mamola's claim that a substantial part of his corpus should be read more aesthetically than thematically is Dick's reflection on his "artistic vision" in his *Exegesis*:

> One vast artistic vision, all the way from "Wub" to *DI* [*The Divine Invasion*], with particular emphasis on *Scanner*, the intro to *The Golden Man*, *VALIS*, "Chains ... Web" and *DI* (This last *my dream*. That sustains me. I cannot be separated from my work ... Me and my own private vision ... *VALIS* is not as important as supernatural revelation about God and suffering as it is about me as a person- unique and individual—and my vision ... Me and my own private vision; this is what we call art ... Therefore it is not theologically meaningful but artistically.[77]

As for the specific parodic aspects of *DI*, among what structures the novel is a parody of the divine covenant that the biblical Jehovah made with the Israelites. Dick articulates that covenant as a parody of James Joyce's *Ulysses*. Mimicking Leopold providing breakfast in bed for Molly in Joyce's novel is *DI's* Herb Asher bringing his ailing wife Linda breakfast in bed. And to alert the reader, the parodic structure shaping the novel is explained by Asher:

> In the Covenant that God made with the Israelites that the strong protect the weak and the weak give their devotion and loyalty to the strong in return; it is a mutuality. I have a covenant with Linda Fox [Herb's favorite singer, a stand-in for Linda Ronstadt in *DI*], and it will not be broken ever, by either of us. I'll fix breakfast for her he decided.[78]

While the parody of a covenant theology in *DI* is Dick's way of distancing himself from the god of the "*Old* Testament," it is in his *Do Androids Dream of Electric Sheep* that Dick develops a parody of the "*New* Testament." Siding with Nietzsche's contempt for a version of Christianity as a slave morality, Dick writes (in *The Exegesis*):

> Nietzsche is right about Christianity. It's a fucking hair shirt syndrome: always made me feel shame, guilt, always responding to duty and obligations to others—I view myself as weak, at the beck and call of others, obligated to them. Bullshit, "I am a man:—as that book of Judaism puts it, I need no one's

permission anymore, I need not account to anyone, I owe them nothing; they are pushing old buttons, long out of date. I have proved my worth and earned my reward."[79]

As is the case for Nietzsche, parody is Dick's primary way of distancing himself from orthodox Christianity. Nietzsche's parodic writing—counter-songs in a writing genre Deleuze refers to as a "counter-philosophy"[80] (most notably in *The Gay Science* and *Thus Spoke Zarathustra*)—bears comparison with Dick's, which in Dick's case is widely distributed in his fiction but is especially apparent in his invention of the Christ surrogate, Mercer, in *Do Androids Dream of Electric Sheep*. Dick's Nietzsche effect in his parodic writing is in accord with his self-description as a "fictionalizing philosopher," which applies well to Nietzsche's late texts, especially his *Zarathustra*, which is composed as a philosophical novel.

Dick's *Androids* takes place in a dystopic future in which a dystopic radioactive world is a nuclear war legacy. There's cross-traffic as those whose mentalities have not attenuated seek to emigrate to an off world, while Androids from an off-world head to earth in search of a way to modify their programmed short-life span. Among the protagonists are Rick Deckard, whose job is to "retire" rogue Androids that have breached the boundary between earth and the off world and John Isadore, a "chicken head" (one classified as mentally deficient and is thus stuck on earth). The novel's plot hinges on a complicated identity matrix. To distinguish himself as a human rather than an Android, Deckard wants to own a real pet (rather than the electric sheep he owns) to prove his humanity because Androids lack empathy and would not therefore bond with an animal. To acquire one, Deckard reassigns himself to Android retirement in order to earn enough for the purchase.

However, rather than pursuing that part of the novel's structure, I am focusing on Deckard and Isadore because both involve themselves—albeit in different ways—in the neo-Christian media religion, Mercerism. To elaborate: in the novel, Dick turns to a contemporary medium. He invents a Christ-like character, Mercer, the god/protagonist in a television religion. In contrast with his perspective on radio as a liberating technology (e.g., in his *Time Out of Joint* and *Radio Free Albemuth*), television for Dick perpetuates fraud rather than providing counter-hegemonic messaging; it reinforces orthodox

Christian theology. His Mercer mimics Christ's suffering for "our sins" on Buster Friendly's daily television show, which viewers access through their empathy boxes. However, instead of struggling with carrying a cross up toward Golgotha, Mercer ascends a hill while being stoned. Moreover, in contrast with the way biblical texts serve to assemble believers with persuasive proclamatory discourse, Dick's surrogate divinity, accessed by viewers both visually and tactilely, is encouraged to merge with Mercer and have an embodied experience of his suffering. That provides a Calvinist turn to Dick's representation of Mercerism; Calvin insisted, "'As long as Christ remains outside us', his suffering 'remains useless and of no value to us.' To benefit from Christ's suffering, 'he has' to become ours and dwell within us."[81]

Inventing a futuristic technology, Dick gives the "within" a sensory effect. As Buster Friendly's daily television show dramatizes the god-like Mercer, his suffering is literally felt by those who tune into their television sets with empathy boxes. They both see his suffering and feel the way he feels as he toils up a barren hill. Accordingly, as John Isadore tunes in to the Buster Friendly show, what he sees and feels is:

> One single figure, more or less human in form, [who] toiled its way up the hillside: an elderly man wearing a dull, featureless robe ... Wilber Mercer prodded ahead, and as he clutched the handles [of his empathy box], John Isadore gradually experienced a waning of the living room in which he stood ... he found himself, instead, ... entering into the landscape of the dull hill, drab sky. And at the same time ... His own feet now scraped, sought purchase, among the familiar loose stones; he felt the same old painful, irregular roughness beneath his feet.[82]

(Wilber) Mercer's repetitive eternally repeated climb promises to offer his viewers (and bodily co-experiencers) eternal life. Explaining the nature of immortality that Mercer's climb represents and imparts, the character, Hannibal Sloat says, "Wilber Mercer is always renewed. He's eternal. At the top of the hill, he is struck down; he sinks into the tomb world but then rises inevitably. And us with him. So we're eternal too."[83] However, Mercer himself debunks the myth of salvation, telling Rick Deckard that he cannot save anyone because he cannot save himself: "Don't you see," he says, "*There is no salvation.*"[84] And subsequently, Mercer is exposed as a fraud. Rather than a god-like figure, he is actually an elderly alcoholic named Al Jarry, a former actor from Indiana whom Buster Friendly uses by patching in "a series of [Jarry's] short fifteen-minute video films ... Wilber Mercer is not human, does not in fact exist. The world in which he climbs is a cheap, Hollywood sound stage."[85] Buster Friendly, whose indefatigable presence—running his "unending show"—indicates that he's an android, exposes Mercer's fraud. The contention between the two is a battle between fake deity and fake media pitchman for the "psychic selves" of the viewers (where what is psychic includes the physiological part of consciousness).

Dick goes on to extend his parody of the resurrection, applying it to the persistence of those who want to believe in it. Despite Buster Friendly's disclosure about Mercer, the human believers continue to seek to merge with him; they want to believe in Mercerism, even though it is exposed as artificial. Because of the strength of their will to believe, their attachment to the pseudo-Christian version of the divine that "Mercer" (aka Al Jarry) performs is unshaken by the revelation. Dick's parody is therefore deployed on the steadfastness of belief in a debunked myth as well as on the Christ story. His character John Isadore exemplifies the zealous believer, maintaining his Mercer allegiance, reaching out to him, and seeking his advice despite Mercer's/Jarry's admission of who he actually is.

In contrast with Isadore, Deckard's connection with Mercerism is vicarious. His Mercer connection is mainly through his wife Iran, a devotee who draws Deckard into a machine-aided empathy practice (they both use Penfield mood organs). Yet there is one direct conversation between Deckard and Mercer, who at one point stands before him with "his weary, pain drenched eyes" and reports, *"there is no salvation."* When Deckard asks, "then what's this for," the response is, "to show you that you are not alone. I am here with you ... you must do your task, even though you know it's wrong."[86] That conversation resonates with two of Dick's commitments, his view that the divine provides no clear moral guidelines and his will to community, which he figures (as I have noted) as the turning of one's *idios cosmos* into a *koinos cosmos*. If theology is to have positive value, that is, the way Dick seems to regard its mission. However, as I have suggested, to develop his empathy-oriented religion surrogate, he must detach himself from conventional theology, a detachment he achieves parodically, very much the way Nietzsche used parody to detachment himself from conventional

Christianity. Moreover, to achieve that detachment, Dick must also adopt a Nietzschean philosophical frame that eschews reliance on the traditional philosophical binary, appearance versus reality.

Spiritual Healing PKD with Nietzsche

In addition to sharing Nietzsche's parodic rendering of orthodox Christianity, Dick shares one of Nietzsche's metaphorical displacements for critically encountering allegiance to the divine, a symptomatology or health-illness binary. It's a discursive frame that articulates Nietzsche's critical challenge to the canonical philosophical tradition. Deleuze provides a good summary:

> Nietzsche substitutes the correlation of sense and phenomena for the metaphysical duality of appearance and essence and for the scientific relation of cause and effect. All force is appropriation, domination, exploitation of a quantity of reality. Even perception, in its diverse aspects, is the expression of forces which appropriate nature.[87]

Nietzsche's "symptomatology," which migrates (in Nandita Melamphy's words) into a "political-psychological perspective" and is "attentive to the problem of 'health' and 'illness,'" resonates with the religious ethos articulated in much of Dick's literary corpus.[88] Applying that binary to himself, Dick writes that his "pink light" experience "brought psychological wholeness to a partitioned, splintered mind ... a transcendental symbol & realization healed me, & by and large I am still healed."[89] Although "healed," Dick persisted, as he undertook the writing of his religious trilogy, to use his period of illness (more or less a nervous breakdown) to figure one's exploration of the divine. As one of his Dick stand-ins, Horselover Fat, observes in *Valis*, "People suffering nervous breakdowns often do a lot of research, to find explanations for what they are undergoing."[90]

Heeding Fat's reference to "research," it's evident that with respect to a relationship with the divine Dick evinces more of a will to knowledge than a will to believe. It is also evident that the energy driving that will is "mental illness." Paranoid schizophrenia, which Fat, a self-described paranoiac explicitly theorizes, is a route to reality: "What we do not know ... is that it [paranoia] is sometimes an appropriate response to reality to go insane."[91] Given that "the ideational structure of paranoia [as Freud noted] is that of a ruthless hermeneutic,"[92] we can see Dick (through his characters) as a zealous knower. To figure the critical aspect of Dick's epistemic method in which illness is intrinsic, we can designate it, after Sarah Mann-O'Donnell's conception, as "chronic critique," a critical knowledge practice she ascribes to Nietzsche (and a Nietzsche-influenced Deleuze and Guattari).[93]

As she elaborates that epistemic figuration, Mann-O'Donnell refers to a "reevaluation of health as a condition of chronic critique, a condition that wraps itself around illness to keep itself critical."[94] There are many places in his texts where Nietzsche, representing illness as a crucial knowledge vehicle, practices that form of critique. One that effectively captures it is in his *Genealogy of Morals*: "We have no doubt that sickness is instructive, much more instructive than health ... Does this not make us every day more questionable but also more worth questioning, perhaps more worthy to be alive?"[95] And in the Preface to his *Human All Too Human*, he writes that he cannot "dispense even with sickness as a means and a grappling hook of knowledge."[96] Ultimately, for a sickness-driven, knowledge provoking convalescence to end in a restoration of health for Nietzsche, to as he puts it, "effect [his] cure and self-recovery," he needs "faith," not theological faith but a form of critical hermeneutic faith: "faith enough ... not to look at life from a singular point of view."[97] That perspective is resident in his texts; "Great health ... more audacious, and gayer than any previous health" is achieved by Nietzsche through the way he writes, i.e., through parody.[98]

Dick employs a similar sickness health narrative, seeing the paranoid mind as an effective engine of inquiry on the one hand but in need of an ultimate cure on the other. However, unlike Nietzsche, for whom healing requires a retreat from transcendence and metaphysics, Dick "was not, in his late novels, ready to give up the healing potential and artistic possibility of metaphysics and transcendence."[99] And whereas Nietzsche dug into biblical scriptures to create an anti-theological parody of adherence to divine transcendence, employing "theological terms" to construct himself as "an enemy and challenger of God," one who takes "pleasure in externals, superficialities, the near, the accessible,"[100] Dick's theological parodies reorder scriptural technology to insert the divine in a different communicational relationship with believers.

Crucial to that new medium in which the divine is transmitted is how it encourages reception. Valis is in effect a sci-fi realization of the concept Peter Brown describes in his *The Making of Late Antiquity* (treated in Chapter 1), interpreting signs to discern if someone is intimate with the divine. However, in *Valis*, the two Dick stand-ins Horselover Fat and Phil Dick are dealing with a divine that is not the esoteric deity—i.e., one hidden behind ambiguous signs—with which late antiquity Christians were faced. In *Valis*, as the acronym Vast Active Information System implies, what must be interpreted is exoteric. The traditional hermeneutics of suspicion, for which revealing or uncovering is the appropriate methodological metaphors, must be refigured to make sense of Dick's rendering of the divine. His characters have to interpret an assaultive revelation, a "divine invasion" (the title of his follow-up novel in his religious trilogy) rather than engage in an uncovering.

I'm reminded of a parodic travel agency advertisement I saw in Aleppo Syria in 1964 at a time when the "Arab World" was struggling to contain what they regarded as a dangerously expansive enemy: "Visit Israel before Israel visits you." Similarly, the implication of Dick's divine assault in his *Valis* is the requirement of a religious hermeneutics in which one must sort and interpret an ambiguous—either emancipating or endangering—"visit" (allegedly) from the divine rather than discovering it. As a result Dick's approach to a phenomenology of religious experience is effectively captured by a metaphor for mentality with that of divine broadcasts; as the text states, "The Universe keeps jabbing us with tropisms over which we have no control … but we are part of the playback equipment."[101] To the extent Dick's *Valis* embraces a form of piety, it is a pious hope that the divine is reachable by one's susceptibility to stimuli. A knowledge junky, Dick wanted to maximize rather than avoid sensation; he wanted to feel and interpret it incessantly. "Think of the possibilities," he wrote, "if our brains could handle twenty images at once, think of the amount of knowledge which could be stored in a given period."[102]

Once Dick's theological parody moves from *Valis* to *The Divine Invasion*, he has developed technological prostheses to expand and externalize that brain—new apparatuses and metaphors for representing and animating mentality, a computer-like "Information Slate" and a "Holoscope," both of which are physical and metaphorical apparatuses that render the mind as a reading machine. With the latter device, "scripture is released by this [latter] device from the linearity and flatness of text on page and translated into a vibrant multidimensional state that more closely approximates the immaterial existence of information in the mind."[103] Where Luther had invented a reading congregation that experiences the divine through standard textual mediation (all reading the same Scripture, made available in vernacular language), in Dick's version of mind-as-reading machine, the text becomes plastic rather than fixed and univocal. It functions in accord with Nietzsche's above-noted commitment "not to look at life from a singular point of view." As it is put in the novel, "The total structure of Scripture formed, then, a three-dimensional cosmos that could be viewed from any angle and its contents read ... Thus scripture yielded up an infinitude of knowledge that ceaselessly changed."[104]

Nevertheless, despite the striking accord one can observe between Nietzsche's and Dick's uses of illness-recovery narratives and their similar embrace of interpretive multiplicity, Dick's religious texts are more Pauline than Nietzschean. Apart from his already noted affinity to Paul (a remark quoted from his *Exegesis*), the Pauline presence in *The Divine Invasion* becomes apparent if we heed Paul's Second Letter to the Thessalonians where he evokes the Katechon, a withholding of the Parousia. Massimo Cacciari provides a convenient summary of Paul's warning:

> Paul—or the faithful disciple who interprets or tries to explain his thought—returns in *The Second Letter to Thessalonians* to the eschatology of *The First Letter to Thessalonians* in order to warn that the Lord Jesus will not return until the work of his Adversary (*Antikeimenos*) is complete. His Day must be preceded by the full unfolding of *apostasy* (*discessio*), of the *mystery of anomia* (*mysterium iniquitatis*); the mystery that is the epiphany of Christ is followed by the apocalypse according to the force of Satan, of iniquity, of the one who *pretends* to be God and demands to be worshipped as God. The day of the Lord must be *awaited* during the passage through this time of immense devastation.[105]

The narrative of *The Divine Invasion* combines a parody of the biblical story of an endangered Christ child who must be hidden during the famous "slaughter of the innocents" and Paul's warning about waiting for the Katechon, the withholding of the Parousia until pretenders to divine end time can be vanquished. Without going into all the aspects of a fraught set of relationships among the characters, I will point to the novel's contest for divine hegemony. The god Yah, born in human form has to challenge the evil fallen angel Belial, who has ruled Earth for 2000 years. The characters, Herb Asher and Rybys Rommey, who are Joseph and Mary surrogates and thus protectors of the newborn "savior," Emmanuel, must shield him from the forces of evil until Belial is defeated. Salvation can come only to those who have chosen the savior rather than Belial.

"Theology, a Packaged Fraud"[106]

By the time Dick's religious speculations move to the third novel in the trilogy, *The Transmigration of Timothy Archer*—clearly the most sophisticated book in the trilogy, both philosophically and aesthetically—it has become even more evident that "Dick was very importantly a Pauline,"[107] even though as I have already suggested, he is more driven by a will to knowledge than a will to believe, a searcher rather than an apostle. Moreover, the way he is Pauline is parodic. While Paul's "event" is the crucifixion, for Dick's narrator, Angel Archer, an atheist, it is the death of John Lennon. Even her father, Bishop Timothy Archer, initially deeply involved with Paul's premise "that we are saved through grace and not by works,"[108] begins to doubt the validity of the Christ story and remarks, "I'm not sure I'm a Christian. I'm now not sure there is in fact such a thing as Christianity."[109] As Dick mobilizes his aesthetic subjects to carry on the drama in the novel's interpersonal matrix, they also serve as what Deleuze and Guattari call "conceptual personae" which "*show thought's territories.*"[110] In addition to animating the plot, they are the biopolitical vehicles through which the novel thinks. If we ask *how* it thinks. We can observe it replicating the "undecidability of 'subjective' and 'objective' causality,"[111] exhibiting a simultaneous embrace and abjection of traditional theological commitment. As a result, another feature of Deleuze and Guattari's conceptual personae becomes apropos. Referring to conceptual personae who stammer, they ask "'What is this thought that can only stammer'?" and go on to suggest, "This is not two friends who engage in thought; rather it is thought itself which requires this division of thought between friends."[112] Their notion of stammering thought accords well with the way Dick divides himself among his characters—for example Horselover Fat and Phil Dick in *Valis* and Bill (Timothy Archer's schizophrenic son) and Angel (his daughter-in-law who narrates the novel and, as was the case for Dick himself, has worked in a records store). He is distributed among characters who exist in ideational states of tension, engaging in *"thought-events,"* as they seek to manage "the epoch or historical milieu in which they appear."[113]

Archer (as is the case with his other novels) is therefore an essay as well as a drama, where an essay (as famously developed by Montaigne) "is an experiment in the community of truth and not a packaging of knowledge ruled by definitions and operations. The essay is a political instrument inasmuch as it liberates the writer and reader from the domination of conventional standards of clarity and communication [it's an] expression of literary initiative ... accomplished against the limits of received language."[114] Accordingly, throughout the novel its language transgresses the boundary between fiction and reality as, through its conceptual personae, it ponders questions about human destiny in a situation of ontological uncertainty. As regards its theological content, Dick plays with it—rejecting it at some moments and indulging it at others—in what appears as an intellectual version of what Freud famously called a *"fort da"* (away, here) game, which in Dick's case has a more Lacanian than Freudian manifestation, i.e., it is about the subject's "radical vacillation" rather than its seeking of mastery.[115] In any case, Dick seems more attuned to his writing genre than to theology. As he has confessed,

> God, as a topic in science fiction, when it appeared at all, used to be treated polemically, as in *"Out of the Silent Planet."* But I prefer to treat it as intellectually exciting ... Science fiction, always probing what is about to be thought, become, must eventually tackle without preconceptions a future neo-mystical society in which theology constitutes a major force as in the medieval period.[116]

Inquiry rather than allegiance thus dominates Dick's theological speculations. And insofar as he has a theology, it is "bound less to transcendence that to immanent contradiction"[117] which is very much at play in the inability of the two Archers, Timothy and Angel, to achieve a theological accord.

As for its parodic element, as I have suggested the novel deifies musical icons, e.g., John Lennon, whose shooting death, as I've noted, is a seeming substitute for Paul's Christ event. Thoroughly musically punctuated, as the narrator, Angel Archer distributes musicians and composers throughout her commentary, the novel testifies to the way music was central to Dick's "creative world."[118] *Archer* extends the musical idiom developed in *The Divine Invasion*, which is also musically punctuated through its focus on the popular singer, Linda Fox (a stand-in for Dick's obsession with Linda Ronstadt) who serves as an object of faith that assists the protagonist, Herb Asher to expunge his demon. As is the case with *DI*, philosophical referents accompany the pervasive musical referents throughout *Archer*, the former mostly articulated through Timothy Archer and the latter through Angel Archer's narration, as she and Timothy conversationally challenge each other. Their interactions recreate the ways that Dick philosophically and culturally mediates his skepticism (through Angel) and theological speculations (through Timothy).

Repeating the way Dick invests himself in his protagonists throughout his writing, the *Archer* encounters articulate the speculations that express Dick's vacillating relationship with the divine. Ultimately therefore, Dick's *Archer* expresses his commitment to *thinking*. That he's a thinker rather than a believer (as I have been suggesting) is a conclusion that is available when we heed the last PKD surrogate, Angel Archer. Near the end of the novel, after Angel has resisted Timothy's request to accompany him to Israel (and he dies in the desert while in search for ancient manuscripts), Angel is back working in her record store, arguably the closest approximation to a church in musically attuned Dick's life. Asked by a guru, whose seminars she is attending, if she will allow the character Bill Lundborg (hospitalized after insisting he has become an incarnation of the late Timothy Archer) to move in with her, she says, "I'll have to think a long time about that." Asked why, she adds, "Because that's how I do things like that." That's precisely how Dick did things (to which his stories, novels, and his long rambling *Exegesis* testify). He spent his life thinking and steadfastly opposing ideational hegemonies, for example, the one to which Palmer Eldritch aspired in *Three Stigmata*. In his lifelong speculations about how people might share a world empathically, whether through a shared spirituality or otherwise, he raised questions rather than imposing answers, leaving conclusions, provisional or definitive, to his readers. It's an ethical posture he develops early in his writing career—in his 1965 story "Not by Its Cover,"[119] to which I now turn.

The Phenomenology of Reception According to PKD

Dick's story "Not by Its Cover" arguably provides his view of the phenomenology of reading.[120] In the story, Dick brings back his slovenly but very philosophically articulate pig-like wub (who discusses mythological figures and Odysseus's travels with his owner on a space ship and then takes over the body of a ship's captain who ingests it in the earlier story).[121] In this later story, wubs exist as book covers. Five thousand copies of a book are covered in wub fir, *"the most elegant, expensive material we could locate,"* according to Mr. Masters, "The Elderly, cross-tempered president of Obelisk Books."[122] The publisher is visited by a scholar who points out an error in Obelisk Book's publication of the Dryden translation of Lucretius's *De Rerum Natura*. There's a quatrain that "preaches a message diametric to that of the entire book … Dryden didn't write it … Lucretius didn't," according to the scholar (Mr. Brandice). It's discovered that a wub fir-covered publication of Paul's letters to the Corinthians has also been altered, which gives rise to another Dick theological parody, in this case of Paul's promise that the Christ event has conquered death. A character in the story, Snead, says, "What occurs to me is this. The wub hasn't merely learned to avoid death; it's actually done what it preaches. By getting killed, skinned, and its hide—still alive made into book covers—it has conquered death." As the bookstore conversation goes on, the theological parody continues. Another character, Saperstein ponders what wubs do, "Being the binding of a book; just lying there supine, on a shelf year after year, inhaling minute particles from the air." Snead answers, "They think theology … they preach." That preaching goes on in another publication, the *Britannica*, to which the wub covering has "added whole articles … on the soul, on transmigration, on hell, damnation, sin, or immortality; the whole twenty-four volume set became religiously oriented."[123]

While much of the story is a religious parody, what it also conveys is a critically oriented phenomenology of reading that challenges the privilege of authorial intent. In changing the texts, the wubs "act is analogous to that of the reader," a reader who "approaches a text from a certain stance or belief and reacts to the text, in part, through that belief, often changing what is read (what the author meant to have read, that is) to suit the particular reader's framework."[124] There are two important implications of Dick's depriviledging of authorial intent in his "Not by Its Cover." One is well captured in Thomas Mann's novelistic version of the story of Joseph in the Hebrew bible. At the beginning of the third volume of his novelistic tetralogy, *Joseph and His Brothers*, Mann has Joseph remark (to the nomadic Ma'onites who pull him from the pit where his brothers had left him to die), "Where are you taking me?" One of them, Kedeema, responds, "You have a way of putting yourself in the middle of things," and goes on to point out that they are headed somewhere and that Joseph happens to be with them; they have no reason to regard themselves as part of his story: "Do you suppose that we are journeying simply so that you may arrive somewhere your god wants you to be."[125] Edified by Kedeema's remarks, Joseph admits that "the world has many middle points," but insists nevertheless that at least he stands in the center of *his* circle.[126] As the story continues, Joseph loses that conceit as well, as Mann (very much like Spinoza) re-inflects a sacred text in an intervention that challenges authorial privilege and thereby the textual basis of institutionalized theology.

The second implication of the story is the space Dick creates for reader reflection. His "Not by Its Cover" can be read as an invitation to the reader to share Dick's mentality, i.e., his speculative thinking about theology (and about the meaning of life in general). The story, like much of his writing, is "writerly," in the sense that Roland Barthes has attributed that style to the "new" as opposed to the classical novel. Unlike the "readerly text," which creates a passive reader, one who is the receiver of a fixed, pre-determined, text, "The writerly text is a perpetual present, upon which no *consequent* language (which would inevitably make it past) can be superimposed; the writerly text is *ourselves writing*."[127] In short, the space afforded to Dick's readers is the space commandeered by the wubs in "Not by Its Cover." However, it's not enough to merely state that Dick invites his readers to share his mentality because "mentality" can stand for a wide variety of aspects of cognition. To conclude I want to refer to those complications in order to provide a bridge to a final chapter which engages William James's lifelong efforts to sort the complications while at the same time seeking to save one of his valued elements of mentality, religious belief, from the forms of skepticism that neurological research encouraged.

The Cognitive Locus of PKD's Ethos

In bringing to his literary feast a host of aesthetic and philosophical figures that inhabit his enormous compendium of writings, what Philip K. Dick puts on display challenges the reader to sort what Dominic Pettman refers to as "a baroque tangle of affect, ethics, interpellation and obligation."[128] What adds to the challenge are the intricate ways that Dick interweaves technology and mentality, complicating the locus of intelligibility. Accordingly, in anticipation of Chapter 5's exploration, focused on the philosophical and psychological musings of William James, as they articulate aspects of mentality—believing, thinking, willing—I want to reemphasize Dick's tendency to locate mentality outside humans, e.g., as radio broadcasts that invade brains rather than embracing a model in which human brains express themselves, i.e., turning the inside toward an outside. In a stunning passage concerned with the role of the telephone in the ideational struggles precipitating the Second World War, William T. Vollmann locates mentality inside a telephone:

> Consciousness [he writes] may indeed derive ... from entirely mechanical factors: Within the bakelite skull of the entity [telephone] hangs, either nestled or strangled in a latticework of scarlet-colored wires, a malignantly complex brain not much larger than a walnut. Its cortex consists of two brown-and-yellow lobes filamented with fine copper wire. It owns ideas as neatly, numerously arrayed as Poland's faded yellow eagle standards: *The camp of counter-revolution ... German straighforwardness ... the slanders of the opposition ... the soundness of Volkish theory.*[129]

As Vollmann implies, the telephone is more than a simple prosthesis, it, much as has been the case with the other twentieth-century technologies (e.g., gramophones, films, and typewriters as Friedrich Kittler has famously pointed out[130]), has a mentality of form. Dick well understood how technological devices have redistributed the locus of consciousness, altered the ethics and politics of interpersonal association, and challenged theologies and other ontological commitments. As technological advances in this century bring increasingly "smart" technologies that alter the locus of thinking, we can continue to learn from Philip K. Dick's writing style, which distances us from institutionalized approaches to intelligibility, and from his speculations, the ethico-political questions, theological and otherwise, that they raise.

William James: Theology's "Anchorage" in Mentality

The James Pulpit

There's much to unite the ethico-political conceits of Philip K. Dick and William James. Apart from their shared ambivalence toward theology—both alternating between acceptance of a divine presence and deep skepticism—is their shared commitment to unqualified empathy. While Dick's testimony about it is implicitly developed in his stories and novels, James stated it directly with extraordinary eloquence in his 1898 essay, "Human Immortality":

> The heart of being can have no exclusions akin to those which our poor little hearts set up. The inner significance of other lives exceeds all our powers of sympathy and insight. If we feel a significance in our own life which would lead us spontaneously to claim its perpetuity, let us be at least tolerant of like claims made by other lives, however numerous, however unideal they may seem to us to be. Let us at any rate not decide adversely on our own claim, whose grounds we feel directly, because we cannot decide favorably on the alien claims, whose grounds we cannot feel at all. That would be letting blindness lay down the law to sight.[1]

What is expressed in that passage is similar to what Slavoj Žižek attributes to the ethical sensibility of William's brother, the novelist Henry James. After asserting that "there is no ethical substance which provides fixed coordinates of our ethical judgment in advance, that such a judgment can emerge only from our own work of ethical reflection with no eternal guarantee," Žižek proceeds to identify the obligation that implies, discernible in Henry James's novels. It's an ethical imperative that accords with the one his brother William's ethical position: "The lack of a fixed frame of reference, far from simply condemning us to moral relativism, opens up a new 'higher' field of ethical experience: that of intersubjectivity, the mutual dependence of subjects, the need not only to rely on others, but also to recognize the ethical weight of others' claims on me."[2]

I would like to be able to regard that passage in William James's "Human Immorality" as the essence of what he contributed to the conversation about our obligations to each other and to life in general. However, William James, whose "oppositional" style contrasts with Henry James's "immanent" mode of ethical expression, was extraordinarily prolix and ambiguous about his views on the cognitive basis of ethics, spirituality, and inter-personal obligation.[3] Consequently, much of that essay heads in different directions to pursue a different aim. James, who in an address eight years later will have disparaged theodicies (by "stall-fed officials of an established church"[4]), delivers one in this address to provide reassurance to those who have a "real passion" for the matter of immortality. Among what James claims is that new knowledge of the physiology of the brain (contrary to what some scientists suggest) has no bearing on justifications for God's existence and therefore on one's hope for immorality.

It's not the only time James had delivered a reassuring, sermon-like address to Christian believers. In an earlier speech to a Unitarian assemblage, he performed a similar task, the rhetorical rhythms of which also suggest a Philip Dick comparison. Specifically, the intellectual *fort/da* game I ascribed to Dick's approach to theology in Chapter 4's discussion of his last novel, *The Transmigration of Timothy Archer*, structures a James theodicy in a lecture delivered prior to his "Human Immortality." His address, "Reflex Action and Theism," to the Unitarian Ministers' Institute of Princeton, Massachusetts (in 1881), which seems to promote the reality of the divine at some moments and suggest skepticism at others, delivers an injunction that is quite similar to one in Paul's First Epistle to the Corinthians. Just as Paul disparages the Greek tendency to approach the divine by seeking wisdom (1: 22), telling them, "your faith should not stand in the wisdom of men (2: 5)," James counsels a similar diremption between wisdom and faith. In an eloquent piece of sophistry, in which he alternatively summons and dismisses the reality of God, James tells his audience that scientific approaches to mentality do not compromise their theological commitments.

However, in contrast with Paul's confident assertion of his calling ("Paul, called to be an apostle, of Jesus Christ," 1 Corinthians 1: 1), James apologizes for his. He begins with self-effacing humility: "Let me confess to the diffidence with which I find myself standing here to-day ... it was as a teacher of physiology that I was most unworthily officiating when your committee's invitation reached me." Thereafter, in a speech punctuated throughout by god talk, he issues reassurances that contemporary physiological science, within which "reflect action" is the main concept, poses no challenge to their theology.[5] As for the "perlocutionary force" of his address (John Austin's expression for persuasive locutionary effects, appropriately delivered in his 1955 "William James" lecture at Harvard[6]), rather than like Paul summoning his audience to theological commitment, he is legitimating that to which they are already committed. As a contribution to a political theology, his remarks align him precisely with what Žižek refers to as a philosophy of "(re)normalization," one that "would, on the one hand, promote scientific research and technical progress and, on the other hand, contain its full socio-symbolic impact, i.e., prevent it from posing a threat to the existing theologico-ethical constellation."[7]

Nevertheless, there is considerably more than mere reassurance and legitimation in the address. Throughout the body of his remarks, James exercises, with characteristic *"muscular elegance,"*[8] his initially developed physiologically informed approach to psychology (which he later altered as he recognized that all psychologies are infused with metaphysics)[9] and his already developing philosophy, which was to emerge as both his pragmatism and his radical empiricism. With respect to the delivery of its philosophical dimension, the style of the address is didactic. One has to be reminded that what is doctrinal with respect to James's support of theology, in which he naturalizes and anchors subjectivity, is contradicted by the way his radical empiricism treats both subjects and objects as unanchored and "in transition."[10]

James's "Reflex Action and Theism" is therefore a propitious text with which to begin an engagement with the way James mobilizes his perspectives on mentality to defend theology as he ponders and instructs on how, as volitional beings, we confront the life world, even though with respect to theology, his personal commitment to the existence of a divine transcendence is uncertain. The divine for James was as much a matter of intellectual speculation as it was an object of religious allegiance. His attachment to Christian theology paled in comparison with his passion for advancing knowledge. As he remarked in the "immortality" essay, "The whole subject of immortal life has its prime roots in personal feeling. I have to confess that my own personal feeling about immortality has never been of the keenest order, and that, among the problems that give my mind solicitude, this one does not take the very foremost place."[11] He put it more definitively years later (1904) in a letter written to James H. Leuba: "The Divine, for my active life, is limited to impersonal and abstract concepts which, as ideal, interest and determine me, but do so but faintly in comparison with what a feeling of God might effect, if I had one."[12]

Despite James's claim that his own mindfulness is ordinarily deployed on other things, throughout his address to Unitarian Ministers, he naturalizes and universalizes that "personal feeling" (which weighs much less heavily on him than on his addressees). He refers to "God ... if he did exist [as] ... the most adequate possible object for minds framed like our own as lying at the root of the universe."[13] As the address develops, despite the sermon-like atmosphere in which it is delivered, the style is more that of an intellectual than a believer. Committed to ideas in a pragmatic sense—concerned not with what an idea is but its consequences for thinking and acting[14]—James sees beliefs similarly, i.e., in terms of how they dispose one to act, for example, to participate in a shared-belief religious assemblage. Within that pragmatic sensibility, belief evolves into faith because for James, belief leads one to act to the extent that it is held with "confidence" (where he interpolates confidence as "faith").[15]

There is thus no duplicity in the reassurance James is offering his audience; his remarks accord with his philosophical views. Although all the god talk may have seemed to align him with his audience's predilections, what James delivers is an essayistic sermon. While it likely provided reassurance, its main audience was arguably James himself, seeking with a complex signifying structure to reconcile his scholarly proclivities – his deep immersion in the disciplines of physiology, psychology, and philosophy—and his religious sensibility, an oft-repeated conviction that the universe holds higher powers, "something beyond awareness"[16] and thus inaccessible to our ordinary knowledge practices. Hence an assessment of what James offers to a conversation about the viability of religious belief in that address requires attention to both his rhetorical strategy, which I will render as the semiological codes that punctuate the address, and its ideational legacies, the "thought worlds" and style-shaping genres on which he drew. I begin with the former.

The Textual Structure of "Reflex Action and Theism"

To venture a critical engagement with the overwhelming extravagance and richness of James's presentation to the Unitarians, one is well-advised to practice what Walter Benjamin referred to as an "ascetic apprenticeship," which in his case preserved his objectivity when he engaged a different extravagant and rich literature, German tragic drama. As he put it,

> Only by approaching the subject from a distance and, initially foregoing any view of the whole, can the mind be led, through a more or less ascetic apprenticeship, to the position of strength from which it is possible to take in the whole panorama and yet remain in control of oneself.[17]

James's address to the Unitarian assemblage is a pervasively epistemological text. I suggest that it yields its persuasive effect—a vindication of religious belief—if it is parsed with resort to a textual analysis developed by Roland Barthes, who treated texts as what he called "methodological fields."[18]

In the textual exercise most relevant to my application, Barthes breaks a novelistic text, Balzac's *Sarrasine*, into fragments he refers to as "lexia," which are a series of semiological codes that comprise its signifying structure.[19] Applying that approach to the text of James's address, I draw on an adaptation of that aspect of Barthes's method that I used in an earlier investigation to analyze one of Freud's texts, his case study, *The Wolfman*, which I broke into a series of "epistemological codes."[20] Specifically, I noted the way Freud achieves epistemological warrants for an application of his psychoanalytic method by evoking empirical, hermeneutic, narrative, and polemical codes. James's text deploys a similar strategy. It is open to textual analysis because what was once an event—a speech whose meanings were controlled by an interlocutory context—is now a text. No longer dialogic, once it has moved from speech to writing, the text has, in Paul Ricoeur's terms, "free[d] itself, not only from its author, but from the narrowness of the dialogic situation."[21] It is thus available to as many contexts as readers may decide to evoke. Mine follows.

After beginning with an observation on the tendency of theologians to "hearken to the conclusions of men of science," James invokes an empirical code to note that the actions to which such "men" (always "men" throughout the address) refer as "reflex actions" are what all educated people *know* [i.e., it has been empirically well-established] about how the brain operates from its 'nervous centers.'[22] That appeal to established research-based knowledge is followed by a turn to a hermeneutic code with which James locates 'all action' as 're-action' within what he refers to as the 'structural unit of the nervous system.' James renders that 'system' – the whole within which action moments make sense – as a 'triad' with 'sensory impression … awaking the central process of reflection' [which] exists only for the sake of calling forth the final act.[23]

James then adds nuance to complicate that picture of the brain by invoking a narrative code in which willing (the consistently privileged aspect of cognition for James) is activated prior to the functioning of other aspects of brain activity; it's the engine driving other cognitive functions: "The willing department of our nature dominates both the conceiving department and the feeling department; or, in plainer English, perception and thinking are only there for behavior's sake."[24] At that moment James is effectively rehearsing the perspective on mentality, rendered as the cognitive dynamics of mind, to which he himself had contributed. With obvious pride he extols the science he has outlined, noting what a "great contribution physiology has made to psychology of late years."[25] However, at this point I am on edge because I am alert to James's title and to the nature of his audience. I sense that the address is going to veer in a new direction. Sure enough; James follows his synopsis of the contributions of physiology to modern psychology with a polemical code, the substance of which must have greatly pleased his theology-invested audience.

The audience-friendly direction toward which James follows his focus on psychological science begins with the suggestion that the knowledge he has outlined has "influence" that extends "beyond the limits of psychology, even to those of theology herself."[26] Having opened his address with an observation about the "eagerness" with which theologians "hearken to the conclusions of men of science,"[27] he goes on with heavy sarcasm to disparage "writers" who "say that reflex action and all that follows from it give the coup de grâce to the superstition of a God" and refers to a time "when the existence of reflex action and all other harmonies between the organism and the world were held to prove a God. Now, they are held to disprove him. The next turn of the whirligig may bring back proof of him again."[28]

Having implied that those thinkers who belong to the disproving side of the debate have no warrants for their position other than an attitude, which has proven to be historically labile, James (without conceding that he himself is a believer) offers a theology-supporting "thesis" in an ambiguous prose passage that captures the discursive rhythms with which he both disparages resistance to the existence of God and at the same time casts doubt on "his" existence:

> Into this debate about his existence, I will not pretend to enter. I must take up humbler ground, and limit my ambition to showing that a God, whether existent or not, is at all events the kind of being which, if he did exist would form the most adequate object for minds framed like our own to conceive as lying at the root of the universe. My thesis, in other words [doubtless by now his perplexed listeners crave "other words"] is this: that some outward reality of a nature defined as God's nature must be defined, is the only ultimate object that is at the same time rational and possible for the human mind's contemplation.[29]

Quite aside from the *fort/da* game to which James treats his listeners—the here he is, there he goes, now he's back playing with the reality of God's existence—is his venturing of what he regards as "theism." As is the case with much of James's oeuvre, it's all about mentality: "Theism, whatever its objective warrant, would thus be seen to have a subjective anchorage in its congruity with our nature as thinkers."[30] Accordingly, what I want to explore next are the conditions of possibility—the aesthetic and ideational legacies—upon which James's remarks about "our nature as thinkers" depend.

Borrowing Immanuel Kant's expression, I offer a "transcendental exposition"[31] to expose what James presupposes as a non-experiential principle of (historical) judgment in order to demonstrate actual experiences that have theological plausibility. I begin with James's observations about the aesthetic supplement of his analytic thinking, specifically the way he figures himself as a writing subject (whose writing style mediates what he claims to discover about mental states) and the way he figures mental states, the primary objects of his thinking. However, I must note a qualification. An assiduous run through James's *Principles* reveals that "after more than fourteen years of research and two thousand pages of psychological writings which fall ostensibly under the natural-scientific program, James confessed that he did not know what a mental state is [or] … what could count as a mental state."[32]

Figuring Subjectivity

As I have pointed out in Chapter 3, theatricality shapes Ingmar Bergman's line of flight from theology. However, while Bergman's theater metaphor points to a world without transcendence, the "small world," which his cinematic scenarios suggest we should assume is our only world, James turns to theater to figure the dynamics of mentality. *His* theater abides within subjectivity. It's one among the many artistic metaphors with which he figures his primary contributions to a science of mentality, the "stream of consciousness": "The mind is a kind of theatre, where several perceptions successively make their appearance; pass, repass, glide away and mingle in an infinite variety of postures and situations." Lest we assume that the subject is a director in control of that theater, James hastens to add that there is much mindlessness in that theatrical mindfulness: "The comparison of the theatre must not mislead us," he suggests, "for we are not wholly aware of the provenance of the successive perceptions … that constitute the mind"; we have only "the most distant notion of the place where these scenes are presented [and] of the material of which it is composed."[33] Catherine Malabou (whose view of the brain is introduced below) has a similar insight: "The brain is a work, and we do not know it. We are its subjects-authors and products at once—and we do not know it."[34]

Because James's rendering of mentality involves an encounter of compositions, an analysis of his views must heed the way his written compositions engage the process of cognitive composition he ascribes to mentality. Not surprisingly, James turns to another artistic genre for an aesthetics of the writing subject, painting. As one who had trained to be a painter before he turned to psychological science, James had painting continually on his mind. Although career-wise he turned from art to science, mentality-wise he never abandoned art. As a result, in the philosophical compositions that emerged late in his career, he likened the compositional aspect of writing to the process of adding shape and color to a painter's canvass. In his *Pragmatism*, for example, he compares philosophical argumentation to painting, stating that philosophers "paint" their "views."[35] His attachment to painting also emerges in his own writing style. To follow the way a James essay develops is to witness an author who resembles a patient painter, one like Paul Cézanne for example, whose painting process likens him to an essayist: "Graduated sequences of hues, dark and light, warm and cool, situated first by regular blocky strokes, then by freer more irregular ones, become the abstract designators of position. Through color difference, otherwise known as color interval, [Cézanne] build[s] the space."[36]

Similarly, James's views of mentality in general and spirituality specifically emerge as he writes, gradually applying figuration and illustration as he slowly builds a picture of how persons experience worlds (the "multiverse" as he famously puts it). For example, while elaborating the dynamics of that building process, James adds another artistic genre; he follows his theatre metaphor with, sculpture: "The mind ... works on the data it receives very much as a sculptor works on his block of stone."[37] However, painting is James's more frequent artistic figure. With spirituality in the forefront of his concerns, he uses a painting analogy to refer to the way the materiality of paint becomes part of a mental picture when it is transferred from a "pot" where it is merely "so much saleable matter" to the canvass, where "with other paints around it, it represents, on the contrary, a feature in a picture and performs a spiritual function."[38]

If spirituality and theological commitment—what James calls theism— has a "subjective anchorage,"[39] i.e., are seated in the mind-as-stream-of-consciousness, how does James support that inference? One of his many answers is available if we turn back to his "Reflex Action and Theism" address where he follows his remark about theism's subjective anchorage with a reference to its "congruity with our nature as thinkers."[40] That claim raises the question of how such a nature arose. James's answer is that there is a historical warrant. Invoking the "psychological gain" that accrues from the congruity to which he refers, James invokes "the natural history of the mind" and adds, "as a matter of such natural history, God may be called the normal object of the mind's belief."[41] He is therefore telling the assemblage of Unitarian ministers that theism (yours but not necessarily mine) comes about naturally as a result of the way the natural history of mentality orients one toward belief in God.

A commitment to "Natural history," which is a major part of what I have called James's ideational heritage, is therefore one of the conditions of possibility for what emerges from James's mouth and pen (even though that version of "history" was already a very much contested anachronism). Admittedly, throughout his *Principles of Psychology* James treats the "natural history of the mind" empirically, seeing it as an enabling accumulation of habit. Nevertheless, it's a perspective that neglects the effects of mind-influencing media and the changing discourses that generate ideational contingency rather than licensing a linear model of historical accumulation. As Michel Foucault's archaeological investigation of the history of epistemes discloses, by the time James was invoking natural history, it was part of an epistemological paradigm that had been surpassed.[42] Apart from what subtle differences may obtain between the historical episteme and James's reference, Foucault offers an instructive methodological insight, which requires only a slight modification in wording to challenge James's perspective on an "object of the mind's belief." Displacing "mind" with language practices (i.e., discourse), Foucault refers to the "rules of formation" of objects:

> Natural history was not simply a form of knowledge that gave a new definition to concepts like 'genus,' or 'character,' and which introduced new concepts like that of the 'natural classification' ... above all, it was a set of rules for arranging statements in a series, an obligatory set of schemata of dependence, of order, and successions, in which the recurrent elements that may have value as concepts were distributed.[43]

Treating the implications of holding onto historical perspectives that embrace and naturalize continuities—mind-forged or otherwise—Foucault refers to such histories as a "privileged shelter for the sovereignty of consciousness."[44] Although that charge may apply to James's reliance on consciousness as the locus of experience, the mode of "sovereignty" James applies to consciousness is unstable. Consciousness for James is plastic and pragmatic; it adjusts along with changing interests and alterations in surrounding systems of recognition rather than maintaining an inflexible authoritarian reign over experience.

Nevertheless, the picture James paints of theism's "anchorage" in consciousness in his *Theism* essay, which is a simple version of what becomes more complex as his *Principles* ponders selfhood's plurality, naturalizes what can be treated more critically. Turning to one of Foucault's remarks about criticism, I want to suggest that one way to implement that phrase "more critically" is to think in terms of events rather than continuities. Foucault suggests that instead of looking for "formal structures with universal value [we investigate] … the events that have led us to constitute and to recognize ourselves as subjects of what we are doing, thinking, saying."[45] Put succinctly, "the objective of [Foucault's] work is to develop a thinking adequate to events and thus permit the 'introduction into the very roots of thought of notions of chance, discontinuity and materiality.'"[46] And crucially, rather than building the kind of picture with which James is concerned in his address, Foucault's historical analyses deal with a different temporality and a different knowledge issue; his investigations are focused on the conditions under which certain forms of knowledge became possible and on the forces surrounding apparatuses of implementation.

To provide an illustration of such a critical alternative, I want to step away from the content (the neuro-psychological details) of James's address to the Unitarian assemblage and heed what is historically peculiar about that encounter. The very fact that a religious assemblage is being addressed by a physiological psychologist says something about the historical moment in which theologians are soliciting such an encounter. It is a moment experienced as a crisis in which an ideational event (a movement toward secularism) is happening in theology-challenging ways. Such moments are endemic to theology. As Jacob Taubes points out: "The hour of theology is come when a mythical configuration breaks down and its symbols that are congealed as canon come into conflict with a new stage … in [human] consciousness."[47]

At a point in his investigations in which Foucault understood his historical work as genealogical—thinking in terms of transformative events rather than continuities (a focus on the changes in the will to knowledge in contrast with James's concern with the enduring will to believe)—he provides a relevant and instructive intervention in the crisis moment of the theologians-James encounter. The event Foucault describes is an encounter in a nineteenth-century courtroom in which psychological expertise has been solicited. In an analysis of an episode in a discontinuous history of "the will to truth," he analyzes what he refers to as the problem of the "dangerous individual in 19th-century legal psychiatry" and points to "the gradual emergence in the course of the nineteenth century of [an] additional character, the 'criminal.'" Whereas in previous centuries courts countenanced only crimes and penalties (no knowledge practices were applied to the mentalities of those involved in committing crimes), the nineteenth century witnessed the emergence of the criminal as a new object of knowledge, surveilled and interrogated by professional knowledge agents. Among what resulted were new conversations in juridical settings in which medical professionals participated. Rather than simply an object of retaliation through which sovereign power is reactivated, the accused had become someone whose motivations and thinking had to be understood. It was a historical period in which the problem of governance had shifted from a preoccupation with the life of the sovereign to a concern with the life of the population as a whole. As part of that shift, psychiatry had entered the courtroom as one among many parts of a new medical *dispositif*, focused on "a sort of public hygiene" applied to a new target of governance, the social order.[48] Their intervention follows a series of them that began in the middle of the eighteenth century when, as Foucault notes, "the species body" is governed and supervised by various regulatory agencies, operating as part of what he calls "a biopolitics of the population."[49]

Like James's, "Reflex Action and Theism," Foucault's text, "About the Concept of the 'Dangerous Individual' in 19th-Century Psychiatry," is pervasively epistemological. However, rather than framing the knowledge issue the way James does—asking for example about the extent to which mentality can achieve a "harmony between [its] faculties and the truth [of a divine presence]"[50]—Foucault's question is about why mentality is being analyzed and why that particular knowledge issue is being pursued at a particular historical moment. As a moment when criminals are asked to speak and knowledge agents (forensic psychiatrists) are asked to evaluate what they say about themselves, what is analytically important to Foucault is not the particular theories the psychiatrists embraced (He doesn't concern himself as does James with the nuances of psychological perspectives) but the very fact that psychiatrists were involving themselves in an interrogation of a type of mentality at a particular historical moment.

Whatever the psychiatrists' particular views of the unconscious might have been, it was their entry into an official role as knowledge agents that a genealogical history concerns itself with. They were part of a complex apparatus serving a newly institutionalized *political* mentality, a "governmentality" whose biopolitical problem had shifted from the body of the sovereign to a newly recognized collective body, the "population." Criminal danger was seen as impacting on the health of the population, which had become something that governance must manage: "'population' as an economic and political problem: population as wealth, population as manpower or labor capacity, population balanced between its own growth and the resources it commanded. Governments perceived that they were not dealing simply with subjects, or even with a 'people' but with a population."[51] However, rather than pursuing a James-Foucault contrast in knowledge problematics further—in some ways there is conceptual convergence (e.g., Foucault saw himself pursuing "the pragmatics of the self"[52])—I want at this point to heed the way James ultimately painted from a different pallet, as his mentality idiom shifted from psychology to philosophy and as a result his *Principles of Psychology* took on a phenomenological character. As Bruce Wilshire discerns, "Phenomenology enters *The Principles of Psychology* exactly at the point where the explicit program of the work [the scientific correlation of 'mental states with brain states' with which he regaled the Unitarians] breaks down."[53]

William James's Phenomenology

An inspection of the phenomenological elements that emerge in James's *Principles* bears comparison with some materialist or object-oriented versions of phenomenology, for example, that of the Czech philosopher, Jan Patočka, which offers an active model of subjectivity but at the same time holds the world responsible for the sensations and ideas that arise in mentality.[54] At a point at which James is referring to one's "immediate sensorial attention," he introduces duration and draws first on the history of what has imposed on the mind—in his words, the way "[w]e are 'evolved' so as to respond to special stimuli by special accommodative acts"—and adds, "We don't bestow it, the object draws it from us. The object has the initiative, not the mind."[55] To the extent that the mind takes the initiative for James, it involves more than simple discharges (one of his frequent figurations) in response to objects; it evokes a complex "mental geography" combining concepts with the percepts as the subject builds an ideational and affective territory, which is presupposed in the way it imagines its world and (crucially for James's privileging of volition) the way it pursues its interests, preparing to act.[56]

It is the concept of interest with which James's *Principles of Psychology* articulates his version of phenomenology (which ultimately influenced the more canonical versions, e.g., that of Husserl whose notion of intentionality was explicitly inspired by James's text). In a telling metaphorical passage, which resonates with Nietzsche's reference to "the great dice game of existence,"[57] James invokes his concept of interest while describing his phenomenology:

> The performances of a high brain are like dice thrown forever on the table. Unless they be loaded, what chance is there that the highest number will turn up oftener than the lowest? … Can consciousness increase its efficiency by loading the dice? Such is the problem. Loading the dice would mean bringing a more or less constant pressure to bear in favor of those performances which make the most permanent interests of the brain's owner; it would mean a constant inhibition to stray aside. Well just such pressure and such inhibition are what consciousness seems to be exerting all the while. And the interests in whose favor it seems to exert them are its interests and its alone, interests which it creates and which, but for it, would have no status in the realm of being whatever.[58]

James's references to "pressure" and "interests" instantiate the inter-articulation of his pragmatism with his phenomenological psychology and at the same time gesture toward what he regards as the privileged cognitive faculty, will. Although there is much more one can say about James's phenomenology (and many have elaborated it well),[59] what will occupy my analysis next is the way the concept of will shapes and energizes James's defense of theology.

James and the Will to Believe

In *The Will to Believe*, the prototype of which was his address by the same title to the Philosophy Clubs of Yale and Brown University, James reengages the question he pursues in his "Reflex Action and Theism." However, this time his sermon-like address is less convoluted. Promising "something like a sermon on justification by faith," James launches a full-throated attack on skepticism, in which he dismisses faith-vetoing scientific skepticism but at the same time uses a scientific idiom (mainly in the many references to hypotheses) in full support of his theism (clearly *his* as well as theirs this time, for he states, "we all of us believe in … Protestant Christianity"). Continuing with a "we" grammar, he goes on to state, "We want to have truth" but are faced with an adversary, whom James refers to (literally in incendiary terms) as a pyrrhonistic sceptic, who he has asked "*how we know*" all this, can our logic find a reply? "No, certainly it cannot," he says. it is "one volition against another,—we willing to go in for life upon a trust or assumption which he, for his part does not care to make."[60]

After proceeding to disparage "scientific absolutists," few of whom are willing to warrant such parapsychological phenomena as telepathy (because lacking a pragmatic perspective, they ask whether it yields truth rather than seeing what it can do), he invokes "our 'non-intellectual nature'" which supports our "convictions" and refers to the belief-fostering effects of our "passional tendencies and volitions which run before others." Those references serve as a prologue to his statement of his thesis.

> The thesis I defend is … this: *Our passional nature not only lawfully may, but must, decide an option between propositions, whether it is a genuine option cannot by its nature be decided on intellectual grounds; for to say, under such circumstances "Do not decide, but leave the question open," is itself a passional decision – just like deciding yes or no – and is attended with the same risk of losing the truth.*[61]

What James then mounts is a defense of religion within two discursive practices. Combining pragmatic (or what Rose Ann Christian calls "prudential"[62]) and epistemological arguments, within the latter he asserts that the existence of God is a "live hypothesis" and within the former he asserts that "we are better off … if we believe [the] affirmation of [the 'live hypothesis'] to be true."[63] In contrast, addressing himself to that same "religious hypothesis," Nietzsche evokes a "will to blindness [that] dominates the founders of religion," and adds that the "hypothesis of a god of 'eternal values,'" amounts to a denial of the

"I will." It contains the assumption that because "the task has already been accomplished," there is no necessity to strive actively to give meaning to life.[64] Paradoxically, despite his equivocal defense of God's existence, associated as it is with an eternal model of temporality, James like Nietzsche does not see the task as already accomplished. He accompanies the language of hypotheses with the position that the question of god, like all questions, should remain always open. After saying, "I am ... myself a complete empiricist so far as the theory of human knowledge goes," James adds,

> I live, to be sure, by the practical faith that we must go on experiencing and thinking over our experience, for only thus can our opinions grow more true ... we find no proposition ever regarded by any one as evidently certain that has not either been called a falsehood or at least had its truth sincerely questioned by some one else.[65]

How can we represent the effects of James's equivocations, which carry on throughout his *The Will to Believe* and other writings? For example, the same James who at moments sounds like a traditional moralist, referring to the way the natural history of the mind makes God its normal object, writes, "visible nature is all plasticity and indifference,—a moral multiverse, and not a moral universe."[66] To situate the unexpected arrests and reversals in the ideational flow of James's text, we can recall the affinity between his writing style and painting and draw on an instructive treatment of a Vermeer landscape by Georges Didi-Huberman, who finds among the iconic details in Vermeer's canvasses blotches of paint, non-mimetic elements that do not participate in the paintings' representational effects. Didi-Huberman suggests that those enigmatic signs, which do not have a descriptive role, create a "catastrophic commotion" in the onlooker.[67] Similarly there are unexpected ideational punctuations within James's text. His occasional expression of an openness to an endless quest for truth at one moment creates a catastrophic commotion for the reader, given the overall aim of the text—an eternity-embracing treatise—and thus the expectations it solicits by its main theme, summarized in James's religious hypothesis: "Religion says essentially two things. First she says that the best things are the eternal things, the overlapping things, the things in the universe that throw the last stone so to speak, and say the final word ... an affirmation which obviously cannot yet be verified scientifically at all."[68] He then adds a pragmatic justification for that hypothesis, referring to a "second affirmation of religion ... that we are better off even now if we believe her first affirmation to be true."[69]

Responding first to James's epistemological argument, I want to suggest that the way he poses the options brings to mind Foucault's remarks on the blackmail of the enlightenment. In his review and re-articulation of the Kantian inspiration for his position on criticism, Foucault writes, "I think that ... we must free ourselves from the intellectual blackmail of 'being for or against the enlightenment.'" Enacting a similar blackmail, James articulates a for or against choice with respect to the religious hypothesis. He asserts that "religion is a live hypothesis which may be true."[70] Although that assertion is accompanied with an injunction that seems recalcitrant to his main theme, that each of us should respect the others "mental freedom," e.g., the right to choose to turn one's "back altogether on God,"[71] a statement that makes his position seem non-coercive, one of his earlier remarks renders his position as a version of "intellectual blackmail." Drawing the reader into what Wittgenstein would doubtless call a coercive "language game,"[72] James constructs the prospective believer as one having the choice of accepting the hypothesis or not and presumes that the "not" option is motivated by a fear of being wrong: "To preach skepticism to us as a duty until 'sufficient evidence' for religion be found, is tantamount to telling us, when in the presence of a religious hypothesis, that to yield to our fear of its being error is wiser and better than to yield to our hope that it may be true."[73] Certainly, one could be wholly indifferent to the religious hypothesis and the language game within which James presents it. One could for example be indifferent to the hypothesis or be skeptical, not out of fear of error but because one regards religious ontologies as implausible and/or because one thinks that belief in transcendence is a misleading superstition. As many have recognized, professed atheism "retains the essence of what it negates,"[74] so it is with skepticism, which retains what it doubts. There is however the non-skeptical option of evading a language game rather than taking up a position within it. In short, as J-F Lyotard points out, "the social bond [is a] multiplicity of games ... each with its own pragmatic efficacy and its capability of positioning people in precise places in order to have them play their parts."[75] James's theatrical production is not the only place to audition for roles.

As for James's pragmatic or "prudential" argument that we are better off if we believe religion's first affirmation ["that the best things are the more eternal things"] to be true,[76] it recalls Charles Taylor's position (described in Chapter 2), which restricts wellbeing—what he calls a richer more full version of life—to an acceptance of a divine transcendence. If we resist that language game as well as the epistemological version that James proffers, we are able to freely negotiate vitality, i.e., to practice the resistance to closure to which (the equivocal) James himself is occasionally committed (for example, in his above-quoted remark, "we must go on experiencing and thinking over our experience"). In short, if we don't capitulate to the discursive claustrophobia inherent in James's two affirmations in which the choice is to accept a transcendent version of the divine or reject it, we are enfranchised as thinkers rather than cast as willing versus recalcitrant believers and can therefore open ourselves to a wide variety of language games in which the meaning and value of life are on the agenda.

To illustrate a concrete alternative, I want to reflect on George Canguilhem's suggestion that instead of viewing life through the lens of theology's preoccupation with death as the primary negation ("the negation of life by the non-living" in his words), we can situate life within a different "vital counter-value … monstrosity," which he describes as "the accidental and conditional threat of incompleteness or distortion in the formation of form; it is the limitation from within, the negation of the living by the non-viable."[77] Monstrosity "disconcerts," he suggests, because it tells us that life is capable of failures.[78] As a result, monstrosity encourages us to think about life not on the basis of acceptance of the traditional "positivist formula, which defines a world as a system of laws" but to embrace "the opposite maxim, one which science excludes but the imagination applies … an anti-cosmos … a chaos of exceptions without laws."[79] Ultimately, then, what distinguishes Canguilhem's perspective from James's is both his ontology of disorder and his focus on the discontinuous forces that provoke thinking rather than the continuities than encourage believing, especially his emphasis on the "singular histories" within which knowledge of life is continually contested and altered.[80]

James also concerned himself with singularities. However, his units of analysis are not historical moments but personal religious experiences. When he delivered his famous Gifford lectures, published as *The Varieties of Religious Experience*, he distinguished the ways individuals have religious experiences from religion as it is constructed by the church institutions that deliver the corporate version of Christianity, which consist in the ritual practices that provide religion-as-unreflective habit. Proposing to ignore "the institutionalized branch entirely ... the ecclesiastical organization ... and to confine [himself] ... to personal religion,"[81] James proceeded on the basis of this perspective: "If religion is to mean anything definite for us, ... we ought to take it as meaning [an] added dimension of emotion [an] enthusiastic temper of espousal."[82]

However, as was the case with his *Principles*, James constructs experience with resort to symbolism. As he puts it in *Principles*, "The object of every thought is neither more nor less than all that the thought thinks, exactly as the thought thinks ... and however symbolic the manner of the thinking may be."[83] And in *Varieties* he suggests that what "the intellect does" is operate in a domain of object/symbols, where an important one "awakens our devotion."[84] That claim is perplexing in light of James's privileging of an active mentality, where (to repeat a phrase) "the willing department" is controlling, and it is even more perplexing in light of his "radical empiricism" in which he seeks to destabilize and enlarge assumptions about the self-evidence of experience itself,[85] In *Varieties*, James locks experience into a way of experiencing things that concedes experience to (religious) object/symbols that provoke will. A more active and critical view of how consciousness derives experience— e.g., the one Walter Benjamin develops in his treatise on German tragic drama—displaces the symbol with the allegory. For Benjamin, an allegory "discloses the truth of the world far more than the fleeting glimpses of wholeness attained in the Romantic symbol." A phenomenology shaped by "the allegorical intention" is one in which consciousness performs creatively as "a kind of writing."[86] Arguing that "the knowledge sought in the symbol is a 'resplendent' but ultimately non-committal one" because it countenances a "unity of the material and transcendental object'.[the material and the transcendental]," Benjamin turns to allegory to challenge a view of mentality that "could not tolerate the self-combating tension ... within allegory, a tension ... characterizing human life."[87]

Nevertheless, whatever the extent to which he evacuated the tensions that Benjamin's view of allegory restores, religion for James, as he outlines it throughout *Varieties*, is derived from a well-articulated phenomenology of "life," as an individual experiences it—in his words, one's "total reaction upon life."[88] The lectures are often profound. As they develop, we witness a James combining his impressive capacity for empathy, which is well-expressed earlier in the quotation from "Human Immortality," with what Charles Taylor refers to (with a pious exaggeration) as his "unparalleled phenomenological insights."[89] Although Taylor is occasionally critical of James in the process of "working out an exchange"[90] with him, for the most part, he carries on the James legacy, especially in his claim (mentioned in Chapter 2) that "life" is richer and more full when it is infused with a sense of divine transcendence.

I resist that claim in Chapter 2 and want to test it again here. Edified by the way many of Ingmar Bergman's autobiographically inspired characters have found divine intentionality enigmatic and disconcerting rather than fulfilling, I want to end this chapter (and my investigation as a whole) with analyses of two artistic interventions, a Thornton Wilder novel *The Bridge of San Luis Rey* and a Paul Schrader film *First Reformed*, both of which respond (like Bergman) to that enigma with texts that think critically as they dramatize struggles with the aporias of divine intention. Their dramatizations of the issue constitute their individual phenomenological perspectives on theology. To put it figuratively, as imaginative playwrights (the model for an aesthetically oriented phenomenology I introduced in Chapter 1), they stage the way they see the problem. In the case of Wilder, even his version of theology, which evokes the redemptive power of love, is mediated continually throughout the novel with theatricality. For example, when his character Uncle Pio professes his enduring love to the actress Camila Perichole, she responds, "You don't seem to learn as you grow older, Uncle Pio. There is no such thing as that kind of love … It is in the theater you find such things."[91]

"The Bridge": "All You Need Is Love."

The passion of love … transforms the value of the creature loved as utterly as the sunrise transforms Mont Blanc from corpse-like gray to a rosy enchantment.

William James, *The Varieties of Religious Experience*

Thornton Wilder's novel begins with a simple factual sentence: "On Friday noon, July the twentieth, 1714, the finest bridge in all Peru broke and precipitated five travelers into the gulf below."[92] In the Foreword to a new edition of the 1927 novel, Russell Banks, referring to the "will" concept (which pervades the thinking of William James), quotes Wilder's reference to the novel's main question, "Is there a direction and meaning in lives beyond the individual's own will?"[93] Characterizing the novel as a "moral fable," Banks observes the "underlying assumption of the novel ... that any one of us could have been on that bridge when it collapsed and threw five people into the abyss" and points to the novel's other "abyss." It is an abyss between "faith" and "the facts" with which a Franciscan missionary, Brother Juniper, struggles after having observed the event. Presuming that everything that occurs "has divine purpose," the Franciscan seeks to discover the divine rationale behind the occurrence.[94] Undertaking the task of discerning the workings of a divine will, his aim is to find out why God decided to end the lives of those particular five people.

The novel treats the presence of Brother Juniper at the scene of the collapse as another co-incidence, thus raising the same question that the Franciscan decides to pursue: "By a series of coincidences so extraordinary that one almost suspects the presence of some Intention, this little red-haired Franciscan from Northern Italy happened to be in Peru converting the Indians and happened to witness the accident."[95] In search of clues to the divine intention, Brother Juniper, having committed himself to the heretical position "that it was high time for theology to take its place among the exact sciences," attempts to recover the biographies of the victims of the collapse.[96] His attempt turns out to be seriously flawed. For example in the case of his research on one of the victims, Doña Maria, Marquesa de Montemayor, the novelist interjects, "Any Spanish schoolboy is required to know more today about [her] ... than Brother Juniper was to discover in years of research."[97] However, what the Franciscan fails to discover is ably dramatized by the novelist, who invents and stages episodes in the lives of the Marquesa and the other victims: the Marquesa's maid Pepita, a teenage orphan Esteban, Don Jaime, the son of the actress Camila Perichole, and Camila's mentor, Uncle Pio. Nothing in the narratives of the victim's lives testifies to the divine intention that Brother Juniper presumed to unite them in the coincidence of their appearing on the bridge at the moment of its collapse.

However, there is an apparent authorial intention, which the novel effectively articulates. If we ask what Wilder, who is referred to as a "Christian humanist" in a commentary on his novels, does in *The Bridge* to illustrate the vagaries of life, and how he does it,[98] the answer is that by narrating the life experiences of the character/victims he juxtaposes Brother Juniper's delusional and heretical quest for a scientific understanding of divine intention with a Bergman-like emphasis on the passions deployed by the characters in their everyday lives, rendered as commitments to love.[99] Recalling Bergman's remark about his view of theology (quoted in Chapter 3), "love as the only thinkable form of holiness,"[100] it is shown to operate as well in lives of each of the victims in Wilder's novel.

Providing a series of portraits, a less pious version of the traditional lives of the saints, Wilder, in Part One, "Perhaps an Accident" (which precedes the portraits of the victims), figures the alternative positions as pure caprice versus assiduous intentionality. "Some say that we shall never know and that to the gods we are like the flies that the boys kills on a summer day, and some say, on the contrary, that the very sparrows do not lose a feather than has not been brushed away by the finger of God."[101] That passage is effectively doubled by the novel's structure. Juxtaposed to Part One's "Perhaps an Accident" is Part Five, "Perhaps an Intention." In between those parts, love rather piety prevails as it pervades each portrait, led off in the Marquesa chapter with a meta statement on the purpose of literature. Although he ascribes that purpose to the Marquesa's love letters to her indifferent daughter, Wilder is doubtless expressing his affective connection with his own writing. He writes that the Marquesa's son-in-law, upon reading the letters, enjoyed the style but had missed "the whole purpose of literature which is the notation of the heart. Style is but the faintly contemptible vessel in which the bitter liquid is recommended to the world."[102]

Having poured out her heart in her letters to her daughter, the Marquesa confronts "[t]he knowledge that she would never be loved in return. [It] acted upon her ideas as a tide acts upon cliffs. Her religious beliefs went first, for all she could ask of a god, or of immortality, was a gift of a place where daughters love their mothers; the other attributes of heaven you could have for a song."[103] After the portraits of the other victims are drawn, we learn that each of them also achieves a measure of moral regeneration through love. However, it's another character, the Abbess Madre Marta del Pilar, Pepita's protector and moral mentor (described as longing "to be back in the simplicity of love"),[104] who states what is arguably Wilder's implicit theological commitment. Although his novel does not attempt to choose between "accident" and "intention"—As Wilder has stated, "The business of literature is not to answer questions, but to state them fairly."[105]—it does deliver an ontology. At the end of the novel, the Abbess's rendering of the meaning of the disaster embraces neither accident nor intention. Instead she says, "Love will have been enough, all those impulses of love return to the love that made them. There is a land of the living and a land of the dead and the bridge is love, the only survival, the only meaning."[106]

First Reformed: Cinema Confronts Theology

A Bergman-like sensibility, which structures Wilder's "moral fable," provides a more explicit framing for Paul Schrader's film *First Reformed* (2017). Although the film draws part of its ideational problematic from Robert Bresson's *Diary of a Country Priest* and has a "character lineage"[107] (from Schrader screenplays) between the Reverend Toller (Ethan Hawke) and *Taxi Driver's* Tavis Bickle (Robert De Niro), both of whom are troubled characters destined for a violent explosion, its plot at the outset is a quotation of the encounter in Bergman's *Winter Light* between the pastor Tomas Ericsson and Jonas Persson, a suicidal parishioner. While Bergman's anxious parishioner is brought by his wife to see the pastor because his fear of nuclear annihilation has made him suicidal, in Schrader's film, Michael's (Philip Ettinger) wife Mary (Amanda Seyfried) asks the Reverend Toller to meet Michael (at their home) because his fear of the ecological destruction of the planet has made him suicidal.

Schrader's biography is similar to Bergman's inasmuch as he like Bergman is an ideational refugee. Motivated in part by a Bergman film, Schrader extracted himself from a strict religious upbringing:

I was a product of the Christian Reformed Church in Grand Rapids, a Calvinist denomination which at that time proscribed theater attendance and other 'worldly amusements.' So naturally I was drawn to the forbidden. I wanted to square my love of movies with my religious upbringing. Through a Glass Darkly (1961) was the point of entry; Viridiana (1961) was the counterpoint of entry … [later he notes] I was in Los Angeles in full pursuit of the profane. Calvin College was a memory.[108]

The intertextual nature of Schrader's film, which begins as a quotation of Bergman's *Winter Light*, derives much of its critical effect from the phenomenology of reception. Mikhail Iampolski's analysis of cinematic intertextuality makes that case well: "*The quote is a fragment of the text that violates its linear development.*"[109] Accordingly, it "interrupts the linearity of the text because it fractures the mind of the viewer—causing him or her to enact an alternative, yet simultaneous mode of thought."[110] However, the critical effect of quotation's impact on the viewer is one among many ways Schrader's film thinks, and with its compositional ingenuity, activates thinking about how theological commitments affect one's management of life's hopes and despairs.

Because it distills and deepens all the themes implied in the title of this investigation—it is philosophically inclined, it emphasizes religious media, and it exemplifies the advantages of the cinematic art for critical thinking—an engagement with the film provides a fitting conclusion. Schrader's *First Reformed* implements what he refers to as a "transcendental style," by which he means not something that reaches toward the divine but rather the way the implementation of slowness, in the form of delaying edits and other stylistic cues, creates an uneasiness that "the viewer must resolve [coping with 'shocks to thought' in Deleuze's language]." What then results is "an acceptance of parallel reality—transcendence."[111]

Before reproducing the Bergman-like encounter between the suicidal parishioner and the clergyman, the story told by the camera at the outset of the film is about the media-religion connection. The opening shots, which explore the exterior of Reverend Toller's church, recall an insight of the Russian filmmaker, Sergei Eisenstein. Inspired by his reading of architectural treatises, especially August Choisy's *Histoire d' architecture*, Eisenstein decided that a building such as the Acropolis is better investigated with "a montage sequence" than by walking among the buildings.[112] He therefore made architecture one of the underlying motifs in [his] films, working always "to find practical answers to the problem of how to film a building, how to transform it from a passive setting of action, into a major agent of the plot."[113] Schrader's "solution" is ideational as well as practical. As the film opens the camera moves toward the church building, locating it in the center of the square frame (with no surrounding landscape that might distract attention). As the camera closes in, it tilts upward toward the cross on top of the steeple, implying something about the spiritual aspiration that the church embodies (Figure 5.1). However, because the approach is slow and deliberate, it suggests as well the kind of hesitation that turns out to characterize Toller's belief quandaries, which are featured as central to the film's plot. Moreover, as Schrader explains, when a film's slowness results in "taking longer than we have been conditioned to expect,"[114] the film creates "a sense of unease," and as a result, the viewer's thinking is activated.[115]

Following that long take of the church, the camera cuts to a placard on the front lawn, which informs us of the church's venerable pedigree: "The oldest continuing church in Albany County. Organized in 1767 and built in 1801 by settlers from West Friesland led by Dominie Gideon Wortendyk"[116] (doubtless weighing heavily on Toller's reflections about his responsibility to the church's legacy). The camera then cuts back to a side view of the church,

Figure 5.1 Reverend Toller's church in *First Reformed*. Directed by Paul Schrader. Copyright Lionsgate 2017. All rights reserved.

again from a low angle aimed upward, repeating the spiritualizing effect by making the church seem to loom skyward. That shot is followed by one of the church's front doors. After a pause, the viewer is finally brought into the interior where there's an immediate media shift. What is on view when the camera first enters the church is a section of Reverend Toller's body with his hand in the foreground, writing in a diary, a quotation of the opening scene in a film Schrader much admired, Robert Bresson's *The Pickpocket* (1959) which opens with the protagonist Michel (Martin LaSalle) writing in a diary.

However, there's another more dramatic media effect that surrounds the move from the outside to the interior of the church. It is aural rather than visual. Outside the church at the outset of the first scene, birds can be heard chirping. They are the positive signs of the life world outside—what Schrader refers to as "abundance" (in his analysis of the cinema-spirituality relationship). That aural abundance is juxtaposed to the quiet austerity of a church interior (in Schrader's word, a "sparseness"). As Schrader points out (and doubtless implemented the insight in the film), "One way to determine the 'spiritual quality' of a cinematic style … is to examine the manner in which it disposes of its inherent abundant means and substitutes sparse means."[117] Schrader marks his concept of abundance in two ways early in the film. While Toller is conversing with his organist about a problem with a leaking toilet, the organist asks if he has contacted the plumbing service named "abundant life." Subsequently, when Mary Mansana asks him to talk to her suicidal husband, Toller asks her if she's sure that she doesn't want instead to try a counseling service named "abundant life."

The abundance-sparseness couplet is elaborated once we're taken from the aural exuberance outside to the inside of the church to observe a conflicted body within that austere ("sparse") interior. Reverend Toller is involved in expressing his moralizing angst, as he pledges a merciless self-appraisal. Surrounding what we see while observing our first scene of the tense Reverend Toller's struggle to "set down all [his] thoughts," choosing words assiduously, while scratching out some that seem to disturb a fidelity to his demand on himself for "complete transparency," is an implicit narrative that is more general; the film is offering a survey of theological media. After shots of Toller's writing hand, there's a cut to shelves near the church entrance displaying religious pamphlets. Then, when the camera enters Toller's bedroom, it shows a stack of bedside theological studies, among which is Thomas Merton's *A Life in Letters*. Other media manifest themselves with Toller's body, his clerical vestments, his location at a podium above his parishioners, and his voice with which he delivers the liturgy.

Nevertheless, the primary medium in the early part of the film is architecture, which can be construed as a "narrative medium,"[118] when we recognize that buildings are what Bernard Tschumi calls "event spaces."[119] In the film the building is a narrative thread as it organizes the experience of worship. There is for example the singular stance of the clergyman at a podium from which he speaks. As we observe the church as an "event space," nothing happens until the moment when Toller enters from a side door and stands at the podium to begin the service, his credentials marked not only by his vestments but also by the cross behind him, in full view of the parishioners, whose location in rows of pews facing the altar encourages passivity.

Given the intertextual connection between Bergman's *Winter Light* and Schrader's *First Reformed*, the architectural feature that stands out more than the props associated with the role of the clergyman is the church windows, which are the source of much of the interior lighting in churches. As a historian of religion points out, "Throughout the history of religion, light's symbolic role has been related to the sacred," and has as a result has "profoundly affected the design of ... religious buildings ... [in which] light has been used to not only to provide the necessary visual condition for the religious acts to be performed but also to evoke mystical and spiritual feelings and strengthen the belief."[120] However, when the light-theology effect is being mediated by film, light performs a dual role, articulating its historical religious architecture function on the one hand and participating in the mood surrounding the personal stories on the other.

Bergman's *Winter Light* is appropriately named. Filmed using only the natural light available in the film's venue, the light pervading Pastor Tomas Ericsson's church matches the quality of the light outside the church. In contrast with Schrader's opening shots, tightly centered on the church and eschewing the surrounding landscape, Bergman's opening shows the church in the midst of the grayness of a bleak landscape (Figure 5.2), which the camera emphasizes by pulling back from its first shots of the church to include more of the surroundings. The quality of the light inside matches what is outside,

Figure 5.2 Pastor Tomas's church in *Winter Light*. Directed by Ingmar Bergman. Copyright Svensk Filmindustri (SF) 1957. All rights reserved 1963.

rendering the bleak landscape as a metaphor for what turns out to be a demoralized pastor, performing ritualistically in a bleak looking interior. The winter light turns out to be a protagonist as well as a title.

The light effect is very different in *First Reformed*. While Toller is performing the liturgy in preparation for the congregation's march up to the podium to take communion, there's a shot from the side of Toller that frames him in front of a typical church window on his left. In this case, the brightness of the light outside emphasizes an exterior that contrasts with the dreariness of the small humble group of worshipers in the church's austere interior, exposed to a ritualistic performance by a clergyman who has lost his spiritual motivation. The window shot of a venerable architectural feature of churches reemphasizes the disjuncture between a vibrant ("abundant") life world outside, which had earlier been aurally expressed by chirping birds, and the quiet, cloistered ("sparse"), and ideationally constricted one inside. And as Schrader says about the effect of light in transcendental films, in which the sparse visual depictions in the film refer "to something stretching beyond the frame into infinity,"[121] "Light is stronger than the story,"[122] because, "Images [are] preferred over dialogue."[123]

The largely dialogue-free, media-saturated scene at the church at the beginning of Schrader's film is a prelude to a telling media confrontation thereafter, which *is* fundamentally dialogic. Once Toller is seated in the couple's home, in preparation to fulfill his promise to Mary to speak with her husband Michael, there's an encounter between incommensurate media that recalls the one Bergman stages in *Winter Light*. However, in contrast with the nearly silent Jonas, whose panic has resulted from what he's learned from print media about an impending nuclear catastrophe (and is met with Tomas's god talk to which he has no response), Michael is a garrulous conduit from the data he's gleaned from diverse media to an expectation of catastrophe, while Toller says relatively little in response. Michael also envisions a doomed world, in his case from environmental degradation rather than the nuclear holocaust that Bergman's Jonas fears. Expecting an unlivable planet in the not-too-distant future, he's reluctant to welcome a child, whose pregnant wife will soon be delivering.

The body postures in that conversation in *First Reformed* differ dramatically from their placements in the conversational choreography of *Winter Light*. In the latter, Pastor Tomas is on camera most of the time, even when he turns his back on Jonas as he drones on about his disappointment in the "echo god" whose silence oppresses him (Figure 5.3). There are only a few reverse shot moments for Jonas's brief responses along with close-ups of his anxious face. In contrast, Toller and Michael are filmed mostly from the side in a give-and-take conversation (Figure 5.4). Moreover, Michael dominates the dialogue, producing a wealth of data, not only about the personae with whom he's concerned—e.g., his age, the age his future daughter would be in a dystopic world of 2050—but also about the consequences of a warming climate. He mentions among other things the "irreversible impacts" of a three-degree centigrade rise in temperature on crops. Accompanying his remarks are shots of video footage on his home monitor that shows the progressive effects of the climate change to which he's referring. While those are in view, he utters the main consequence on his mind; if his wife resisted an abortion and instead gave birth, his daughter would be "an endangered species."

Figures 5.3 Tomas and Jonas in *Winter Light*. Directed by Ingmar Bergman. Copyright Svensk Filmindustri (SF) 1957. All rights reserved 1963.

Figure 5.4 Toller and Michael in *First Reformed*. Directed by Paul Schrader. Copyright Lionsgate 2017. All rights reserved.

When Toller has a turn, his media presentation consists in well-worn biblical allusions, for example, "Jacob wrestling all night long with the angel." His sparse media presentation is greeted by Michael's elaborate, data-driven responses about the names of the many environmental activists "killed last year for their beliefs." Toller's ultimate attempt at solace, "Now Michael, I can promise you that whatever despair you feel about bringing a child into this world cannot equal the despair of taking a child from it" (that from a man whose own despair is unremitting), is unconvincing. Although unlike *Winter Light's* Pastor Tomas, Reverend Toller directs his remarks to his parishioner's despair rather than his own, the outcome is the same. Like Jonas, Michael ends up committing suicide. However, the ways in which the two clergymen resolve their own despair are markedly different. Tomas Ericsson carries on with his liturgical duties. As the film ends, the focus is on an ineffectual theological vocation that has robbed its protagonist of a capacity for intimacy and empathy (apart from small emotionally sparse gestures), and, ultimately, love.

Toller shares Tomas's wretched loneliness, owed like Tomas's to his inability to maintain a belief in God's care for the world and his seemingly pointless duty to ritualistically convey that care to his sparse congregation. As is the case for Tomas, the religious media within which he dwells—biblical, architectural, embodied—provides no solace. However, unlike Tomas, rather than carrying on ritualistically, he blows up violently (reminiscent of another Schrader character whose loneliness turns him toward apocalyptic violence; Toller is "Tavis Bickle in a clerical collar" as one commentator puts it).[124] After tacking back and forth among three tasks: the mundane chores that keep the church physically viable (e.g., working with a plunger to clear a toilet), performing the Christian liturgy at services to keep the church spiritually viable, and writing in his diary to keep himself personally viable—all to no avail—there's a radical turn away from his tasks. He becomes a zealot strapping on a suicide vest as he readies himself for martyrdom (Figure 5.5).

However, quite apart from the film's apocalyptic ending is what Schrader provides with what he calls a transcendental style in cinema (which he ascribes to Ozu, Bresson, and Dreyer). Through its temporal rhythms—emphasizing pauses and long takes rather than narrative to challenge the viewer's narrative expectations—the film implies not (viz. Bergman and Wilder) that what one needs by way of spirituality is love but rather what one needs (also by way of spiritualty) is to be distanced from one's habitual expectations by being

Figure 5.5 Toller in suicide vest in *First Reformed*. Directed by Paul Schrader. Copyright Lionsgate 2017. All rights reserved.

shocked into thinking. That effect, according to Deleuze (whose cinema books Schrader read avidly), is the way cinema [has] manifested "spiritual life," because "Cinema puts movement not just in the image; it puts it in the mind."[125] In a remark about the brain's "cerebral circuits," Deleuze evinces a model of mind that comports with the way James construes it; the brain, Deleuze writes, makes "connections [that] do not preexist the stimuli and corpuscles, or particles that trace them."[126]

What radically distinguishes Deleuze from James is his approach to habit. Deleuze endorses textually based thinking practices that disrupt habitual structures of recognition to activate critical convention-resistant thinking, while James offers maxims for developing good habits (even though he advocates abandoning old habits once a new one has found its way securely into one's life). Nevertheless, as always seem to be the case when one tries to locate James's ideas and sentiments, the same James who appears to advocate inertia is also one who advocates overcoming it. For example, at the same time when he encourages reinforcing habits, he endorses "plasticity … in the wide sense of the word ... the possession of s structure weak enough to yield and influence, but strong enough not to yield all at once," i.e., the maintenance of ongoing phases a "stable ... equilibrium."[127] James's reference to plasticity is a soft, equivocal version of the concept compared with Catherine Malabou's, which she uses to challenge conventional models of subjectivity. Nevertheless, their most fundamental question is more or less the same; "what is the adequation of brain and world"?[128] Rather than provide an overview of Malabou's use of the concept of plasticity, I want to close this investigation with the way she applies it to what has framed James's view of subjectivity, the brain as neuroscience has modeled it. And, considering the way she foregrounds a normative orientation toward the brain, I want to note an accord between Malabou's and William Connolly's ethically and politically attuned attention to contemporary neuroscience.

Although Malabou approaches the brain with a James-like interest in neuroscience and a James-like question, "how an individual brain can respond to challenges in the social environment,"[129] she does so with a more politically attuned appreciation of the ideational influences within one's milieu on the brain. And in contrast with James's effort to accommodate religious observance within the realities of the brain-world relationship, Malabou has a more political agenda (expressed in ironically toned theological imagery): "to visualize the possibility of saying no to an afflicting economic, political, and mediatric culture that celebrates only the triumph of flexibility, blessing obedient individuals who have no greater merit than that of knowing how to bow their heads with a smile."[130]

Coda: "Any Vision of the Brain Is Necessarily Political"[131]

There is a conceptual convergence between Malabou and Deleuze and Malabou and Connolly. As she reflects on the ethico-political implications of plasticity and ponders "the poetical and aesthetic force that is the fundamental, organizing attribute of plasticity: its power to configure the world," Malabou notes that "Deleuze had perfectly analyzed this power by seeing in it the cinematographic function par excellence," and proceeds to identify Alain Resnais as "a filmmaker of the brain," whose films, like those of Stanley

Kubrick, display "the identity of the brain and world." It's doubtless an insight that applies to Paul Schrader as my analysis of his *First Reformed* implies. At the same time, there's an apparent conceptual *di*vergence between Malabou and James. Invoking a "naturalization effect," Malabou accords to "the power of plasticity" resistance to confounding "the neuronal function … with the natural function of the world, as though neuronal plasticity [is] anchored biologically,"[132] and goes on to implicate a James effect, referring to those who connect "biology and society … on the basis of a physiological metaphor … of the neuronal with its networks and flows."[133] Malabou substitutes a normative model of plasticity, insisting that what "we" should do with our brain is "To refuse to be flexible individuals who combine a permanent control of the self with a capacity to self-modify at the whim of fluxes, transfers, and exchanges."

However, much of that divergence from James's approach to mentality is apparent only if we read one James and neglect another. Malabou ultimately frames her brain-world question in a James-like way. Even though she is more alert than James to the legitimating effects of presuming a brain with natural proclivities, her "what should we do with our brain" inflects the brain-world problem in a pragmatic direction. As William Connolly has discerned, James also sponsored an activist agenda, which in his case conflicted with his occasional intellectual migration into a version of naturalistic thinking that rendered mentality compatible with divine transcendence. In its more critical moments, James's view of mentality, Connolly suggests, "captures … the layered process of thinking" that is open to novelty and can "bring new things into the world not already allowed or disallowed by an authoritative transcendental field."[134] Importantly, for purposes of distinguishing Connolly from James, that "field" derives from what Connolly calls "immanent naturalism," where by naturalism, Connolly means "that all human activities function without the aid of a divine or supernatural force."[135] Whereas Connolly's naturalism is clearly Spinoza-inspired, the democratic ethos he derives from it is Humean. Like Hume (and to some extent James who privileges our "passional selves"), Connolly privileges affect. After identifying his version of naturalism, he goes on to connect the "visceral attachment to life" as a prelude to a cultivation of "more generous identifications, responsibilities, and connections."[136] That suggestion accords well with what I have noted elsewhere as "the Humean insistence that it is 'affective circumstance' that guide people's ideas (because the principles of passion; control ideational inclinations) [so that] association within the social domain becomes a matter of modes of partiality."[137] "As a result, the problem of the social that Hume derives from his privileging of affect is ... one of how, as Deleuze puts it, 'to pass from 'limited sympathy' to an 'extended generosity'."[138]

Finally, Connolly and Malabou exhibit a similar normative mentality with respect to neuroscience. Connolly mobilizes his analysis of neuropolitics to translate the micropolitics of affect into a view of democracy which he renders as "deep pluralism."[139] Similarly, Malabou translates her neuroscience-inspired plasticity into a democratic ethos. Insisting that the question about what we should do with our brain is not about simply sorting intellectual positions, Malabou's version of plasticity encourages "everyone" to anticipate a trans-individual global, anti-hegemonic future, "disengaged from ... ideological presuppositions."[140] I endorse what that implies; there is no transcendent basis for exclusivity with respect to who is eligible to enter the inexhaustible conversation about how to experience life.

Notes

Preface

1   Gilles Deleuze, *Spinoza: Practical Philosophy*, trans. Robert Hurley (San Francisco, CA: City Lights, 1988), 4.

2   In what is arguably his most important remark about critical thinking, Deleuze writes, "Something in the world forces us to think. This something is not an object of recognition but a fundamental *encounter*." Gilles Deleuze, *Difference and Repetition*, trans. Paul Patton (New York: Columbia University Press, 1994), 139.

3   Deleuze, *Spinoza*, 123.

4   Jorge Semprun, *The Second Death of Ramon Mercader*, trans. Len Ortzen (New York: Grove Press, 1973), 13.

5   Deleuze, *Spinoza*, 26.

6   For a review of that aspect of Spinoza's philosophy, see Simon Duffy, "The Joyful Passions in Spinoza's Theory of Relations," in Dimitris Varoulakis, ed. *Spinoza Now* (Minneapolis: University of Minnesota Press, 2011), 51–64.

7   The quotations are from Warren Montag, "Interjecting Empty Spaces: Imagination and Interpretation in Spinoza's *Tractatus Theologico-Politicus*," in Varoulakis, ed. *Spinoza Now*, 162.

8   See Spinoza, *Principles Concerning Cartesian Philosophy* in *The Complete Works of Spinoza*, trans. Samuel Shirley (New York: Hackett, 2002), 197. That position on life as immanent is articulated effectively in a Justin Cartwright novel *The Song before It Is Sung* (London: Bloomsbury, 2007), which I treat in Chapter 2.

9   Deleuze, *Spinoza*, 129.

10 The quotations are from J. Samuel Preus, *Spinoza and the Irrelevance of Biblical Authority* (Cambridge, UK: Cambridge University Press, 2001), 33.

Chapter 1

1   Jacques Rancière, "Contemporary Art and the Politics of Aesthetics," in Beth Hinderliter et al., eds. *Communities of Sense: Rethinking Aesthetics and Politics* (Durham, NC: Duke University Press, 2009), 31.

2   Gayatri Spival, *An Aesthetic Education in the Era of Globalization* (Cambridge, MA: Harvard University Press, 2012), 317.

3   M. M. Bakhtin, "Epic and Novel," in *The Dialogic Imagination*, trans. Caryle Emerson and Michael Holqvist (Austin: University of Texas Press, 1981), 15.

4   *Ibid.*, 39.

5   See M. M. Bakhtin, "Discourse in the Novel," in *The Dialogic Imagination*, trans. Caryl Emerson and Michael Holquist (Austin: University of texas Press, 1981), 259–434.

6   Michael J. Shapiro, *Methods and Nations: Cultural Governance and the Indigenous Subject* (London: Routledge, 2004), 66.

7   Morrison, *Paradise* (New York: Vintage, 2014), 86.

8   I am borrowing the expressions from Jacques Rancière *The Flesh of Words*, trans. Charlotte Mandell (Stanford, CA: Stanford University Press, 2004), 159.

9   Immanuel Kant, "Was ist Aufklarung," ("What is Enlightenment") reproduced in Michel Foucault, *The Politics of Truth,* trans. Lysa Hochroth and Catherine Porter (New York: Semiotexte), 2007), 33.

10 Philip Dick, "The Android and the Human," in Lawrence Sutin, ed. *The Shifting Realities of Philip K. Dick* (New York: Pantheon, 1995), 190–1.

11 Morrison, *Paradise*, 86.

12 Kant, "What Is Enlightenment," 33.

13 Jacob Taubes, "On the Nature of the Theological Method: Some Reflections on the Methodological Principles of Tillich's Theology," *The Journal of Religion* 34: 1 (January 1954), 13.

14 Marc-Alain Oaknin, *The Burnt Book: Reading the Talmud,* trans. Llewellyn Brown (Princeton, NJ: Princeton University Press, 1995), 159.

15 *Ibid.*, 282.

16 Morrison, *Paradise*, 217.

17 Peter Brown, *The Making of Late Antiquity* (Cambridge, MA: Harvard University Press, 1976), 11–12.

18 *Ibid.*, 12.

19 *Ibid.*, 13.

20 Peter Brown, "The Saint as Exemplar in Late Antiquity," *Representations* 1: 2 (Spring 1983), 2.

21 *Ibid.*, 7.

22 Brown, *The Making of Late Antiquity*, 14.

23 *Ibid.*, 6.

24 *Ibid.*

25 Brown, "The Saint as Exemplar in Late Antiquity," 6.

26 The expression belongs to Gilles Deleuze's characterization of Proustian consciousness. See his *Proust and Signs,* trans. Richard Howard (Minneapolis: University of Minnesota Press, 2000), 75.

27 Brown, "The Saint as Exemplar in Late Antiquity," 6.

28 W. G. Sebald, *The Rings of Saturn*, trans. Michael Hulse (New York: New Directions, 1998), 80.

29 Deleuze, *Proust and Signs*, 26.

30 Robert Coover, *The Origin of the Brunists: A Novel* (New York: Grove Press, 1966) and *The Brunist Day of Wrath* (Ann Arbor, MI: Dzanc Books, 2014).

31 Quotations drawn from: http://danteworlds.laits.utexas.edu/textpopup/inf15001. html.

32 Brian Massumi, *Semblance and Event* (Cambridge, MA: MIT Press, 2011), 16.

33 I am quoting from Jacques Derrida, "Of an Apocalyptic Tone Recently Adopted in Philosophy," trans. John P. Leavey *Semeia* 23 (1982), 64.

34 Coover, *The Origin of the Brunists*, 48.

35 *Ibid.*, 86.

36 *Ibid.*, 80.

37 *Ibid.*, 85.

38 The quotations are from Wolf-Daniel Hartwich, Aleida Assmann, and Jan Assmann, "Afterword," in Jacob Taubes, ed. *The Political Theology of Paul,* trans. Dana Hollander (Stanford: Stanford University Press, 2004), 116.

39 Birgit Brandar Rasmussen, *Queequeg's Coffin: Indigenous Literacies and Early American Literature* (Durham, NC: Duke University Press, 2012), 1.

40 Michael J. Shapiro, *The Political Sublime* (Durham, NC: Duke University Press, 2018), 141.

41 Brian Moore, Preface to *Black Robe* (New York: Fawcet Crest, 1985), viii.

42 Gore Vidal, *Live from Golgotha* (New York: Random House, 1992), 5.

43 Alain Badiou, *Saint Paul: The Foundation of Universalism,* trans. Ray Brassier (Stanford, CA: Stanford University Press, 2003), 31.

44 See Taubes, *The Political Theology of Paul,* 54.

45 Friedrich Nietzsche, *The Will to Power,* trans. Walter Kaufman (New York: Vintage, 1968), 101.

46 Coover, *The Origin of the Brunists*, 141–2.

47 *Ibid.*, 140.

48 *Ibid.*

49 *Ibid.*, 207.

50 *Ibid.*, 241.

51 *Ibid.*

52 *Ibid.*, 261.

53 Edward Shils, "Primordial, Personal, Sacred and Civil Ties," in *Center and Periphery: Essays in Macrosociology* (Chicago: University of Chicago Press, 1975), 111.

54 Coover, *The Brunist Day of Wrath*, loc. 2366.

55 Roslyn Weaver, "The Shadow of the End," in John Wallis and Kenneth G. C. Newport, eds. *The End All around Us: Apocalyptic Texts and Popular Culture* (New York: Routledge, 2014), 177.

56 The expression belongs to Georg Lukács, *The Theory of the Novel,* trans. Anna Bostock (Cambridge, MA: MIT Press, 1971), 84.

57 Coover, *The Brunist Day of Wrath*, loc. 451.

58 *Ibid.*, loc. 2216.

59 *Ibid.*, loc. 307.

60 *Ibid.*, loc. 275.

61 *Ibid.*, loc. 1175.

62 *Ibid.*, loc. 607.

63 *Ibid.*, loc. 339.

64 It should be noted that Luther's intervention into the church's orthodoxies was not a singular event. In relatively close historical proximity to Luther's assault on the "brand" were other challenges in cities all over Europe (a cartography of ideational contention): Jan Hus in Prague, Huldrych Zwingli in Zurich, John Calvin in Geneva, and Erasmus in Rotterdam and Deventer, all preceded (and influenced to a degree) by John Wycliffe in Oxford. For an account of the religious ferment among those alternatives to Luther's rebellion, see Michael Massing, *Fatal Discord: Erasmus, Luther and the Fight for the Western Mind* (New York: HarperCollins, 2018).

65 Mark U. Edwards, Jr., *Printing, Propaganda, and Martin Luther* (Berkeley: University of California Press, 1994), 23.

66 *Ibid.*, 7.

67 *Ibid.*, 15.

68 Andrew Pettegree, *Brand Luther: 1517, Printing, and the Making of the Reformation* (New York: Penguin, 2015), 5.

69 Fredric Jameson, *The Ancients and the Postmoderns: On the Historicity of Forms* (New York: Verso, 2017), 3.

70 Thomas G. Kirsch, "Ways of Reading as Religious Power in Print Globalization," *American Ethnologist* 34: 3 (2007), 511.

71   Elizabeth L. Eisenstein, *Divine Art, Infernal Machine: The Reception of Printing in the West from First Impressions to the Sense of an Ending* (Philadelphia: University of Pennsylvania Press, 2011), 46.

72   Edwards, *Printing, Propaganda, and Martin Luther*, 109. Edward's points out that Luther had made his German translation of scriptures reader-friendly by adding "aids to its interpretation [with] forewords, and introductions, marginal glosses [and] polemical illustrations" (111).

73   The expression belongs to Peter L. Berger, who describes a "cognitive minority" as those who still believe in some version of the supernatural. See both his *The Sacred Canopy: Elements of a Sociological Theory of Religion* (New York: Doubleday Anchor, 1969) and *A Rumor of Angels: Modern Society and the Rediscovery of the Supernatural* (New York: Doubleday Anchor, 1970).

74   The quotation is from Bernard Stiegler, *Technics and Time 3: Cinematic Time and the Question of Malaise* (Stanford, CA: Stanford University Press, 2011), 91.

75   Philip Dick, *The Three Stigmata of Palmer Eldritch* (London: Orion, 1964), 41.

76   *Ibid.*, 193.

77   Michel de Certeau, *Practice of Everyday Life*, trans. Steven Rendall (Berkeley: University of California Press, 1988), 178.

78   *Ibid.*

79   Graham Ward, "The Weakness of Believing: A Dialogue with de Certeau," *Culture, Theory and Critique* 52: 2–3 (2011), 242.

80   *Ibid.*, 16.

81   Friedrich Nietzsche, *The Gay Science,* trans. Walter Kaufman (New York: Vintage, 1974), 189.

82   *Ibid.*, 196.

83   *Ibid.*, 2.

84   See Jacques Rancière, *The Emancipated Spectator*, trans. Gregory Elliott (New York: Verso, 2009), 75.

85   Mieke Bal, *Death & Dissymmetry: The Politics of Coherence in the Book of Judges* (Chicago: University of Chicago Press, 1988), 231.

86   Friedrich Nietzsche, *Human All Too Human*, trans. R. J. Hollingdale (Cambridge, UK: Cambridge University Press, 1996), 121.

87   See Sigmund Freud, *Moses and Monotheism* (New York: Vintage, 1955).

88   Harold Bloom and David Rosenberg, *The Book of J* (New York: Grove Weidenfeld, 1990).

89   I am quoting from my earlier reading of the Bloom-Rosenberg text: Shapiro, *Methods and Nations*, 28.

90 See Idan Dershowitz, "The Secret History of Leviticus," *The New York Times*, on the web at: https://www.nytimes.com/2018/07/21/opinion/sunday/bible-prohibit-gay-sex.html.

91 As Rancière puts it, "Everything revolves around the as if: "The Aesthetic Dimension: Aesthetics, Politics, Knowledge," *Critical Inquiry* 36: 1 (Autumn 2009), 16.

92 Michel Foucault, *The Government of Self and Others*, trans. Graham Burchell (New York: Palgrave Macmillan, 2010), 3.

93 In a later chapter I read the trajectory from Nietzsche to Foucault on the will to knowledge against William James's above-mentioned treatise on "The Will to Believe" in which he mounts a two-pronged argument in defense of belief in a transcendent God, one pragmatic and the other epistemological.

94 Michel Foucault, *Lectures on the Will to Know*, trans. Graham Burchell (New York: Palgrave Macmillan, 2013), 197.

95 *Ibid.*, 196.

96 See the William James section from his *Essays in Radical Empiricism* in John McDermott, ed. *The Writings of William James* (Chicago: University of Chicago Press, 1978), 169.

97 From *Winter Light*, directed by Ingmar Bergman. Copyright Svensk Filmindustri (SF). All rights reserved 1957.

98 Tobias Wolf, "Winter Light," *The New Yorker*, June 9 and 16, 2008, on the web at: https://www.newyorker.com/magazine/2008/06/09/winter-light.

99 The quotation is from M. M. Bakhtin, "Author and Hero in Aesthetic Activity," in *Art and Answerability*, trans V. Liapunov (Austin: University of Texas Press, 1990), 13.

100 Michel Foucault, *Remarks on Marx: Conversations with Duccio Trombadori*, trans. R. James Goldstein and James Cascaito (New York: Semiotext(e), 1991), 27.

101 Michel Foucault, *The Government of Self and Others: Lectures at the College De France 1982–1983*, trans. Graham Burchell (New York: Palgrave Macmillan, 2010), 255.

102 *Ibid.*, 31.

103 *Ibid.*

104 From Bertold Brecht's *Fatzer-Fragment*, translated and quoted in Judtih Wilke, "The Making of a Document: An Approach to Brecht's 'Fatzer' Fragment," *TDR* 43: 4 (Winter 1999), 127.

105 *Ibid.*

106 Jan Luc Nancy, *The Inoperative Community*, trans. Peter Connor, Lisa Garbus, Michael Holland, and Simona Sawhney (Minneapolis: University of Minnesota Press, 1991), 75.

107 *Ibid.*, 76.

108 Michael J. Shapiro, *For Moral Ambiguity: National Culture and the Politics of the Family* (Minneapolis: University of Minnesota Press, 2001), 120.

109 See William E. Connolly, *Pluralism* (Durham, NC: Duke University Press, 2005).

Chapter 2

1 Cal Hiaasen, *Lucky You* (New York: Alfred A, Knopf, 1991), 2.

2 *Ibid.*

3 Leonardo Padura, *The Man Who Loved Dogs*, trans. Anna Kushner (London: Bitter Lemon Press, 2009), 103.

4 *Ibid.*, 75.

5 *Ibid.*, 76.

6 *Ibid.*, 209.

7 Jean Paul Sartre, *The Family Idiot: Gustave Flaubert 1821–1857,* trans. Carol Osman (Chicago: University of Chicago Press, 1989), 127.

8 Tara Isabella Burton, "The Religious Hunger of the Radical Right," *The New York Times*, August 16, 2019, A23.

9 The description and quotations are from Garry Wills's account of Saul's zealous violence against Christian believers before his subsequent shift to Paul the apostle; see his *What Paul Meant* (New York: Penguin, 2007), ebook loc. 395.

10 Eugene Thacker, *After Life* (Chicago: University of Chicago Press, 2010), 1.

11 Gilles Deleuze and Felix Guattari, *What Is Philosophy?* trans. Hugh Tomlinson and Graham Burchell (New York: Columbia University Press, 1994), 51.

12 *Ibid.*, 145.

13 The latter quotations are from Deleuze, *Difference and Repetition*, 136.

14 Martin Heidegger, *The Phenomenology of Religious Life*, trans. Matthas Fritsch and Jennifer Anna Gosetti-Ferencei (Bloomington: Indiana University Press, 2010), 55.

15 The expression belongs to John D. Caputo, "Introduction," in John D. Caputo and Linda Alcoff, eds. *St. Paul among the Philosophers* (Bloomington: Indiana University Press, 2009), 2.

16 M. M. Bakhtin, "Forms of Time and the Chronotope in the Novel: Notes toward a Historical Poetics," in *The Dialogic Imagination,* trans. Caryl Emerson and Michael Holquist (Austin: University of Texas Press, 1981), 84.

17 *Ibid.*

18 *Ibid.*

19 Elizabeth A. Castelli, "Introduction: Translating Pasolini Translating Paul," in Pier Paolo Pasolini, ed. *St. Paul: A Screenplay,* trans. Elizabeth A. Catelli (New York: Verso, 2014), ebook loc. 133. Castelli is drawing for that perspective on George Aichele, "Translation as De-Canonization: Matthew's Gospel According to Pasolini," *CrossCurrents* 54: 4 (Winter 2002), 524–34.

20 Caputo, "Introduction," 14.

21 Badiou, *Saint Paul,* 2.

22 For a discursive practice-oriented reading of Paul's epistles, see Elizabeth Castelli, *Imitating Paul: A Discourse on Power* (Louisville, KY: Westminster/John Knox Press, 1991).

23 Slavoj Žižek, *Event: A Philosophical Journey through a Concept* (Brooklyn, NY: Melville House, 2014), ebook loc. 114.

24 Ivan Klima, *No Saints or Angels,* trans. Gerald Turner (New York: Grove Press, 2001), 20.

25 In quotations because the characterization belongs to Badiou, *Saint Paul,* 19.

26 *Ibid.*

27 *Ibid.,* 58. It is in 1 Corinthians 1: 19-21 that Paul inveighs against epistemology: "For it is written, I will destroy the wisdom of the wise and bring to nothing the understanding of the prudent…in the wisdom of God the world by wisdom knew not God…[whom] it pleased…to save them that believe."

28 *Ibid.,* 59.

29 Caputo, "Introduction," in *St. Paul among the Philosophers,* 4.

30 Gilles Deleuze, "Nietzsche and Paul, Lawrence and John of Padmos," in *Essays Critical and Clinical,* trans Daniel W. Smith and Michel A. Greco (Minneapolis: University of Minnesota Press, 1997), 37.

31 See Carl Schmitt, *Political Theology: Four Chapters on the Concept of Sovereignty,* trans. George Schwab (Cambridge, MA: MIT Press, 1985).

32 For a discussion of the way Schmitt's exception operates (having the law recede temporarily), see Arne De Boever, *Against Aesthetic Exceptionalism* (Minneapolis: University of Minnesota Press, 2019), 13.

33 For his analysis of heteroglossia, see Bakhtin, "Discourse and the Novel," in *The Dialogic Imagination.*

34   Heidegger, *The Phenomenology of Religious Life*, 55.

35   Berel Lang, "Space, Time, and Philosophical Style," *Critical Inquiry* 2: 2 (Winter 1975), 266.

36   See J. L. Austin, *How to Do Things with Words* (Cambridge, MA: Harvard University Press, 1962).

37   Heidegger, *The Phenomenology of Religious Life*, 70.

38   Paul's difficulties with the Corinthians are described in Duane Litfin, *St Paul's Theology of Proclamation* (New York: Cambridge University Press, 1994), 160–80.

39   The quotations are from Edwin M. Yamauchi, "On the Road with Paul," on the web at: https://christianhistoryinstitute.org/magazine/article/on-the-road-with-paul.

40   Friedrich Kittler, *Discourse Networks 1800/1900,* trans. Michael Metteer (Stanford, CA: Stanford University Press, 1990), 70.

41   See Johanna Drucker, "From A to Screen," in N. Katherine Hayles and Jessica Pressman, eds. *Comparative Textual Media* (Minneapolis: University of Minnesota Press, 2013), 75.

42   *Ibid.*, 76.

43   John L. White, "Saint Paul and the Apostolic Letter Tradition," *The Catholic Biblical Quarterly*, 45: 3 (July 1983),434.

44   *Ibid.*, 436.

45   *Ibid.*, 439.

46   The observation belongs to Daniel Boyarin, *A Radical Jew: Paul and the Politics of Identity* (Berkeley: University of California Press, 1994), ebook loc. 478.

47   Bakhtin "Forms of Time and the Chronotope in the Novel," 250.

48   White, "Saint Paul and the Apostolic Letter Tradition," 437.

49   Jacques Derrida, *The Post Card: From Socrates to Freud and Beyond,* trans. Alan Bass (Chicago: University of Chicago Press, 1987), 11.

50   *Ibid.*, 9.

51   See, for example, Jacques Derrida, "Freud and the Scene of Writing," trans. Jeffrey Mehlman *Yale French Studies* 48 (1972), 74–117.

52   I am borrowing that expression from Gregory L. Ulmer's review of the French version of Derrida's *The Post Card*: "The Post Age," *Diacritics* 11: 3 (Autumn 1981), 47.

53   German expressions cited throughout the text are from Martin Heidegger, *Phänomenologie des religiösen Lebens, Gesamtausgabe*, Volume 60 (Frankfurt: Vittorio Klostermann, 2011).

54   Catherine Malabou and Jacques Derrida, *Counterpath*, trans. David Wills (Stanford, CA: Stanford University Press, 2004), 184.

55 The quotations are from John Phillips, "Reading the Postcard," on the web at: https://courses.nus.edu.sg/course/elljwp/readingthepostcard.htm.

56 White, "Saint Paul and the Apostolic Letter Tradition," 437.

57 Brown, *The Making of Late Antiquity*, 11–12.

58 Robert Jewett, *Saint Paul at the Movies: The Apostle's Dialogue with America* (Louisville, KY: Westminster John Know, 1993), 55.

59 William E. Connolly, *Neuropolitics: Thinking, Culture, Speed* (Minneapolis: University of Minnesota Press, 2002), 135.

60 M. M. Bakhtin, "Discourse in the Novel," 299.

61 Heidegger, *The Phenomenology of Religious Life*, 55.

62 *Ibid.*, 47.

63 For an explication of Heideggerian time, see Felix O Murchadha, *The Time of Revolution: Kairos and Chronos in Heidegger* (New York: Bloomsbury, 2013), 1–50.

64 Heidegger, *The Phenomenology of Religious Life*, 64.

65 *Ibid.*, 65.

66 The quotation is from Bakhtin, "Author and Hero in Aesthetic Activity," 13.

67 M. M. Bakhtin, "Discourse in Life and Discourse in Art," in Peter Elbow, ed. *Landmark Essays on Voice and Writing* (New York: Lawrence Erlbaum, 1994), 3.

68 Mikhail Bakhtin, *Toward a Philosophy of the Act*, trans. Vadim Liapunov (Austin: University of Texas Press, 1993), 16.

69 See M. M. Bakhtin, *Problems of Dostoevsky's Poetics*, trans. Caryle Emerson (Minneapolis: University of Minnesota Press, 1984).

70 Vera Lucas Pires and Adail Sobral, "Implications of the Subject's Ontological Stature in the Bakhtin, Medvedev, Volosinov Circle's Discursive Theory," *Bakhtiniana: Revista de Estudos do Discurso* 8: 1 (January/June 2013), on the web at: http://www.scielo.br/scielo.php?pid=S217645732013000100013&script= sci_arttext&tlng=en.

71 Michael J. Shapiro, "'The Light of Reason': Reading the Leviathan with the Werckmeister Harmonies," *Political Theory* 45: 3 (June 2017), 405.

72 *Ibid.*, 406.

73 See, for example, Heidegger, *The Phenomenology of Religious Life*, 66.

74 *Ibid.*, 74.

75 *Ibid.*, 48.

76 *Ibid.*, 58.

77 *Ibid.*, 64.

78 *Ibid.*, 51. Agamben succinctly characterizes the messianic temporality of Paul's epistles (which Heidegger frames phenomenologically), as an "internal form of

time...*ho nym kairos*, the 'time of the now.'": Giorgio Agamben, *The Church and the Kingdom*, trans. Ldeland de la Durantaye (London: Seagull Books, 2012), 41.

79   Heidegger, *The Phenomenology of Religious Life*, 51.

80   The term belongs to Charles Lock, "Carnival and Incarnation: Bakhtin and Orthodox Theology," *Journal of Literature & Theology* 5: 1 (March 1991), 68.

81   Jacques Rancière, *The Politics of Literature*, trans. Julie Rose (Cambridge, UK: Polity, 2011), 11.

82   Martin Heidegger, *Nietzsche 2: The Eternal Recurrence of the Same,* trans. David Farrell Krell (San Francisco: Harper and Row, 1984), 27.

83   Bakhtin, "Discourse in Life and Discourse in Art," 3.

84   The expression belongs to Juliet Flower MacCannell, "The Temporality of Textuality: Bakhtin and Derrida," *MLN* 100: 5 (December 1985), 972.

85   *Ibid.*, 976.

86   See M. M. Bakhtin, "Author and Hero in Aesthetic Activity," in *Art and Answerability*, 42–56.

87   See Mikhail Bakhtin, *Appendix II*: "Toward a Reworking of the Dostoevsky Book," in *Problems of Dostoevsky's Poetics,* trans. Caryl Emerson (Minneapolis: University of Minnesota Press, 1984), 293.

88   I am quoting Stacy Burton's succinct summary of Bakhtin's view: "Bakhtin, Temporality, and Modern Narrative: Writing the Whole Triumphant Murderous Unstoppable Chute," *Comparative Literature* 48: 1 (1996), 48.

89   Bakhtin, *Problems of Dostoevsky's Poetics*, 203.

90   The quotation belongs to Lock, "Carnival and Incarnation: Bakhtin and Orthodox Theology," 72.

91   I am quoting Gary Saul Morson, "Strange Synchronies and Surplus Possibilities: Bakhtin on Time," *Slavic Review* 52: 3 (Autumn 1993), 477.

92   Bakhtin, "Author and Hero in Aesthetic Activity," 98.

93   On what amounts to an ethico-political injunction to the artist to enrich words, see Bakhtin, "Discourse and the Novel," 281.

94   *Ibid.*

95   The quotation is from Morson, "Strange Synchronies and Surplus Possibilities: Bakhtin on Time," 482.

96   Graham Pechey, "Philosophy and Theory in 'Aesthetic Activity," in Susan M. Felch and Paul J. Contino, eds. *Bakhtin and Religion: A Feeling for Faith* (Evanston, IL: Northwestern University Press, 2001), 49.

97   *Ibid.*

98   Bakhtin, *Appendix II*: "Toward a Reworking of the Dostoevsky Book," 294.

99 Mikhail Bakhtin, *Rabelais and His World*, trans. Helene Iswolsky (Bloomington: Indiana University Press, 1984), 19.

100 Bakhtin, "Forms of Time and the Chronotope in the Novel," 168.

101 Morson, "Strange Synchronies and Surplus Possibilities," 484.

102 Lock, "Carnival and Incarnation: Bakhtin and Orthodox Theology," 79.

103 The grammatical construction, which suggests an ideational accord, is inspired by the title and conceptual style of a Jacques Lacan essay, *"Kant avec Sade"*—in translation, "Kant with Sade," trans. James B. Swenson, Jr. *October* 51 (Winter 1989), 55–75.

104 The quotation belongs to Giuliana Bruno, "Heresies: The Body of Pasolini's Semiotics," *Cinema Journal* 30: 3 (Spring 1991), 31.

105 Lock, "Carnival and Incarnation," 73.

106 Bakhtin, *Rabelais*, 395.

107 Bruno, "Heresies," 36

108 Erich Auerbach, "Odysseus' Scar," in *Mimesis,* trans. Willard R. Trask (Princeton, NJ: Princeton University Press, 1968), 3.

109 *Ibid.*, 6.

110 *Ibid.*, 7.

111 *Ibid.*, 14.

112 *Ibid.*, 15.

113 Alexandra Ganser, Julia Puringer, Markus and Rheindorf, "Bakhtin's Chrnotoipe of the Road: Space, Time, and Place in Road Movies Since the 1970s," *Facta Universitas* 4: 1 (2006), 3.

114 Hélène Cixous, "Fiction and Its Phantoms: A Reading of Freud's Das Unheimliche ('The Uncanny')," trans. Robert Dennome *New Literary History* 7: 3 (Spring 1976), 544.

115 Interview with Pasolini quoted in Gino Moliterno, "Pasolini, Pier Paolo," *Senses of Cinema*, on the web at: http://sensesof.cinema.com/2002/great-directors/pasolini/.

116 Mary Whitlock Blundell, "Western Values, or the People's Homer: *Unforgiven* as a Reading of the *Iliad*," *Poetics Today* 18: 4 (Winter 1997), 534.

117 Robert Jewitt, "The Gospel of Violent Zeal in Clint Eastwood's *Unforgiven*," *Christianity and Literature* 47: 4 (Summer 1998), 429.

118 *Ibid.*, 428.

119 *Ibid.*

120 From *The Unforgiven*, directed by Clint Eastwood. Copyright Warner Brothers. All rights reserved 1992.

121 It's important to note however that while Bakhtin (writing as Volosinov) "saw a generalization of free indirect discourse as an evasion of responsible utterance and the triumph of bourgeois consciousness," Pasolini saw its critical political possibilities, opening texts to a "different source of enunciation and a different reading position." Louis-Georges Schwartz, "Typewriter: Free Indirect Discourse in Deleuze's *Cinema*," *SubStance* 108 34: 3 (2005), 116–17.

122 Pier Paolo Pasolini, *Heretical Empiricism*, trans. Ben Lawton and Louise K. Barnett (Bloomington: Indiana University Press, 1988), 168.

123 *Ibid.*, 178.

124 *Ibid.*, 179–80.

125 I am quoting Deleuze's treatment of Pasolini's cinematic innovation: *Cinema 2*, 148.

126 *Ibid.*, 87.

127 See Noa Steimatsky's summary of Pasolini's concept: "Pasolini on Terra Sancta: Toward a Theology of Film," *The Yale Journal of Criticism* 11: 1 (Spring 1998), 241.

128 I am taking the quotation from Deleuze's, *Cinema 2* in Patricia Pisters's version (which very effectively draws from separate pages of the text): "Arresting the Flux of Images and Sounds: Free Indirect Discourse and the Dialectics of Political Cinema," in Ian Buchanan and Adrian Parr, eds. *Deleuze and the Contemporary World* (Edinburgh, UK: Edinburgh University Press, 2006), 179.

129 *Ibid.*

130 Pasolini, "The Screenplay as a 'Structure That Wants to Be Another Structure,'" in *Heretical Empiricism*, 192.

131 The expression is in Steimatsky, "Pasolini on Terra Sancta," 244.

132 *Ibid.*, 247.

133 The quotation is from a documentary of Pasolini's scouting trip: *Sopraluoghi in Palestina* (Locations in Palestine, 1963), quoted in *ibid.*, 241.

134 *Ibid.*, 244.

135 Castelli, "Introduction," ebook loc. 140.

136 *Ibid.*, loc. 149.

137 Pasolini, *Saint Paul: A Screenplay*, 3.

138 *Ibid.*, 4.

139 *Ibid.*, 6.

140 *Ibid.*

141 Badiou, *Saint Paul*, 37.

142 *Ibid.*, 37–8.

143 Pasolini, *Saint Paul: A Screenplay*, 9.

144 *Ibid.*

145 *Ibid.*, 108.

146 Castelli, "Introduction," loc. 294.

147 *Ibid.*, loc. 234.

148 Pasolini, *Heretical Empiricism*, 170.

149 The quotation is from an analysis that compares the montage styles of Walter
     Benjamin and Pier Paolo Pasolini: Filippo Trentin, "'Organizing Pessimism':
     Enigmatic Correlations between Walter Benjamin and Pier Paolo Pasolini," *The
     Modern Language Review* 108: 4 (October 2013), 1038.

150 Cathy Lee Crane, "On the Road: Pier Paolo Pasolini, St. Paul," *Brooklyn Rail*,
     October 33, 2014, on the web at: https://brooklynrail.org/2014/10/film/on-the-
     road-pier-pablo-pasolini-st-paul.

151 See Walter Benjamin, "Theses on the Philosophy of History," in Hannah Arendt,
     ed. *Illuminations*, trans. Harry Zohn (New York: Schocken, 1969), 253–64.

152 Caputo, "Introduction," to *St. Paul among the Philosophers*, 12.

153 Christine Buci-Glucksmann, quoted in Trentin, "Organizing Pessimism," 1024.
     See her *Baroque Reason: The Aesthetics of Modernity,* trans. Patrick Camiller
     (London: Sage, 1994), 170.

154 William E. Connolly, *The Fragility of Things* (Durham, NC: Duke University
     Press, 2013), 140. See Charles Taylor, *A Secular Age* (Cambridge, MA: Harvard
     University Press, 2007).

155 Connelly, *ibid.*, 140–1. The inner quotations are from Taylor, *A Secular Age.* The
     William James quotation is from his "Postscript," to *The Varieties of Religious
     Experience*, reproduced in McDermott, ed. *The Writings of William James*, 784.

156 *Ibid.*, 141.

157 See Deleuze, *Proust and Signs*, 75.

158 Richard Foreman, *Manifestos and Essays* (New York: Theater Communications
     Group, 2013), ebook loc. 301.

159 Gilles Deleuze, *Cinema 2: The Time Image,* trans. Hugh Tomilinso and Robert
     Galeta (Minneapolis: University of Minnesota Press, 1989), 175–6.

160 Cartwright, *The Song before It Is Sung.*

161 Jane Shilling, "New Depth to a Profound Story," *The Telegraph*, February 18,
     2007, on the web at: https://www.telegraph.co.uk/culture/books/3663076/New-
     depth-to-a-profound-story.html.

162 Cartwright, *The Song before It Is Sung*, 7.

163 *Ibid.*, 2–3.

164 *Ibid.*, 60.

165 *Ibid.*, 78.

166 The expression belongs to Lukács, *Theory of the Novel*, 84.

167 Cartwright, *The Song before It Is Sung*, 268.

168 *Ibid.*, 266–7.

169 Jameson, *The Ancients and the Postmoderns*, 3.

170 See Steven R. Goldzwig and Patricia A. Sullivan, "Post-Assassination Editorial Eulogies: Analysis and Assessment," *Western Journal of Communication* 59: 2 (1995), 126.

171 Bakhtin, "Forms of Time and the Chronotope of the Novel," 168.

172 Lukács, *Theory of the Novel*, 88.

173 François Zourabichvili, *Deleuze: A Philosophy of the Event*, trans. Kieran Aarons (Edinburgh: Edinburgh University Press, 2012), 74.

174 Caputo, "Introduction," in *St. Paul Among the Philosophers*, 14.

175 I am borrowing that phrase from Gianni Vattimo's discussion of what he calls post-Christian hermeneutics: *After Christianity*, trans. Luca D'Isanto (New York: Columbia University Press, 2002), 67.

176 Caputo, "Introduction," in *St. Paul among the Philosophers*, 14.

Chapter 3

1 William Faulkner's address upon receiving the Nobel Prize for Literature, Stockholm, December 10, 1950, in Malcolm Cowley, ed. *The Portable Faulkner* (New York: Viking Press, 1974), 723–4.

2 From *Winter Light*, directed by Ingmar Bergman, Svensk Filmindustri, copyright 1957. All rights reserved.

3 The Hegel quotation is in Theodor W. Adorno, "Parataxis: On Hölderlin's Late Poetry," in Rolf Tiedeman, ed. *Notes to Literature Volume Two* (New York: Columbia University Press, 1991), 110.

4 Linda Haverty Rugg, "'Carefully I Touched the Faces of My Parents': Bergman's Autobiographical Image," *Biography* 24: 1 (Winter 2001), 72.

5 *Ibid.*, 73–4.

6 See William Egginton, *How the World Became a Stage: Presence, Theatricality, and the Question of Modernity* (Albany: State University of New York Press, 2002), 137.

7 Bergman quoted in John Fletcher, "Bergman and Strindberg," *Journal of Modern Literature* 3: 2 (April 1973), 173.

8   Egil Tornqvist, *Between Stage and Screen: Ingmar Bergman Directs* (Amsterdam: Amsterdam University Press, 1995), 14.

9   *Ibid.*

10 Ingmar Bergman, *The Magic Lantern*, trans. Joan Tate (London: Hamish Hamilton, 1988), 38.

11 Fletcher, "Bergman and Strindberg," 175.

12 Ingmar Bergman, "Each Film Is My Last," in Roger W. Oliver, *Ingmar Bergman: An Artist's Journey, on Stage, on Screen*, trans. E. Munk (New York: Arcade, 1995), 8.

13 Gilles Deleuze and Felix Guattari, *A Thousand Plateaus*, trans Brian Massumi (Minneapolis: University of Minnesota Press, 1987), 179.

14 Andrei Tarkovsky, *Sculpting in Time*, trans. Kitty Hunter Blair (Austin: University of Texas Press, 2012), 183.

15 See Pier Paolo Pasolini, "Observations on the Long Take," trans. Norman MacAfee and Craig Owens, *October* 13 (Summer 1980), 3–6.

16 Gilles Deleuze, *Cinema 1: The Movement Image,* trans. Hugh Tomlinson and Barbara Habberjam (Minneapolis: University of Minnesota Press, 1986), 87.

17 Gilles Deleuze and Felix Guattari, *A Thousand Plateaus* … 115.

18 Deleuze, *Cinema 1*, 100.

19 I am quoting Richard Rushton's distillation of Deleuze's perspective: "What Can a Face Do: On Deleuze and Faces," *Cultural Critique* 51 (Spring 2002), 224.

20 *Ibid.*, 228.

21 *Ibid.*, 234.

22 Robin Wood, *Ingmar Bergman* (New York: Praeger, 1969), 102.

23 *Ibid.*, 103.

24 *Ibid.*, 168.

25 See Stig Björkman, Torsten Manns, and Jonas Sima, *Bergman on Bergman: Interviews with Ingmar Bergman*, trans. Paul Britten Austin (New York: Simon & Schuster, 1973), 164.

26 I am borrowing that expression from Milan Kundera, *The festival of Insignificance*, trans. Linda Asher (London: Faber & Faber, 2013), 78.

27 The quoted expression belongs to Denise Ming-yueh Wang, "Ingmar Bergman's Appropriation of Images in *The Seventh Seal*," on the web at: http://hompi. sogang.ac.kr/anthony/mesak/mes171/denisewang.pdf., 58.

28 Susan Sontag, "The Aesthetics of Silence," in *Styles of Radical Will* (New York: Farrar, Straus and Giroux, 1969), 3.

29 *Ibid.*, 4.

30 The expression belongs to Anna Bjartmarsdottir Sveinbjornsson, "Theartical Images of Bergman's Films," MA Thesis in The Department of Theatre, Film and Creative Writing, The University of British Columbia, April 2000, 3.

31 Michel Foucault, "Of Other Spaces," trans. Jay Miskowiec *Architecture/ Mouvement/Continuité*, October 1984 ("Des Espace Autres," March 1967), on the web at: http://web.mit.edu/allanmc/www/foucault1.pdf.

32 From *Fanny and Alexander*, directed by Ingmar Bergman Svensk Filmindustri. Copyright 1982. All rights reserved.

33 Ingmar Bergman, *Images: My Life in Film*, trans. Marianne Ruuth (New York: Arcade, 1994), 22.

34 Törnqvist, *Between Stage and Screen*, 179.

35 Thorsten Botz-Bornstein, *Films and Dreams: Tarkovsky, Bergman, Sokurov, Kubrick, and Wong Kar-Wai* (New York: Lexington Books, 2008), 43.

36 Bergman, *The Magic Lantern*, 2.

37 The quotation is from the film review by Vincent Canby, "Ingmar Bergman's 'Fanny and Alexander'," *The New York Times*, on the web at: https://www.nytimes.com/1983/06/17/movies/ingmar-bergman-s-fanny-and-alexander.html.

38 Quoted in Lynda Bundtzen, "Bergman's 'Fanny and Alexander': Family Romance or Artistic Allegory?" *Criticism* 29: 1 (Winter 1987), 95.

39 Bergman, *The Magic Lantern*, 11.

40 Bundtzen, "Bergman's 'Fanny and Alexander'," 91.

41 The quoted expression is from *ibid.*, 95.

42 The quoted remark is from Philip Mosley, *Ingmar Bergman: The Cinema as Mistress* (London: Marion Boyars, 2000), 65.

43 Lars Malstrom and David Kushner, *Wild Strawberries: A Film by Ingman Bergman* (New York: Simon and Schuster, 1960), 9.

44 For the details, see Alexis Luko, *Music and Sound in the Films of Ingmar Bergman* (New York: Routledge, 2016), 64.

45 Slavoj Žižek, *The Plague of Fantasies* (London: Verso, 1997), 200.

46 Bruce F. Kawin, *Mindscreen: Bergman, Godard, and First-Person Film* (Princeton, NJ: Princeton University Press, 1978), 96.

47 Bergman quoted in Norman N. Holland, "'The Seventh Seal': The Film as Iconography," *The Hudson Review* 12: 2 (Summer 1959), 266.

48 Theodor W. Adorno, "On Some Relationships between Music and Painting," trans. Susan Gillespie, *The Musical Quarterly* 79: 1 (Spring 1995), 70.

49 *Ibid.*, 66.

50 *Ibid.*, 69.

51 The full Chant is at: http://www.preces-latinae.or/thesaurus/HYmn/iesIrae.html.

52 From *The Seventh Seal*, directed by Ingmar Bergman Svensk Filmindustri. Copyright 1957. All rights reserved.

53 Gilles Deleuze, *Francis Bacon: The Logic of Sensation*, trans. Daniel W. Smith (Minneapolis: University of Minnesota Press, 2003), 14.

54 Michael J. Shapiro, *Cinematic Geopolitics* (London: Routledge, 2009), 100. The inner quotation is from *ibid.*, 60.

55 Birgitta Steene, *Ingmar Bergman* (New York: Twayne Publishers, 1968), 97.

56 See M. M. Bakhtin, "Discourse and the Novel," in Michael Holquist, ed. *The Dialogic Imagination*, trans. Caryl Emerson (Austin: University of Texas Press, 1981), 259–422.

57 The expression belongs to Don Delillo, who repeats in two novels, *White Noise* and *Libra*.

58 On that aspect of Bergman's films, see Birgitta Steene, *Ingmar Bergman: A Reference Guide* (Amsterdam: Amsterdam University Press, 2005), 131–41.

59 Fabio Pezetti Tonio, "The Sensation of Time in Ingmar Bergman's Poetics of Bodies and Minds," *Acta Univ. Sapientae, Film and Media Studies*, 8 (2014), 49.

60 See Henri Bergson, *Matter and Memory*, trans. N. M. Paul and W. S. Palmer (New York: Zone Books, 1991).

61 David Gross, "Bergson, Proust, and the Reevaluation of Memory," *International Philosophical Quarterly* 25 (December 1985), 375.

62 Karl Marx, *Economic and Philosophical Manuscripts of 1844,* trans. Martin Milligan (Radford, VA: Wilder, 2011), 75.

63 French and French, *Wild Strawberries*, 19.

64 M. M. Bakhtin "Forms of Time and the Chronotope in the Novel: Notes toward a Historical Poetics," in *The Dialogic Imagination,* trans. Caryl Emerson and Michael Holquist (Austin: University of Texas Press, 1981), 84.

65 Hélène Cixous, "Fiction and Its Phantoms: A Reading of Freud's Das Unheimliche ('The Uncanny')," trans. Robert Dennome *New Literary History* 7: 3 (Spring 1976), 544.

66 Törnqvist, *Between Stage and Screen*, 113.

67 *Ibid.*

68 From *Wild Strawberries*, directed by Ingman Bergman, copyright Svensk Filmindustri 1957. All rights reserved.

69 *Bergman on Bergman* (interviews), trans. Paul Britten Austin (London: Secker & Warburg, 1973), 169.

70 *Ibid.*, 168.

71　From *Through a Glass darkly*, directed by Ingmar Bergman. Copyright Svensk Filmindustri 1961. All rights reserved.

72　Bergman quoted in Peter Cowie, *Ingmar Bergman: A Critical Biography* (New York: Charles Scribner's and Sons, 1982), 199.

73　The quotation is from Robert E. Lauder, *God, Death, Art & Love: The Philosophical Vision of Ingmar Bergman* (New York: Paulist Press, 1989), 141.

74　Törnqvist, *Between Stage and Screen*, 201.

75　Susan Sontag, "Bergman's *Persona*," in *Styles of Radical Will*, 141.

76　Bergman quoted in Birgitta Steene ed. *Focus on the Seventh Seal* (Englewood Cliffs, NJ: Prentice Hall, 1972), 70.

77　The quotation is from William Alexander, "Devils in the Cathedral: Bergman's Trilogy," *Cinema Journal* 13: 2 (Spring 1974), 25. It's a speech in the *Winter Light* screenplay that was omitted from the film.

78　The quotation is from *ibid.*, 32.

79　See, for example, Robert Lauder, *God, Death, Art, and Love: The Philosophical Vision of Ingmar Bergman* (New York: Paulist Press, 1989), 158.

80　Bergman quoted in Lise-Lone Marker, "The Magic Triangle: Bergman's Implied Philosophy of Theatrical Communication," *Modern Drama* 26: 3 (Fall 1983), 252.

81　Bergman quoted in Luko, *Music and Sound in the Films of Ingmar Bergman*, 46.

82　Foucault, "Of Other Spaces."

83　The quotation is from Bergman and Visual Art by Egil Törnqvist, on the web at: https://www.ingmarbergman.se/en/universe/bergman-and-visual-art.

84　From *The Silence*, directed by Ingmar Bergman. Copyright Svensk Filmindustri 1957. All rights reserved.

Chapter 4

1　I am borrowing that apropos phrase from Friedrich Kittler, "Gamophone, Film, Typewriter," in John Johnson, ed. *Friedrich A. Kittler Essays: Literature, Media, Information Systems* (Amsterdam: OPA, 1997), 34.

2　Anthony Ennis, "Media, Drugs, and Schizophrenia in the Works of Philip K. Dick," *Science Fiction Studies* 33: 1 (March 2006), 76.

3　Quotations from Dick's account in Gabriel Mckee, *Pink Beams of Light from the God in the Gutter* (Dallas: University Press of America, 2004), 2–3.

4　Philip Dick, *Radio Free Albemuth* (New York: Vintage, 1998), 38.

5   Philip Dick, *The Divine Invasion* (New York: Mariner, 2011), 192.

6   Philip K. Dick, *Valis* (New York: Houghton Mifflin Harcourt, 1981), 21.

7   Philip K. Dick, quoted in Lawrence Sutin, *In Pursuit of VALIS* (New York: Underwood, 1991), 161.

8   Jams Edward Burton, *The Philosophy of Science Fiction: Henri Bergson and the Fabulations of Philip K. Dick* (London: Bloomsbury, 2017), 158.

9   *Bergman on Bergman*, 169.

10   Quotations are from Umberto Rossi, "The Holy Family from Outer Space: Reconsidering Philip K. Dick's *The Divine Invasion*," *Extrapolation* 52: 2 (2011), 155.

11   One intellectual biography of James explicitly renders him as a becoming subject. See Howard Feinstein, *Becoming William James* (Ithaca, NY: Cornell University Press, 1999).

12   The quotation is from Garrett Barden's analysis of Henri Bergson's method: "Method in Philosophy," in John Mullarkey, ed. *The New Bergson* (Manchester, UK: Manchester University Press, 1999), 37.

13   The expression belongs to Gilles Deleuze, "Literature and Life," in *Essays Critical and Clinical*, trans. Daniel W. Smith and Michael A. Greco (Minneapolis: University of Minnesota Press, 1997), 5.

14   Kim Stanley Robinson, "An Afterword to Philip K. Dick's Valis," on the web at: https://philipdick.com/literary-criticism/essays/an-afterword-to-philip-k-dicks-valis/.

15   Pamela Jackson and Jonathan Lethem eds. *The Exegesis of Philip K Dick* (New York: Houghton Mifflin Harcourt, 2011), 19.

16   Dick, "The Android and the Human," 189.

17   *Ibid.*, 124.

18   See Philip K. Dick, *Do Androids Dream of Electric Sheep* (New York: Del Ray, 1968).

19   Dick, "The Android and the Human," 185.

20   Katherine Hayles, *How We Became Posthuman* (Chicago: University of Chicago Press, 1999), 160.

21   See Yari Lanci, "*Remember Tomorrow*: Biopolitics of Time in the Early Works of Philip K. Dick," in Alexander Dunst and Stefan Schlensag, eds. *The World According to Philip K. Dick* (London: Palgrave Macmillan, 2015), 102.

22   Dick, *Radio Free Albemuth*, 120.

23   This expression is in Immanuel Kant, *Anthropology from a Pragmatic Point of View,* trans. Victor Lyle Dowdell (Carbondale: Southern Illinois University Press, 1978), 40.

24 *Ibid.*

25 *Ibid.*, 154.

26 *Ibid.*, 155.

27 Jackson and Lethem eds. *The Exegesis of Philip K Dick*, 4.

28 See Immanuel Kant, "Perpetual Peace," in *Perpetual Peace Other Essays,* trans. Ted Humphrey (Indianapolis, IN: Hackett, 1983) and in contrast Philip Dick's "Letter of Comment," from *SF Commentary*, February 9, 1970, reproduced in Bruce Gillespie, ed. *Philip Dick: Electric Shepherd* (Melbourne, Australia: Norstrilia Press, 1975), 31.

29 The Nietzsche quotes are from *Twilight of the Idols/The Anti-Christ*, trans. Reginald J. Hollingdale (New York: Penguin, 1990), 49.

30 *Philip Dick: Electric Shepherd*, 31–2.

31 Philp K. Dick, *Valis* (Boston: Mariner Books, 1981), 178.

32 See Bergson, *Matter and Memory.*

33 See Fredric Jameson, quoted in Umberto Rossi, *The Twisted Worlds of Philip K. Dick* (London: McFarland & Company, 2011), ebook loc. 1131.

34 Dick, *Valis*, 137.

35 Friedrich Nietzsche, *The Gay Science Book 5 Paragraph 354.*

36 The quotation is from Alexander Dunst, "Android Gods: Philip K. Dick after Postmodernism," *Textual Practice* 25: 4 (2011), 825.

37 The expression belongs to Adam Hulbert, "Elsewhere, Elsewhen and Otherwise: The Wild Lives of Radios in the Worlds of Philip K. Dick," *Journal of Language, Literature and Culture* 63: 2–3 (2016), on the web at: https://www.tandfonline. com/doi/abs/10.1080/20512856.2016.1244915

38 Auerbach, *Mimesis*, 15.

39 Philip K. Dick, "Exhibit Piece," in *Philip K. Dick's Electric Dreams* (New York: Houghton Mifflin Harcourt, 2017), 13.

40 *The Exegesis of Philip K Dick*, 10.

41 Dick, *Radio Free Albemuth*, 122.

42 *Ibid.*, 113.

43 Umberto Rossi, "Radio Free PKD," *Foundation* 37: 106 (2010), 11.

44 *Ibid.*

45 Philip K Dick, *Time Out of Joint* (New York: Houghton Mifflin Harcourt, 2012 (originally published in 1959).

46 Fredric Jameson, History and Salvation in Philip K. Dick." In Frederic Jameson ed. *Archaeologies of the Future: The Desire Called Utopia and Other Science Fictions* (New York: Verso, 2005), 345.

47   Thomas Pynchon, *Gravity's Rainbow* (New York: Penguin, 2006), 509.

48   David Porush, "Hacking the Brainstem," in Robert Markley, ed. *Virtual Realities and Their Discontents* (Baltimore, MD: Johns Hopkins University Press, 1996), 124.

49   Darko Suvin, "Goodbye and Hello: Differentiating within the Later P. K. Dick," *Extrapolations* 43: 4 (2002), 382.

50   Felix Guattari, *Lines of Flight: For Another Word of Possibilities,* trans. Andrew Goffey (London: Bloomsbury, 2015), 4.

51   *Ibid.*, 15.

52   Dick, *Radio Free Albemuth*, 121.

53   *Ibid.*, 136.

54   Burton, *The Philosophy of Science Fiction*, 16.

55   "Philip K. Dick interview: *Slash,* May 1980, 16 in *Simulacrum* no. 3, on the web at: https://philipdick.com/literary-criticism/interviews/phil-k-dick-interview-slash-may-1980/.

56   Philip K. Dick, "Foreword to *The Preserving Machine*," in R. D. Mullen et al., eds. *On Philip Dick* 40 Articles from *Science-Fiction Studies* (Terre-Haute, IN: SF-TH Inc., 1992), 16.

57   Foucault, "Of Other Spaces."

58   See Hulbert, "Elsewhere, Elsewhen and Otherwise."

59   *Ibid.*

60   Dunst, "Android Gods: Philip K. Dick after Postmodernism," 828.

61   Don DeLillo, *Mao II: A Novel* (New York: Penguin, 1992), 48.

62   Richard Foreman, *The Manifestos and Essays* (New York: Theatre Communications Group, 2013), ebook loc 82.

63   Dick, *Radio Free Albemuth*, 35.

64   *The Exegesis of Philip K Dick*, 19.

65   Philip K. Dick, "My Definition of Science Fiction," in Sutin, ed. *The Shifting Realities of Philip K. Dick* (New York: Vintage, 1996), 99.

66   Deleuze, *Francis Bacon*, 71.

67   The quotations are drawn from Rodolphe Gasché, "Objective Diversions: On Some Kantian Themes in Benjamin's 'The Work of Art in the Age of Mechanical Reproduction,'" in Andrew Benjamin and Peter Osborne, eds. *Walter Benjamin's Philosophy: Destruction and Experience* (London: Routledge, 1994), 197.

68   See Linda Hutcheon, "Parody without Ridicule: Observations on Modern Literary Parody," *Canadian Review of Comparative Literature* 5: 2 (Spring 1978), 201.

69   John Rieder, *Philip K. Dick's Mass Cultural Epistemology* (Middletown, CT: Wesleyan University Press, 2017), 99.

70   Quotation from Hutcheon, "Parody without Ridicule, 206.

71   Gary Shapiro, "Reading and Writing in the Text if Hobbes's *Leviathan*," *Journal of the History of Philosophy* 18: 2 (April 1980), 148.

72   Thomas Hobbes, *Leviathan* (New York: Penguin, 1968), 6.

73   David Albahari, *Globetrotter*, trans. Ellen Elias Bursac (New Haven, CT: Yale University Press, 2014), 50.

74   See Daniel Goldman, "David Albahari's 'Globetrotter,'" *Words without Borders,* October 2014, on the web at: https://www.wordswithoutborders.org/book-review/david-albaharis

75   Gabriel Mamola, "Opus Dei: The Divine Invasion and the Philip K. Dick Canon," *Science Fiction Studies* 46: 2 (July 2019), 308.

76   *Ibid.*

77   Quoted in *ibid.*, 309.

78   Dick's *The Divine Invasion* quoted in *ibid.*, 317–18.

79   Dick, *The Exegesis*, 847.

80   Gilles Deleuze, "Nomad Thought," in David B. Allison, ed. *The New Nietzsche* (New York: Dell, 1977), 149.

81   See John Calvin, "Introduction," in *Institutes of the Christian Religion*, trans. John Allen (Philadelphia: Library of Christian Classics, 1930). The quotation as a whole is from Ralph C. Handcock, *Calvin and the Foundations of Modern Politics* (Ithaca, NY: Cornell University Press, 1989), 158.

82   Dick, *Do Androids Dream of Electric Sheep?* 21.

83   *Ibid.*, 71.

84   *Ibid.*, 164.

85   *Ibid.*, 192.

86   *Ibid.*, 164.

87   Gilles Deleuze, *Nietzsche and Philosophy*, trans. Hugh Tomlinson (New York: Columbia University Press, 1983), 3.

88   The quotations are from Nandita Biswas Mellamphy, *The Three Stigmata of Friedrich Nietzsche* (London: Palgrave Macmillan, 2010), xii.

89   Quoted in Robinson, "An Afterword to Philip K. Dick's Valis."

90   Dick, *Valis*, 20.

91   *Ibid.*, 10.

92   The quotation is from Carl Freedman, "Toward a Theory of Paranoia: The Science Fiction of Philip K. Dick," *Science Fiction Studies* 11: 1 (March 1984), 16.

93 Sarah Mann-O'Donnell, "From Hypochondria to Convalescence: Health as Chronic Critique in Nietzsche, Deleuze and Guattari," *Deleuze Studies* 4: 2 (2010), 161–82.

94 *Ibid.*, 162.

95 Friedrich Nietzsche, *On the Genealogy of Morality and Other Writings*, trans. Carole Diethe (Cambridge, UK: Cambridge University Press, 2017), 64.

96 Friedrich Nietzsche, "Preface" in *Human All Too Human*, trans. Stephen Lehmann (Lincoln: University of Nebraska Press, 1996), section 4.

97 *Ibid.,* section 1.

98 See Nietzsche, *The Gay Science*, 346.

99 Roger J. Stilling, "Mystical Healing: Reading Philip K. Dick's VALIS and the Divine Invasion *as Metapsychoanalytic Novels*," *South Atlantic Review* 56: 2 (May 1991), 102.

100 Nietzsche, "Preface," in *Human All Too Human*, section 1.

101 Pamela Jackson and Jonathan Lethem eds. *The Exegesis of Philip K. Dick*.

102 Philip Dick, "The Electric Ant," in *The Eye of Sibyl and Other Classic Stories* (New York: Citadel, 1987), 233.

103 Stilling, "Mystical Healing," 96–7.

104 Dick, *The Divine Invasion*, 65–6.

105 Massimo Cacciari, *The Withholding Power: An Essay on Political*, trans. Edi Pucci (London: Bloomsbury, 2018), 3.

106 Philip K. Dick, *The Transmigration of Timothy Archer* (New York: Mariner Books, 2011), 6.

107 Scott Lash, *Intensive Culture: Social Theory, Religion & Contemporary Capitalism* (London: Sage, 2010), 187.

108 Dick, *The Transmigration of Timothy Archer*, 41.

109 *Ibid.*, 76.

110 Gilles Deleuze and Felix Guattari, *What Is Philosophy?*, 69.

111 Scott Durham (quoting Peter Fitting), "P. K. Dick: From the Death of the Subject to a Theology of Late Capitalism," *Science Fiction Studies* 15: 2 (July 1988), 176.

112 Deleuze and Guattari, *What Is Philosophy?* 69.

113 *Ibid.*, 70.

114 John O'Neill, *Essaying Montaigne* (Liverpool: Liverpool University Press, 2001), 9.

115 See Jacques Lacan, "Of the Subject Who Is Supposed to Know, of the First Dyad, and of the Good," in Jacques-Alain Miller, ed. *The Four Fundamental Concepts of Psycho-Analysis,* trans. Alan Sheridan (New York: Penguin, 1979), 239.

116 Lord RC, *Pink Beam of Light: A Philip K. Dick Companion* (Ganymedean Slime Mold Productions, 2006), 161.

117 Durham, "From the Death of the Subject to a Theology of Late Capitalism," 183.

118 See chapter 21, "The Creative World (1945–50)," in Greg Rickman, *To the High Castle Philip Dick: A Life 1928–1962* (Long Beach, CA: Valentine Press, 1989), 208–17.

119 See Philip K. Dick, "Not by Its Cover," originally published in *Famous Science Fiction* (Summer 1968), on the web at: http://sickmyduck.narod.ru/pkd035-0.html.

120 That argument is explicitly made by Aaron Barlow, "Chapter Eight: Religion and the Demise of the 'Gray Truth': Philip K. Dick's Our Friends from Frolix 8 (1970) and Valis (1981)," on the web at: https://2010philipkdickfans.philipdick. com/articles/barlow.htm.

121 Philip K. Dick, "Beyond Lies the Wub," in *The Early Stories of Philip K. Dick* (New York: Dover, 2013), 1–8.

122 Philip K. Dick, "Not by Its Cover," [1965], on the web at: http://sickmyduck. narod.ru/pkd035-0.html.

123 *Ibid.*

124 Barlow, "Chapter Eight: Religion and the Demise of the 'Gray Truth': Philip K. Dick's Our Friends from Frolix 8 (1970) and Valis (1981)."

125 Thomas Mann, *Joseph and His Brothers*, trans. John E. Woods (New York: Alfred A. Knopf, 2005), 541.

126 *Ibid.*

127 Roland Barthes, *S/Z: AN Essay*, trans. Richard Miller (New York: Hill and Wang, 1974), 5.

128 Dominic Pettman, *Human Error: Species Being and Media Machines* (Minneapolis: University of Minnesota Press, 2011), 61.

129 William T. Vollmann, *Europe Central* (New York: Viking, 2005), ebook loc. 142–58.

130 See Friedrich Kittler, *Gramophone, Film, Typewriter*, trans. Geoffrey Winthrop-Young (Stanford, CA: Stanford University Press, 1999).

Chapter 5

1 William James, "Human Immortality" (1998), on the web at: https://www.uky. edu/~eushe2/Pajares/jimmortal.html.

2 Slavoj Žižek, "Kate's Choice, or the Materialism of Henry James," in Slavoj Žižek, ed. *Lacan: The Silent Partners* (New York: Verso, 2006), 290.

3 The contrast between "oppositional" and "immanent" is taken from Posnock, *The trial of Curiosity*, 285.

4 William James, "Is Life Worth Living," in *The Will to Believe and Other Essays in Popular Philosophy* (New York: Dover, 1960), 22.

5 William James, "Reflect Action and Theism," in *The Will to Believe and Other Essays in Popular Philosophy* (New York: Dover, 1960), 132–3.

6 See Austin, *How to Do Things with Words*.

7 Slavoj Žižek, *Like a Thief in Broad Daylight* (New York: Allen Lane, 2018), 3.

8 The expression belongs to Bill Vallicella, "On Writing Well: The Example of William James," on the web at: https://maverickphilosopher.typepad.com/maverick_philosopher/2009/09/on-writing-well-the-example-of-william-james.html.

9 For a commentary on how, after the breakdown of James's intention—in his *Principles of Psychology*—to correlate mental states and brain states, he ended with a position that locates thought in the interstices between mind and its objects, so that a mental state includes its object(s), see Bruce Wilshire, "Protophenomenology in the Psychology of William James," *Transaction of the Charles S. Pierce Society* 5: 1 (Winter 1969), 25–43.

10 See William James, *Essays in Radical Empiricism* (Lincoln: University of Nebraska Press, 1996), 25. The quoted expression belongs to Brian Massumi's interpretation of James's position in his, *Semblance and Event* (Cambridge, MA: MIT Press, 2011), 30.

11 William James, "Human Immortality," in *The Will to Believe and Other Essays in Popular Philosophy*, 3.

12 Quoted in G. William Barnard, *Exploring Unseen Worlds: William James and the Philosophy of Mysticism* (New York: SUNY Albany, 1997), 19.

13 James, "Reflex Action and Theism," 137.

14 This formulation of James on ideas is well developed in David Lapoujade, *William James: Empiricism and Pragmatism*, trans. Thomas Lamarre (Durham, NC: Duke University Press, 2020), 27.

15 See *ibid.*, 51.

16 The quotation is from an analysis of James's view of "mystical emotions" by Jeremy Carrette, "William James," in John Corrigan, ed. *Religion and Emotion* (New York: Oxford University Press, 2008), 430.

17 Benjamin, *The Origins of German Tragic Drama*, 56.

18 See Roland Barthes, "From Work to Text," in *Image Music Text*, trans. Stephen Heath (New York: Hill and Wang, 1977), 155–64. My resort to a Barthes-influenced textual analyses is part of *my* "ascetic apprenticeship."

19 Roland Barthes, *S/Z*, trans. Richard Howard (New York: Hill and Wang, 1974).

20 Michael J. Shapiro, "Metaphor in the Philosophy of the Social Sciences," *Cultural Critique* 2 (Winter 1985–6), 191–214.

21 Paul Ricoeur, "The Model of the Text: Meaningful Action Considered as Text," *New Literary History*, 5: 1 (Autumn 1973), 96.

22 James, "Reflex Action and Theism," 134.

23 *Ibid.*

24 James, "Reflex Action and Theism," 135.

25 *Ibid.*, 136.

26 *Ibid.*

27 *Ibid.*, 133.

28 *Ibid.*, 137.

29 *Ibid.*

30 *Ibid.*

31 See Immanuel Kant, *Critique of Pure Reason* §3

32 Wilshire, "Protophenomenology in the Psychology of William James," 26.

33 William James, *Principles of Psychology—Vols 1–2* (Leamington Spa, UK: Pantianos Classics 2017), ebook loc. 5810.

34 Catherine Malabou, *What Should We Do with Our Brain*, trans. Sebastian Rand (New York: Fordham University Press, 2008), 1.

35 William James, *Pragmatism: A New Name for Some Old Ways of Thinking* (New York: Longmans, Green & Co., 1910), 275.

36 The quotation is from Norman Turner, "Cezanne, Wagner, Modulation," *Journal of Aesthetics and Art Criticism* 56: 4 (Fall 1998), 10.

37 James, *Principles of Psychology*, ebook loc. 4674.

38 William James, *Essays in Radical Empiricism* 9.

39 James, "Reflex Action and Theism," 137.

40 *Ibid.*

41 *Ibid.*

42 See Michel Foucault, Chapter 5, "Classifying," in *The Order of Things: An Archaeology of the Human Sciences* (New York: Vintage, 1994), 125–65.

43 Michel Foucault, The Archaeology of Knowledge, trans A. M. Sheridan Smith (NY: Pantheon, 1972), 57.

44 *Ibid.*, 12.

45 Michel Foucault, "What Is Enlightenment," in *The Politics of Truth*, trans. Lyse Hochroth and Catherine Porter (New York: Semiotext(e), 1997), 113.

46 James W. Bernauer, "Michel Foucault's Ecstatic Thinking," in James Bernauer and David Rasmussen, eds. *The Final Foucault* (Cambridge, MA: MIT Press, 1988),

The inner quotation is from Michel Foucault, "The Discourse on Language," in
The Archaeology of Language, 231.

47   Jacob Taubes, "Theology and the Philosophical Critique of Religion,"
CrossCurrents 5: 4 (1995), 324.

48   See Michel Foucault, "About the Concept of the 'Dangerous Individual' in 19th-
Century Psychiatry," *International Journal of Law and Psychiatry* 1: 1 (1978),
on the web at: http://schwarzemilch.files.wordpress.com/2009/02/foucault_
dangerous_individual.pdf.

49   See Michel Foucault, *Lectures on the Will to Know*, trans. Graham Burchell (New
York: Picador, 2014).

50   James, "Reflex Action and Theism," 137.

51   Michel Foucault, *The History of Sexuality Vol I: An Introduction*, trans. Robert
Hurley (New York: Pantheon, 1978), 25. In a subsequent investigation, based
on his lectures under the title, *Security, Territory, Population*, Foucault refers
not only to an emerging governmentality—connected to new techniques
of power focused on managing the new collective object, the "population"
(a collectivity subject to calculations)—but also to the role of the "human
sciences." He shows that at the same time when governance had shifted from a
focus on sovereign power to one of managing the social order, those "sciences"
became concerned with the population's individual subjects, whose living,
working, and speaking had to be comprehended: Michel Foucault, *Security,
Territory, Population*, trans. Graham Burchell (New York: Palgrave Macmillan,
2007), 79.

52   Michel Foucault, *The Government of the Self and Others*, trans Graham Burchell
(New York: Picador, 2010), 5.

53   Wilshire, "Protophenomenology in the Psychology of William James," 25.

54   See Jan Patočka, *Introduction to Husserl's Phenomenology*, trans. Erazim Kohak
(Chicago: Open Court, 2018).

55   James, *Principles of Psychology*, ebook loc. 7536.

56   The observation about concepts and percepts and the quotation are taken from
Lapoujade, who is reading James through a Deleuzian lens: *William James:
Empiricism and Pragmatism*, 28.

57   Nietzsche, *The Will to Power*, 375.

58   James, *Principles of Psychology*, ebook loc. 23932.

59   See, for example, Bruce Wilshire, *William James and Phenomenology: A Study of
the Principles of Psychology* (Bloomington: Indiana University Press, 1968), Ash
Gobar, "The Phenomenology of William James," *Proceedings of the American
Philosophical Society* 1114: 4 (August 1970), 294–309, and James M. Edie,

William James and Phenomenology (Bloomington: Indiana University Press, 1987).

60 William James, *The Will to Believe* (Indianapolis, IN: Aeterna Classics, 2018), ebook loc. 116.

61 *Ibid.*, loc.131.

62 See Rose Ann Christian, "Truth and Consequences in James "The Will to Believe," *International Journal for Philosophy of Religion* 58: 1 (August 2005), 1–26.

63 William James, *The Will to Believe* (Chicago: Hackett, 2018), ebook loc. 313–14.

64 Nietzsche, *The Will to Power*, 510.

65 James, *The Will to Believe*, ebook loc. 176.

66 James, "Is Life Worth Living," in *The Will to Believe and Other Essays in Popular Philosophy, and Human Immortality*, 22.

67 Georges Didi-Humberman, "The Art of Not Describing: Vermeer—the Detail and the Patch," *History of the Human Sciences* 2: 2 (June 1989), 149.

68 *Ibid.*, loc. 298.

69 *Ibid.*, loc. 298–314.

70 *Ibid.*, loc. 326.

71 *Ibid.*, loc. 360.

72 For his concept of the language game, see Ludwig Wittgenstein, *Philosophical Investigations* (New York: Wiley-Blackwell, 2009).

73 Didi-Humberman, "The Art of Not Decribing," loc. 314.

74 Jean Luc Nancy, *Dis-Enclosure: The Deconstruction of Christianity*, trans. Bettina Bergo (New York: Fordham University Press, 2008), 16.

75 Jean-Francois Lyotard and Jean-Loup Thébaud, *Just Gaming*, trans. Wlad Godzich (Minneapolis: University of Minnesota Press, 1985), 99.

76 *Ibid.*, loc. 298–314.

77 Georges Canguilhem, "Monstrosity and the Monstrous," in *Knowledge of Life*, trans. Stefanos Geroulanos and Daniela Ginsburg (New York: Fordham University Press, 2008), 135–6.

78 *Ibid.*, 136.

79 *Ibid.*, 146.

80 The quotation is from Paolo Maratti and Todd Meyers, "Foreword" to Canguilhem, *Knowledge of Life*, xi.

81 William James, *The Varieties of Religious Experience* (New York: Philosophical Library, 2015), ebook loc. 421.

82 *Ibid.*, loc. 665.

83 James, *Principles of Psychology*, loc. 4507.

84 James, *The Varieties of Religious Experience*, loc. 136.

85 I am quoting from Russell J Duvernoy's succinct summary of the approach to experience in James's *Radical Empiricism*: "Pure Experience and Planes of Immanence: From James to Deleuze," *The Journal of Speculative Philosophy* 30: 4 (2016), 430.

86 The quotations are from a commentary on Benjamin's treatment of allegory in his *Origin*. See Bainard Cowan, "Walter Benjamin's Theory of Allegory," *New German Critique* no. 22 (Winter 1981), 112.

87 The outer quotations are from *ibid.*, 111–12. The inner ones are from Benjamin, *The Origin of German Tragic Drama*, 159.

88 *Ibid.*, loc. 482.

89 Charles Taylor, *Varieties of Religion Today* (Cambridge, MA: Harvard University Press, 2002), 22.

90 *Ibid.*, vi.

91 Thornton Wilder, *The Bridge of San Luis Rey* (New York: Harper, 2003), 89.

92 *Ibid.*, 5.

93 Russell Banks, "Foreword," to Wilder, *The Bridge of San Luis Rey*, xi.

94 *Ibid.*, xii.

95 Wilder, *The Bridge of San Luis Rey*, 6.

96 *Ibid.*, 7.

97 *Ibid.*, 13.

98 That designation for Wilder belongs to E. K. Brown, "A Christian Humanist: Thornton Wilder," *University of Toronto Quarterly* 4: 3 (April 1935), 356–70.

99 In the novel, Brother Juniper's obsession with divine intention seals his fate. When the Church discovers the book with his research, he is burned in the public square as a heretic.

100 See Stig Björkman, Torsten Manns, and Jonas Sima, *Bergman on Berman: Interviews with Ingmar Bergman*, trans. Paul Britten Austin (New York: Simon and Schuster, 1973), 164.

101 Wilder, *The Bridge of San Luis Rey*, 9.

102 *Ibid.*, 16–17.

103 *Ibid.*, 17.

104 *Ibid.*, 35.

105 Thornton Wilder, Letter to John Townley, "Afterword," in *ibid.*, 128.

106 *Ibid.*, 107.

107 The expression belongs to Brian Brems, "Hope and Despair: Paul Schrader's 'First Reformed,'" *Vague Visages*, on the web at: https://vaguevisages. com/2019/02/21/hope-and-despair-paul-schraders-first-reformed-screenplay/.

108 Paul Schrader, *Transcendental Style in Film: Ozu, Bresson, Dreyer* (Berkeley: University of California Press, 2018), ebook loc. 93.

109 Mikhail Iampolski, *The Memory of Tiresias: Intertextuality and Film,* trans. Harsha Ram (Berkeley: University of California Press, 1998), 31.

110 The quotation is from Chelsey Crawford's interpretation of the implications of Iampolski on the quote: "The Permeable Self: A Theory of Cinematic Quotation," *Film-Philosophy* 19 (2015), 107.

111 Schrader, *Transcendental Style in Film*, loc. 110.

112 Sergei M. Eisenstein, "Montage and Architecture," trans. Michael Glenny, *Assemblage* 10 (1989), 117.

113 The quotations are from Y. A. Bois, "Introduction to Eisenstein," *ibid.*, 113.

114 Schrader, *Transcendental Style in Film,* loc. 283.

115 *Ibid.*, loc. 121.

116 From *First Reformed*, directed by Paul Schrader. Copyright Lionsgate 2017. All rights reserved.

117 Schrader, *Transcendental Style in Film,* loc. 388.

118 The quoted expression belongs to Christine Bucher, "Architecture as a Narrative Medium," *Electronic Book Review*, May 1, 2002, on the web at: https://electronicbookreview.com/essay/architecture-as-a-narrative-medium/.

119 See Bernard Tchumi, "Violence and Architecture," in *Architecture and Disjunction* (Cambridge, MA: MIT Press, 1994), 121.

120 Theodora Antonakaki, "Lighting and Spatial Structure in Religious Architecture," *Bartlett*, on the web at: @inproceedings{Bartlett2007LIGHTINGAS, title={LIGHTING AND SPATIAL STRUCTURE IN RELIGIOUS ARCHITECTURE: a comparative study of a Byzantine church and an early Ottoman mosque in the city of Thessaloniki 057}, author={The Bartlett}, year={2007}}.

121 Schrader, *Transcendental Style in Film* (quoting Tarkovsky), loc. 379.

122 *Ibid.*, loc. 133.

123 *Ibid.*, loc. 326.

124 See Rand Richard's Cooper, "God's Lonely Man" *Commonweal*, July 6, 2018, on the web at: https://www.commonwealmagazine.org/god%E2%80%99s-lonely-man.

125 Deleuze, "The Brain Is the Screen," 40.

126 *Ibid.*

127 William James, *Habit* (Amazon Kindle version), 5.

128 Malabou, *What Should We Do with Our Brain*, 38.

129 Marc Jeannerod, "Foreword" to Malabou, *ibid.*, xiv.

130   Malabou, *What Should We Do with Our Brain*, 79.

131   *Ibid.*, 52.

132   *Ibid.*, 9. Malabou's reference to a "naturalization effect" is from Luc Boltanski and Eve Chiapello, *The New Spirit of Capitalism*, trans. Gregory Elliott (New York: Verso, 2018).

133   *Ibid.*, 10.

134   Connolly, *Neuropolitics*, 66.

135   *Ibid.*, 85.

136   *Ibid.*, 86.

137   Shapiro, *Cinematic Geopolitics*, 118. The inner quotations are from Gilles Deleuze's reading of Hume: *Pure Immanence*, trans. Anne Boyman (New York: Zone Books, 2005), 45.

138   Shapiro, *Cinematic Geopolitics*, 119; Deleuze, *Pure Immanence*, 46.

139   See Connolly, *Neuropolitics*, 136–7.

140   Malabou, *What Should We Do with Our Brain*, 11.Bloomsbury names00–00

Index Names

Index Words

empathy: for P K Dick 108, 110, 121–3; James on 135, 154

empiricism: James's radical 137; Pasolini's heretical 12

enlightenment: Kant on 2–3; Foucault on 15

epistemology/knowledge: aesthetic 18, 22; Benjamin on 153; for Bergman 86–7 for P K Dick 114, 125; Foucault on 23, 145–7; for James 136, 138, 140, 145–6, 152; for Montaigne 129; for Nietzsche 125, 127, 150; novel as 1; Pasolini and 59; Rancière on 19, 22–3; western 12

epistles 32, 40, 42–3, 50, 62–3; 1 Corinthians 39, 41, 47, 76, 93, 131, 137; 2 Corinthians 38; Galatians 31, 43, 46; Philippians 47; Romans 8–9, 38, 42, 47; Thessalonians 41, 43, 127

ethics 1, 22, 31, 58, 69, 133: in Bakhtin 41; Bergman on 85, 92, 96–7; Connolly on 167; P K Dick's 133; Henry James 135–6; Kant's 111; Pauline 108; for William James 136; Žižek on 136–7.

event(s) 34: ambiguous 104; apocalyptic 7; Bakhtin on 36, 45, 60, 90; Badiou on 34; belief as 11; Christ as 32, 36, 41, 45, 130; in cinema 39; Derrida's 37; deadly, 62; disruptive 4; Foucault on 145; Heidegger on 45; ideational 145; initiating 6, 12; legitimating 48; Luther's 14; Paul's 34; on the road 33, 60, 90; spirituality-relevant 5, 12; structured 12; thought- 129; Tschumi on 161; Žižek on 12

faces: Bergman on 67; in Bergman films 25, 50, 67–70, 80, 88, 92, 95, 97, 99, 102, 163; Deleuze on 68; Pasolini on, 52; Žižek on 80

fatherhood, in Bergman films 24, 69–70, 74, 76, 79–80, 86, 92–8, 100

fiction 1, 20–1: Bakhtin on 1; for Derrida 40; P K Dick on 18, 117–18, 121, 129; Jameson on 112; meta- 117–20; in Nietzsche 113; Spivak on 1; Rancière on 19; P K Dick on, science 15, 118, 129; Thacker on 31

genre(s): Auerbach on 48; Bakhtin on 2, 13, 40, 44; Benjamin on 118; in Bergman 72, 83–4; in Cartwright 62; contemporary 31; in P K Dick 116, 118, 125–6; discursive 35; fictional 1; film 31, 49, 67, 118; in James, 139, 142–3; literary 33, 36, 63; media vii, xi, 13, 30–1, 33, 35, 44, 58, 62, 72, 83; for Paul 36–7, 39, 58; sci fi 116, 118; Thacker on 31; writing 121, 129

grammar: Heideggerian 41; in James 149

hermeneutics 43: Bakhtin's 43; P K Dick's 108, 125; in Freud 139; Heidegger's 44; in James 140; in Nietzsche 125; phenomenological 43; theological 46

history 22: Bakhtin on 33; in Bergman films 89, 97; biblical 22, 36; Brown on 6; in Cartwright's novel 61; of Christendom 8; Derrida on 37; Foucault on 23, 144–7; Hegel's teleological 37; James on 143, 147, 150; in Morrison's *Paradise* 2; natural 143;-144, 150; Padura on viii, 30; in Pasolini's *Gospel of St Matthew* 54; of religion 161; of theology viii; in Wenders' *Paris Texas* 50

immortality: P K Dick on 112, 122, 131; James on 135–8, 154; Wilder on 156:

interpretation(s) 68: Bal's biblical 20, 22; Bloom's biblical 22; Deleuze and Guattari on 68; Freudian 23; productive 63; in Rabelais 46, 63;

language: Bakhtin on 40, 44; Barthes on 132; Deleuze's 158; in James, 150, 152; Luther's vernacular 127; for Montaigne 129; Pasolini on 47, 57; of Romans 4, 38; Semitic 36; and technology 36; Wittgenstein on 151

letters 36, 38: in Bergman films 77, 99, 105; in Cartwright's novel 62; in Christianity's emergence 36; Derrida on 37–8; P K Dick's 109; Greek 36, 39; James' 138; Paul's 31–2, 35, 37–8, 40–1, 43, 56, 58, 127, 131; Taubes on 9; in Wilder's novel 156

Lightning Source UK Ltd.
Milton Keynes UK
UKHW020252100123
415094UK00007B/126